Your God is Too Somber

Your God is Too Somber

CHRISTOPHER DREISBACH

WIPF & STOCK · Eugene, Oregon

YOUR GOD IS TOO SOMBER

Copyright © 2019 Christopher Dreisbach. All rights reserved. Except for brief quotations in critical publications or reviews, no part of this book may be reproduced in any manner without prior written permission from the publisher. Write: Permissions, Wipf and Stock Publishers, 199 W. 8th Ave., Suite 3, Eugene, OR 97401.

Wipf & Stock
An Imprint of Wipf and Stock Publishers
199 W. 8th Ave., Suite 3
Eugene, OR 97401

www.wipfandstock.com

PAPERBACK ISBN: 978-1-5326-5599-9
HARDCOVER ISBN: 978-1-5326-5600-2
EBOOK ISBN: 978-1-5326-5601-9

Manufactured in the U.S.A. 01/16/19

New Revised Standard Version Bible, copyright © 1989 National Council of the Churches of Christ in the United States of America. Used by permission. All rights reserved worldwide.

Scripture quotations marked (NIV) are taken from the Holy Bible, New International Version®, NIV®. Copyright © 1973, 1978, 1984, 2011 by Biblica, Inc.™ Used by permission of Zondervan. All rights reserved worldwide. www.zondervan.com The "NIV" and "New International Version" are trademarks registered in the United States Patent and Trademark Office by Biblica, Inc.™

For my dad, the Reverend Frank Dreisbach,
whose God is *not* too somber.

It is God's will that we seek Him willfully and busily,
gladly and merrily without unskillful heaviness and vain sorrow

—Julian of Norwich

Contents

List of Tables | viii
Preface | ix
Acknowledgements | xiii
Abbreviations | xiv
Introduction | xv

Part I: A Call to Joy | 1
1 Call to Joy: Laying the Foundation | 3
2 Humor as a Means to Truth | 11
3 Humor About vs. Humor Within | 17

Part II: A Theology of Laughter | 25
4 A Little Logic | 27
5 Arguments for Humor in Christianity | 36
6 Arguments against Humor in Christianity | 51

Part III: The Bible as Comedy | 61
7 Humor in the Bible: Overview | 63
8 Humor in the Old Testament | 80
9 Jonah as Comedy | 103
10 Humor in the New Testament | 113
11 Humor in the Parable of the Talents | 136
12 Conclusion | 151

Bibliography | 159
Subject Index | 173
Scripture Index | 187

Tables

Saroglu's Five Religious and Humorous Biases (ch. 6) | 57
Books of the Bible not Considered Otherwise (ch. 12) | 155

Preface

When J. B. Phillips published *Your God Is Too Small* in 1961, he found troubling many Christians' failure to find a "God big enough for modern needs," and their worshipping instead "A childish conception of God which could not stand up to the winds of real life for five minutes."[1] Phillips hoped that his book would "expose the inadequate conceptions of God which still linger unconsciously in many minds, and which prevent our catching a true glimpse of God"; and that his book would "suggest ways in which we find the real God for ourselves."[2]

Phillips starts the book with a list of 17 false conceptions about God, each of which describes a god inadequate to meet contemporary needs and each of which falls short of the New Testament's description of God. Most of these misconceptions ascribe false attributes to God, for example, "meek and mild"; "God in a Box," limiting God's attributes to those distinctive of a particular denomination; and "Perennial Grievance," a disappointing God who is fallen down on the job.[3] Several other misconceptions describe or entail a false and inadequate relationship between God and humanity, for example, "Absolute Perfection," which abhors the imperfection of humans; the "Heavenly Bosom," which limits God to a place for humans to escape; and the "Managing Director" who has no time for puny humans, as He keeps the universe on track.[4] Still other misconceptions of God deny true attributes of God, such as the "Grand Old Man," which describes an old fashioned God that is neither living nor contemporary.[5]

1. Phillips, *Your God is Too Small*, 8.
2. Ibid.
3. Ibid., 26, 37, 48.
4. Ibid., 30, 33, 40.
5. Ibid., 23.

Preface

Phillips then describes an "adequate God" who focuses Himself through the person of Christ and offers a relationship with humans that forgives their sins, offers answers to the most pressing spiritual questions, and negates death.

In describing an adequate God, Phillips declares that

> It is not our intention to build up merely a bigger and better god, who may be just as much an artificiality as any of the unattractive galaxy we have discarded. What we are going to try to do is to open the windows of the mind and spirit—to put it crudely, to enlarge the aperture through which the light of the true God may shine.[6]

Whether Phillips' description of an adequate God is accurate—and adequate—he succeeds in challenging Christians to rethink their frequently incorrect or insufficient conceptions of the God they claim to worship. Whether those Christians accept the challenge is beyond Phillips' control.

Three years after Phillips published *Your God is too Small*, Elton Trueblood published *The Humor of Christ*, whose cover describes the book as "A bold challenge to the traditional stereotype of a somber, gloomy Christ."[7] Whether by design or by coincidence, Trueblood's target is one of Phillips' "unreal Gods": the "Pale Galilean," whom worshippers treat as a negative force in their lives.[8] This God is a scolding, scowling God—the God of the stereotypical Puritan—whose presence is a constant reminder of human depravity and spiritual illness. Looking for some compensation in worshipping such a God, Phillips posits three imagined advantages:

- "The belief that the joy and freedom of those who do NOT subscribe to the worship of the negative god is just an illusion."
- "A certain spiritually masochistic joy in being crushed by the juggernaut of a negative god."
- The comforting idea of being "something special." [9]

---

6. Ibid., 59.

7. Trueblood, *The Humor of Christ*. While Trueblood's book begins a trend of scholarship of this sort, it was not the first to engage this topic. See, for example, Lanyon, *The Laughter of God* (1941); Morison, *The Humour of Christ* (1931); Webster, *Laughter in the Bible* (1960); Wordsworth. *The Laughter of God* (1925): Zuver, *Salvation by Laughter* (1933).

8. Phillips, *Your God is Too Small*, 50.

9. Ibid., 51–52.

Preface

Phillips notes the lines of a traditional hymn that captures this view: "Oh to be nothing, nothing, Only to lie at His feet, A broken and emptied vessel For the Master's use made meet." [10] Phillips claims that what is missing from this inadequate, if not false, image of God is a sense of humor:

> The sense of humor is, of course, suspended by the negative god, or his devotees would be bound to see the absurdity of anyone's ambition being to be "nothing," a "broken" and, not unnaturally, "emptied" vessel lying at God's feet! Better still, the New Testament (a book full of freedom and joy, courage and vitality) might be searched in vain to supply any endorsement whatsoever of the above truly dreadful verse and the conception of God it typifies. If ever a book taught men to be "something, something," to stand and do battle, to be far more full of joy and daring and life than they ever were without god—that book is the New Testament![11]
>
> The question, then, for devotees of this God is "dare they defy and break away from this imaginary god with the perpetual frown and find the One who is the great Positive, who gives life, courage and joy. . .?"[12]

Trueblood offers the same dare and sets the stage for a rich body of scholarship to follow. How, these scholars wonder, can Christians answer the call to joy without having a sense of humor? Ought there to be a theology of joy as an answer to the medieval theology of tears? How much do Christians miss if they fail to see the humor in scripture? How much deeper and more fulfilling is Christian worship when it makes room for humor? How much more can Christians teach if they include humor in their teaching? Christians who worship the Pale Galilean are worshipping a God who is too somber.

This book takes its cue from Phillips' warning not to confine God to our false or inadequate images, and follows Trueblood's lead in focusing on one mistake—denying God and God's worshippers a sense of humor. Through a survey of several scholars' views on the matter, this book builds its argument on three propositions: answering the call to joy is impossible in the absence of humor; a theology of joy is plausible and stands up well logically against a theology of tears; and it makes more sense to regard the Bible as comedy than as tragedy.

10. Ibid., 52
11. Ibid.
12. Ibid., 53.

Acknowledgements

THIS BOOK EMERGES FROM a master's-level course I have taught and most recently co-taught at St. Mary's Ecumenical Institute of Theology. My thanks, therefore, go to former Dean, Dr. Michael Gorman, for giving me the chance to design and teach the course in its first form; and present Dean, The Rev. Dr. Brent Laytham, for trusting me to put the course online, and then to develop a new version of the course based on a rough draft of this book. Thanks to Dr. Rebecca Hancock, biblical scholar, who co-taught the most recent version of this course and who taught me a great deal in the bargain. And thanks to all of the students who have taken the course, for suggesting improvements to course content, and for encouraging this study. Because the most recent student cohort worked with a draft of this book and made many terrific suggestions for improvement, these folks deserve recognition by name: Madison Bolesta, Andrew Brooks, Pat Byrnes, Dana Casey, Elisabeth Flessner, Julia Mitchner, Jenn Pearson, Peggy Shaffer, Amy Shimonkevitz, and John Tant.

Thanks too to my friends and colleagues Dr. Mark Komrad and Kim Komrad who graciously continue to teach me about Judaism and whose wise questions about Christianity continue to enhance my belief and corresponding practice.

And thanks to my wife Rebecca, teacher and scholar, whose honesty in constructive criticism makes this book much clearer and tighter than it would have been otherwise.

For any shortcomings in the book I am solely responsible.

Abbreviations

1 Cor	First Corinthians
1 Kgs	First Kings
1 Sam	First Samuel
1 Thess	First Thessalonians
2 Cor	Second Corinthians
2 Kgs	Second Kings
2 Sam	Second Samuel
Exod	Exodus
Ezek	Ezekiel
Gal	Galatians
Gen	Genesis
Hos	Hosea
Isa	Isaiah
Jer	Jeremiah
Josh	Joshua
Judg	Judges
Matt	Matthew
NIV	New International Version
NRSV	New Revised Standard Version
Num	Numbers
Prov	Proverbs
Ps	Psalms
Rev	Revelation
Wis	Wisdom

Introduction

> For I know that my Redeemer lives,
> and that at the last he will stand upon the earth.
>
> JOB 19:25[1]

> They would have to sing better songs for me to learn to have faith in their Redeemer; and his disciples would have to look more redeemed!
>
> FRIEDRICH NIETZSCHE, *THUS SPOKE ZARATHUSTRA*

EVEN IN THE MIDST of Job's trials, he was able to celebrate his relationship with God. Many a Christian martyr has faced death with optimism and good humor, celebrating their chance to make the ultimate statement of their faith.[2] Most Christians have no greater trial than Job's or the martyrs' and therefore most Christians should have at least as much to celebrate. And what is celebration without humor? Friederich Nietzsche, who famously said God is dead, must have wondered the same things about Christians, noting how unredeemed congregations of Christians often look and act. If Christianity is telling the truth, who has more to celebrate, more to be happy about, than Christians? And again, what are celebration and happiness without humor? Without humor, they are too somber and their God is too somber.

---

1. All biblical quote are from the NRSV unless noted otherwise.
2. Thank you to John Tant for this insight.

Introduction

This book calls out Christian teachings and practices that include humor on different levels and in different varieties. If we look for it, we will find humor in Scripture, in many Christian traditions, in personal and communal Christian experience, and in arguments for the presence of value of humor in religion generally and Christianity in particular. For example, in the Old Testament God laughs, sometimes in enjoyment, other times in mockery, but perhaps joyful mockery. The New Testament has Jesus frequently using irony, paradox, preposterousness, or banter to make his point. These are much more effective when humor accompanies them than when humor is absent. Indeed many biblical stories make the most sense only if we acknowledge certain humorous features within those stories. Two that stand out and that we will consider in more detail in Part III are the entire book of Jonah and the Parable of the Talents.

Many Christian traditions use humor in telling and trying to understand God's truth and the truth of the human condition. There is the humor of joy, celebration, and relief. There is humor as means to describing the personalities of God and Jesus, and to explaining the precepts of the tradition. Sometimes the humor is aimed inward at the tradition and its adherents; sometimes the humor aims at people outside the tradition. Sometimes the humor is contentious or abusive; sometimes the humor is gentle.

The Christian experience ought to include a lot of humor, especially in the form of celebration and delight at the joy of the Gospel. Here again we may find humor of value for its own sake, or humor as a means to telling and understanding the truth.

And it stands to reason that if Christians are to make a joyful noise unto the Lord that they must do so in good humor, lest the noise be inauthentic.

To be sure, not everyone buys into this idea of humor in Christianity. Consider Chrysostom's theology of tears, for example, over and against Karl-Josef Kuschel's theology of laughter, both of which we will consider in this study. Less academically, any of us who have attended church have probably encountered, as Nietzsche may have, moments of solemnity, atonement, and cries about hell fire and damnation. Perhaps critics of Christianity give these moments even more weight in attacking a typical stereotype of puritanical Christians who refuse to have fun and who consign to hell anyone who does not accept their particular brand of Christianity.

But Christians are called to joy and celebration, which are tough tasks in the absence of humor. Thus, a complete study and practice of Christianity must include its humor—theologically and scripturally. This books aims at

Introduction

contributing to such a study by making a case for the value and presence of such humor, by identifying it, and by suggesting implications of the results.

This book argues that it is a mistake to worship a God who is too somber. It begins with the assumptions that being a Christian requires orthodoxy and orthopraxy and that these require proper devotion. The three main parts of the book assert the necessary conditions for proper devotion. Part One, *A Call to Joy*, examines humor in a religious context broadly. Chapter One lays out this context. Chapter Two works out the distinction between humor as a means to truth and humor as end in itself. Chapter Three works out the distinction between humor about religion and humor within religion.

Part Two, *A Theology of Laughter*, considers several arguments for and against humor in religion. Chapter Four offers a primer on logic in preparation for evaluation of arguments for and against the presence and value of humor in Christianity. Chapter Five examines specific arguments for the value and presence of humor in Christianity, and gathers these up in a discussion of a theology of laughter. Chapter Six examines specific arguments against the value and presence of humor in Christianity, and gathers these up in discussion of a theology of tears.

Part Three, *The Bible as Comedy*, explores humor in the Old and New Testaments. Chapter Seven offers an overview of humor in the Bible, including qualities of humor in the Bible, the Bible as comedy, a theology of laughter revisited, and Jesus's use of humor as means to the truth. Chapter Eight explores humor in the Old Testament, including the Torah, the prophets, and the writings. Chapter Nine focuses on the Book of Jonah as a comedy. Chapter Ten explores humor in the New Testament, including the Gospels, Acts and the Letters, and Revelation. Chapter Eleven focuses on the Parable of the Talents as a humorous story.

Chapter Twelve offers a summary of our efforts and a suggestion for next steps.

PART I

A Call to Joy

The first proposition toward the argument against worshipping too somber a God is the call to joy. Acknowledging this call gives the opportunity to examine humor in a religious context broadly. We will do so across three chapters. Chapter 1 lays out this context. Chapter 2 distinguishes humor as a means to truth from humor as end in itself. Chapter 3 distinguishes humor about religion from humor within religion.

1

Call to Joy
Laying the Foundation

Joy is the most infallible sign of the presence of God.
—Pierre Teilhard de Chardin

A cheerful heart is a good medicine, but a downcast spirit dries up the bones.
—Proverbs 17:22

The call to joy is basic to Christianity. Adherents describe God as all-loving, all-good, able to conquer all evil, and in a valuable relationship with worshippers. To be sure, these same adherents may also refer to God as jealous, angry, and vengeful. But even in such characterization there is promise of a joyful relationship for those who are right with God. Thus, it seems inconsistent to worship God without expressing the joy that such worship entails. Hence the two epigraphs above.

If joy is imperative, then so is humor, for humorless joy is an oxymoron. And it is hard, if not impossible, to imagine a sense of humor unaccompanied by laughter, at least in the form of a gentle smile.

Therefore, given this book's plan to talk about the place of humor in Christianity, a good start is the reminder of the call to joy. Since Conrad Hyers, in *And God Created Laughter*, offers a thoughtful and compelling argument for the centrality of joy in Christianity, this chapter focuses on his position.

Hyers seeks to identify the Bible as a comedy, rather than a tragedy. He builds his case on the Christian call to joy.[1] Let's look at his case more closely, considering biblical evidence for this position, and getting clearer on what we mean by joy and its concomitants, including happiness, humor, laughter, play, and comedy.

THE GOSPEL

In arguing that Christianity is about joy, Hyers develops three premises: The Gospels are, following William Tyndale, "joyful tidings," and the rest of the New Testament builds on these tidings; Christ's sacrifice gives us the freedom to laugh; and the Bible in its entirety is contained within comic parentheses.

Joyful Tidings

Regarding us the Gospels as "joyful tidings," Hyers notes Acts 2, which describes the prevailing mood in the early church as joyful. Acts 2:12–15 includes a funny story within the story. The locals, hearing the Christians speaking in tongues, accuse them of having too much wine. Peter retorts loudly that these Christians cannot be drunk, "for it is only nine o'clock in the morning" (v. 2:15b). Perhaps Peter was serious, but this sounds funny nonetheless to the modern ear.

At Acts 2:28 Peter quotes David: "You have made known to me the paths of life; you will fill me with joy in your presence."

Acts 2:46 describes the Lord's Supper as a love feast and a victory feast.

The call to joy is clear here as is the Christians' attempt to answer that call.

---

1. Hyers, *And God Created Laughter*, ch. 2.

Call to Joy

The Freedom to Laugh

From the gospel as glad tidings, Hyers moves to the Christian's freedom to laugh. Noting that "we are not saved by our righteousness or rightness," Hyers concludes that we are therefore "free to laugh and play as children of God."[2] Theologian Eugene Biser makes a similar claim: Christ overcomes the spirit of gravity and frees us to become like a child.[3] Continuing, Hyers offers a formula to which we shall return more than once in this book: "Faith without humor becomes fanaticism; humor without faith becomes cynicism."[4] Further, "The expression of salvation freely given and received is not weeping but laughter."[5]

Although Hyers focuses on the Christian story in his describing the freedom to laugh, he reminds us that most of the psalms are also celebratory. Theologian James Martin agrees, citing Psalm 65.[6] Consider for example, v. 8b: "You make the gateways of the morning and the evening shout for joy." And v. 13: "The meadows clothe themselves with flocks, the valleys deck themselves with grain, they shout and sing together for joy."

Not only does the Bible free us to laugh, the Bible requires it—at the right time.

The Comic Parentheses

Having declared the Gospels to be "joyful tidings" and having argued that Christianity gives us the freedom to laugh, Hyers moves to his primary premise, which is that the Bible exists within comic parentheses. As he notes, the Gospels and the whole Bible begin and end in celebration. Note especially, says Hyers, that Jesus was not the ascetic that John the Baptist was. In Matt 11:18–19, Jesus notes that people accuse John of having a demon because he neither eats nor drinks, but the same people assail Jesus as a glutton and drunkard. So, we can imagine Jesus engaging in celebration from time to time.

---

2. Ibid., 27.
3. Biser, "Scales of the Spirit," 63, 58.
4. Hyers, *And God Created Laughter*, 27.
5. Ibid.
6. Martin, *Between Heaven and Mirth*, ch. 2.

Part I: A Call to Joy

James Martin notes that to believe Jesus is "fully human" is to "believe that he had a sense of humor, which is a constituent part of being 'fully human.'"[7]

Continuing to make the case that the Bible in general and the Christian message in particular exist within comic parentheses, Hyers notes that tragedy in the classical sense moves toward destruction, while comedy in the classical sense moves toward constructive consequences. The Christian message begins in comic absurdity, moves toward tragedy, but ends up redemptive and celebratory.

Anticipating objections to the claim that the Bible is in general a comedy, Hyers reminds us that in comedy everything does not have to turn out all right compared, say, with fairy tales or romances in which there is always a perfectly happy ending. In many comedies the test is to celebrate in less than ideal circumstances. Here, Hyers invokes 1 Thessalonians 5, especially vv. 16 and 18: "Rejoice always . . . give thanks in all circumstances, for this is the will of God in Christ Jesus for you."

Later in this book we will take a closer look at the notion of the Bible as comedy, adding the view of several scholars that it has a U-shaped structure, rather than the inverted U of a tragedy. For now let us acknowledge the plausible hypothesis that the Bible is a comedy rather than a tragedy, at least in the classical sense.

JOY AND ITS CONCOMITANTS

Joy

Having considered Hyers's argument for the presence and central importance of joy in the Christian message, let's consider some related concepts and definitions. First, as to joy itself, James Martin nicely describes a variety of ways we can think about joy, including the difference between joy in a theological sense and joy in a more conventional sense. According to the dictionary, joy is simply a kind of happiness.[8] Theologically, "joy is a deep-seated result of one's connection to God . . . religious joy is always about a relationship. Joy has an object and that object is God."[9] Joy also is "what

---

7. Ibid., 57.
8. Ibid., 16.
9. Ibid., 25.

we'll experience when we are welcomed into heaven."[10] Continuing, Martin notes St. Thomas Aquinas's claim that "joy is the noblest human act, not just a feeling."[11] Joy, notes Martin, is a traditional fruit of the Holy Spirit, and according to Karl Barth, "joy is the simplest form of gratitude."[12]

The biblical call to joy, therefore, requires discernment about what joy is. It may be different for different people at different times, but the call to joy is something all Christians have in common.

Happiness

Many theologians who write about joy distinguish between joy and happiness. For example, chaplain and humorist Cy Eberhart holds the two to be different members of the same family: "Joy is the more substantial. Happiness is fleeting, temporary. To be found wanting of joy is to be lacking something essential."[13]

C. S. Lewis says that joy is not in our power; it is a kind of want, whereas happiness is a fleeting, temporary fulfillment of a want and is in some respects within our power.[14] James Martin suggests that one can be joyful without being happy all the time.[15] We will encounter this distinction again. For now, we might consider whether joy and happiness are distinct in our own lives.

Humor

There is no joy without humor. James Martin suggests that humor and laughter have the same religious and nonreligious meanings, unlike joy.[16] We may not know for sure what causes humor or what causes laughter, but we know it when we see it, says Martin. And unlike joy, it tends to have the same meaning whether or not we are speaking of it theologically.

---

10. Ibid., 12.
11. Ibid., 28.
12. Ibid., 138.
13. Eberhart, *In the Presence of Humor*, 14.
14. Lewis, *Surprised by Joy*, 18.
15. Martin, *Between Heaven and Mirth*, 171.
16. Ibid., 20.

Part I: A Call to Joy

Many authors writing about humor suggest three possible causes of humor: a sense of superiority; incongruity or surprise; or some sense of relief. Biblical scholar Mark E. Biddle holds that humor is basically the recognition of incongruity and that its corollaries are catharsis and an uncontrollable response, often in the form of involuntary laughter.[17]

In any event, where joy is described variously as a condition, a state, an act, or a feeling, humor is generally considered to be a quality or an attribute. *Merriam-Webster's Dictionary* claims that words related to "humor" include "comedy," "drollery," "funniness," "hilariousness," and "uproariousness."

Note that we will not attempt an analytic definition here, that is, a definition of the form, "humor = X." Sometimes such definitions are possible, as in "a bachelor = an unmarried man." Other times we have to settle for a dictionary definition; a stipulative definition (definition by consensus); or an ostensive definition, that is, definition by example. Since we tend to know humor when we see it, let's let an ostensive definition of humor suffice for our purposes.

At present the Christian call to joy is our major impetus, and as we have already noted, it seems impossible to answer that call absent a sense of humor. Thus, humor is a central focus. James Martin suggests eleven and a half reasons for having good humor.[18] First, it evangelizes. Second, it is a tool for humility. Third, it can help us recognize reality. Fourth, it speaks truth to power. Fifth, it shows courage. Sixth, it deepens our relationship with God. Seventh, it welcomes. Eighth, it is healing. Ninth, it fosters good relations. Tenth, it opens our minds. Eleventh, it is fun. And only worth half a point, says Martin, is that humor at times can be practical.

For our present purpose, it is enough to note Martin's reasons without debating them, but readers may want to pause here and consider whether they have experienced humor in any or all of the ways Martin suggests. The opportunity for such consideration will occur again over the course of our study.

We have briefly considered the nature and types of humor. In the next chapter we will consider the function of humor, especially as a means to the truth.

---

17. Biddle, *Time to Laugh*, 3.
18. Martin, *Between Heaven and Mirth*, ch. 4.

Laughter

In addition to joy, happiness, and humor, laughter and play are concepts important to our study. We have mentioned both already and will return to both time and again throughout the book. For now, consider Andrew Greeley's observation that we often laugh at solemn occasions, usually for either of two reasons: the pretensions of the abrupt indignities within such occasions and the laughter that comes with the humor of faith, given that the sacred is a form of play.[19]

Consider also theologian Jacqueline Bussie's concept of tragic laughter.[20] For Bussie, tragic laughter is "a mode of social critique, theological critique, and means of resistance to oppressive systems."[21] Old Testament scholar Juliana Claassens invokes this idea in suggesting that underlying comedic elements in Jonah "are traumatic memories of the devastating violence caused by empires."[22] For Claassens, tragic laughter emerges out of this trauma as a means of "interrupting a system of oppression and thus serving as a form of resistance and protest and fostering hope."[23]

Recognizing different types of and reasons for laughter in Christianity will help us see the broad framework within which humor is a possibility, even where it seems unlikely at first blush.

Play

Laughter is often an indicator of playfulness. Born of faith, laughter may well indicate, as Greely claims, "that the sacred is a form of play." A reluctance to look for or find humor in Christianity may stem from a fear of not taking it seriously enough, but play can be quite serious. Play, after all, is the vocation of children, and Jesus warns us to be as children if we want to get into the kingdom.

---

19. Greeley, "Humor and Ecclesiastical Ministry," 134–40.
20. Bussie, *Laughter of the Oppressed*.
21. Ibid., 16.
22. Claassens, "Rethinking Humour in the Book of Jonah," 655.
23. Ibid.

Part I: A Call to Joy

Comedy

Joy. Happiness. Humor. Laughter. Play. And finally, comedy. All of these matter to the study of the role of humor in religion. We have gotten a taste of Hyers's argument that the Bible is a comedy; we will take a closer look at his argument in the sequel. For now, note that comedy is often said to be synonymous with humor and remember that in a classical sense, a comedy is a story with a constructive ending, as opposed to the destructive ending of a tragedy.

2

Humor as a Means to Truth

Humor is a prelude to faith, and laughter is the beginning of prayer.
—Reinhold Niebuhr

I believe God has a great sense of humor. Sometimes he gives you something like a nudge and says, "Don't take yourself so seriously!"
—Pope Benedict XVI

We do well to study humor in religion, because we are called to joy in relationship with God and joy without humor is unimaginable. Having considered the call to joy in the previous chapter, let's look more closely at humor as a means to the truth, especially God's truth. We will do this in two steps. First, we will consider humorous elements in truth telling, focusing especially on the arguments of Elton Trueblood and of Rolf and Karl Jacobson. Then we will look at some arguments for the use of humor in preaching.

PART I: A CALL TO JOY

HUMOR IN TRUTH TELLING

There is a handful of key elements in religious efforts to tell the truth through humor. A cursory introduction to these might include the following. First, there is an attack on vanity, self-righteousness, pompousness, and arrogance. Then there is the use of irony; paradox; preposterousness; and exaggeration, including overstatement and understatement. Then there are the humor of the unexpected, the humor of repetition, the humor that comes with certain types of misunderstanding, and the humor of puns and other word play.

Trueblood's View

There are four elements in Trueblood's argument for the presence and value of humor as a means to religious truth. First is Jesus's universal humor. While certain types of humor are contextual or otherwise relative to a particular culture or time, Trueblood insists that Jesus's humor cuts across cultures and times. Offering Matthew 23 as exhibit A, Trueblood notes that "swallowing a camel while straining a gnat is funny in any language."[1]

The second element is the child's spirit, which Jesus invokes in all who heed his warning that we must be like children to inherit the kingdom (Matt 18:3). Trueblood notes Søren Kierkegaard's frequent references to this spirit, as exemplified in the observation that "the child laughs because he has not yet been brainwashed and thereby blinded to the truly amusing."[2] The implication is that adults are blinded to the amusing and need help to restore their sight. Jesus's use of humor, says Trueblood, has that effect on those who get his humor.

Third, Trueblood notes the use of paradox by religion in general and Jesus in particular. Paradox is humor when it makes connections that people do not ordinarily see otherwise. For Trueblood, "Christ's use of paradox is dazzling. The entire process of finding similarity in apparent difference, which makes parable possible, is deeply paradoxical."[3] Examples include Jesus's notion of the blind leading the blind, and the list of paradoxes that comprise the Beatitudes. But Trueblood cautions that paradox is humorous

---

1. Trueblood, *Humor of Christ*, 34.
2. Ibid., 35.
3. Ibid., 43.

only when it cuts down to size and does not involve real tragedy or unmerited suffering.

The fourth of Trueblood's four initial elements is preposterousness: "Of all the mistakes which we make in regard to the humor of Christ, perhaps the worst mistake is our failure, or unwillingness, to recognize that Christ used deliberately preposterous statements to get his point across."[4]

Trueblood posits two ingredients in Jesus's use of the preposterous: surprise and inevitability. Jesus often connects them in a paradoxical way, using preposterous imagery, such as the rich man and the needle's eye (Mark 10:26) or casting pearls before swine (Matt 7:6).

Jesus's purpose in the use of the preposterous is to clarify and increase understanding, not to be funny for the sake of being funny, nor to hurt anyone.

The Jacobsons' View

Trueblood's seminal and influential position on Christ's use of humor to tell the truth gets support from theologians Rolf and Karl Jacobson.[5] As they put it, humor is essential to human nature, so "speaking the truth, including the biblical truth, seems to require the use of humor. Humor exposes our flaws and opens us to new vistas—or in theological terms, it preaches both law and gospel."[6]

In short, the church must speak the gospel appropriate to its context, which includes humor. Contrary to Trueblood, the Jacobsons believe that people may be more willing to consider the role of humor in religion today than they once were. As an example of whence we have come on the matter, they cite the *Rule of Benedict*, especially chapter 4, #54 and #55, written in the sixth century, which includes the commands not to speak useless words or words that move to laughter and not to love much or boisterous laughter.[7]

Charting, in their words, the basic dimensions of humor, the Jacobsons claim that humor is universally and exclusively human. Thus, to lack humor is to be less than fully human. What's more, they claim, humor is a

---

4. Ibid., 46–47.
5. Jacobson and Jacobson, "Everyone Who Hears," 107–16.
6. Ibid., 107.
7. Ibid.

form of human intelligence and humor helps us both perceive and tell the truth about the world.

For the Jacobsons, one truth that is necessary to tell, especially in the Old Testament, is the truth of God's law. Humor is a useful means to this end. For those of us not accustomed to looking for humor in the Old Testament, we might be surprised to find it in Amos and Hosea, two of the Jacobsons' examples.

Amos 4:4–5 reads: "Come to Bethel and transgress; to Gilgal and multiply transgression; bring your sacrifices every morning, your tithes every three days; bring a thank offering of leavened bread, and proclaim freewill offerings, publish them; for so you love to do, O people of Israel! says the Lord God."

For the Jacobsons, Amos is using "wicked sarcasm" to parody "the priestly call to worship a typical Israelite might have heard at one of the worship centers."[8] Citing the Psalms as an example, the Jacobsons note that "the reasons for praise are usually something about God, such as that God is . . . a great God. In Amos, however, the prophet turns the form on its head, and uses it to accuse the people: 'For so you love to do.' The passage is a parody that is bitterly ironic."[9]

Hosea 4:7–8 reads: "The more [the priests] increased, the more they sinned against me; they changed their glory into shame. They feed on the sin of my people; they are greedy for their iniquity."

Here the Jacobsons regard Hosea as mocking "the priestly practice of offering animal sacrifices of atonement for the people's sins."[10] Priests fed themselves on the sacrificed food, which was meant as means for people to follow the law and thus not to sin. Hosea mocked this priestly conflict of interest: "They feed on the sin of my people; they are greedy for their iniquity." The result, Hosea said, was that the more priests there were, the more—rather than less—sin there was in the land.[11]

In short, "humor is particularly apt at unmasking pretensions, exposing flaws, and drawing attention to the inconvenient truths we would rather ignore."[12]

---

8. Ibid., 110.
9. Ibid.
10. Ibid., 111.
11. Ibid.
12. Ibid.

HUMOR IN PREACHING

Concerning the appropriateness of humor in preaching, there are three possibilities: it should be prohibited, it should be permitted, or it should be obligatory. If humor is a useful means to the truth and preaching is about the truth, it stands to reason that humor can be useful in preaching. So it should be permitted and possibly be required, but with caveats.

Let us finish this chapter by thinking about some aspects of humor in preaching. As theologian Jason Byassee notes, Cicero's oft-followed directions for good rhetoric include a three-part task: inform, delight, and move.[13] Humor is obviously useful to delighting and moving, and arguably useful to informing.

Biblical scholar Mary Hinkle Shore promotes humor in preaching for three reasons: biblical texts often contain humor; humor can create a connection between speaker and hearer; and humor in the sermon participates in the play that characterizes faith.[14]

Homiletics professor Ruthanna Hooke adds several premises to the argument that Mary Hinkle Shore has started.[15] Humor in preaching is valuable, because "it may help bridge the gulf between preacher and hearer that can develop with a monologue." Humor allows teller and hearer to "establish and signal a connection with each other." Humor helps take down people's defenses against God. "Humor calls us into the space of play." Humor lowers our resistance to hearing the message. And "humor connects us to grace, by reminding us of our absurdities, but leading us to laugh at them rather than despair over them—given God's love for us."[16]

In *Lectionary Levity* Ian Markham, dean of Virginia Theological Seminary, and the Reverend Samantha Gottlich, Episcopal priest, work through the Revised Common Lectionary, suggesting ways to weave humor into preaching the gospel. They do so on the ground that humor, properly used, will help people to listen better and thus to relax and be "more receptive to what will follow."[17] For them, it is not necessary for the preacher always to be funny, but the preacher should give herself permission to use humor

---

13. Byassee, "Stand and Deliver," 20–23.

14. Shore, "Leave Them Wanting More," 124–31. See also Masarik, "Use of the Joke," 491–96; and Stark, "Are Laurence Sterne's Sermons Funny?," 456–70.

15. Hooke, "Humor in Preaching," 187, 189.

16. Ibid., 189.

17. Markham and Gottlich, *Lectionary Levity*, xiii.

where it will enhance the preaching and understanding of the gospel, especially given Jesus's "wonderful sense of humor."[18]

Homiletics professor Christopher Smith takes a different and more succinct tack. For him, the foolishness of the gospel is inherently humorous. And "Jesus is the first fool and preachers are his assistant jesters."[19]

The concept of Christian foolishness is important to this study. For now it is enough to note the value of homiletic humor given the concept of the fool for Christ.

Note some caveats about humor in preaching. Mary Hinkle Shore offers three: humor is sometimes offensive in ways the speaker does not intend; preaching is not about the preacher's cleverness; and most of us aren't as funny as we think we are.[20] Christopher Smith adds that while humor in preaching is essential, jokes are not.[21] Markham and Gottlich agree, claiming that "it is inappropriate for a preacher to just tell a joke that is unrelated to the subsequent sermon."[22]

It is difficult to imagine a categorical imperative for using humor in homiletics, but in light of the foregoing it is just as difficult to imagine the wisdom of forbidding such use, especially where it will enhance our Christian understanding and sensibilities.

---

18. Ibid.
19. Smith, "Humor in Preaching," 188.
20. Shore, "Leave Them Wanting More," 125.
21. Smith, "Humor in Preaching," 188.
22. Markham and Gottlich, *Lectionary Levity*, xiv.

3

Humor About vs. Humor Within

> At its core the piety of the people is a storehouse of values that offers answers of Christian wisdom to the great questions of life. [This storehouse] . . . provides reasons for joy and humor even in the midst of a very hard life.
>
> —CATECHISM OF THE CATHOLIC CHURCH

THIS CHAPTER DISTINGUISHES HUMOR about religion from humor within religion. Humor about religion may be abusive or contentious, or non-abusive or non-contentious. And this humor may come from Christians or non-Christians.

Humor within religion may turn inward, that is, on oneself, or outward, that is, toward others.

We will round out this chapter with a brief acknowledgment of scholarship in two areas. First, scholarship on famous writers and thinkers and their views on humor in religion. Second, scholarship on religious humor in non-Christian religions and cultures.

HUMOR ABOUT RELIGION

Two aspects of humor and religion interest us here: humor *about* religion and humor *within* religion. Both may aim at some truth, but each puts humor in a different framework relative to the religion involved. We look at humor about religion first. In doing so we consider humor that is abusive or contentious and humor that is not abusive or contentious.

Humor about religion may take either of two forms, abusive or contentious and non-abusive or non-contentious. In either form, four scenarios are possible: Christian humor about other Christians; Christian humor about non-Christians; non-Christian humor about Christians; and non-Christian humor about non-Christians.

We are especially interested in humor that involves Christians either as the givers or the receivers of the humor, whether abusive/contentious or not.

Contentious/Abusive Humor

Contrary to the charitable image most Christians would like to project, Christians have been known to aim their humor contentiously or abusively both at fellow Christians and at non-Christians. Note that we should not regard "abusive" and "contentious" as synonyms. To be contentious is to be argumentative or "itching for a fight." To be abusive is to misuse one's authority or position to unjustly lash out at someone or something, verbally or physically. For the time being, we may consider contentious humor and abusive humor to be of the same class under the more general concept of negative humor. Sometimes the humor is meant to be corrective or edifying; other times, it is just plain mean.

Consider two examples. First, theologian and philosopher Chris Huebner presents Stanley Hauerwas's engagement with the Mennonites as an extended joke that is contentious, if not abusive, but with a Christian purpose.[1] Huebner believes that Hauerwas's target is not the Mennonites as such, but any Christians who take themselves too seriously. Such Christians fail to acknowledge their follies and assume that they have more control over their existence than they have. For Hauerwas, Christianity is serious business but is properly engaged in only with a deep sense of the humor in God's willingness to be in relationship with humans. The fundamental problem with many humans is pride. In Huebner's words, "Hauerwas both articulates and practices a conception of theological laughter that is essential to his overall theological project. [Also, he] encourages us to laugh at

---

1. Huebner, "Make Us Your Laughter," 357–73.

ourselves and, in so doing, to recognize the folly of our temptation to put ourselves in place of God."[2]

Concerning Mennonites specifically, Huebner suggests that Hauerwas sees in Mennonite theology a prideful temptation to "elaborate the distinctions and differences that are said to give expression to a particular Anabaptist or Mennonite identity."[3] What's more, Huebner says the Mennonites do not appear to get the joke.

Now is not the time to decide whether this is a fair characterization of the Mennonites or even whether Huebner has described Hauerwas accurately. It is enough for now to recognize the foregoing as an example of contentious or abusive humor from one Christian about another group of Christians.

A second example of Christian humor that is contentious or abusive, aiming this time at non-Christians, is the Landover Baptist Church's Muslim Jokes website. It is an egregious example of humor that is mean without redeeming value. This book's bibliography contains the URL to Landover's website, but it does so with the proviso that the site is extremely offensive. As such, it is a clear example of abusive Christian humor.

Two examples of non-Christian humor toward Christians are comedian Bill Maher's movie *Religulous* and a controversial remark by NPR commentator Andrei Codrescu. Jason Byassee offers a useful critique of Maher's mockumentary in which he attacks Christians as scientifically naïve or antagonistic buffoons.[4] As Byassee notes, Maher focuses on some of the more controversial positions of certain Christians, and Maher offers up science as uncritically as he accuses Christians of being. But the movie is a representative example of non-Christian humor aimed contentiously or abusively at Christians.

Here is another example of abusive or contentions non-Christian humor aimed at Christians: on December 19, 1995, Andrei Codrescu, offering his regular commentary on NPR's *All Things Considered*, noted the belief of four million Christians in the rapture. He responded that "the evaporation of 4 million people who believe this crap would leave the world an instantly better place."[5] The broadcast was widely condemned and NPR offered an apology about a month later.

2. Ibid., 357.
3. Ibid., 366.
4. Byassee, "Zealous Skeptic," 13.
5. "Christians Get Apology from NPR," *Baltimore Sun*, December 23, 1995, 2D.

Part I: A Call to Joy

Rounding out our brief look at abusive or contentious humor about religion is an example of a non-Christian jab at a non-Christian religion. As David Feltmate, professor of religion, puts it: "A generic cult stereotype has developed over time in mass media and is reproduced in these programs for comedic effect."[6] Feltmate offers a conventional formulation of the cult stereotype involving, for example, confining members or depriving them of personal freedoms, charismatic leadership, extreme authoritarianism and discipline, and apocalyptic beliefs. He then discusses three episodes from three different animated sitcoms that poke fun at the stereotype. Feltmate asks and answers the question, why subject the stereotype to biting humor? Recognizing the three grounds of humor to be incongruity, superiority, and relief, Feltmate says, "Cults believe weird things (incongruity), we 'know' they are wrong because they are fraudulent—unlike our real religions—(superiority), and by laughing we relieve the tension that arises from our fear that cults lurk within our midst, waiting to brainwash us or cause some unspeakable act of violence (relief). However, the cultural dynamics that led to portraying cults in animated sitcoms run deeper than a simple equation such as this."[7]

Non-abusive/Non-contentious Humor

From abusive or contentious humor about religion we turn to non-abusive or non-contentious humor. Again, the humor may come from a Christian or a non-Christian and aim at Christians or non-Christians.

One example of Christian non-abusive humor aimed at Christians is Janet Letnes Martin and Suzann Nelson's *You Know You Are a Lutheran If . . .* It teaches that you are a Lutheran if: "You know perfectly well why there is no Lutheran Church named Good Works Lutheran"; "You really have a tough time with the idea that pastors and missionaries procreate"; and "You secretly wonder just who goes downtown to the local liquor store to buy the Communion wine."[8]

An example of Christian non-abusive humor about, if not aimed at non-Christians, concerns a classic joke about the Children of Israel. Joey, an inquisitive Christian child, asks Mr. Goldblatt, a Jew, whether the Bible says that the Children of Israel crossed the Red Sea, beat up the Philistines,

---

6. Feltmate, "Humorous Reproduction of Religious Prejudice," 201.
7. Ibid., 211.
8. Martin and Nelson, *You Know You Are a Lutheran If,* 12, 15, 40.

built the temple, and fought the Romans. When Goldblatt answers, "Yes," Joey asks, "What was all the grown-ups doin?"[9]

An example of non-Christian, non-abusive humor aimed at Christians is this Muslim joke:

> The legendary Maulana Rehmatullah Kairanwi of India was once involved in a debate with a Christian missionary. The missionary in his opening statement asked the Maulana, "Maulana Sahib, why didn't God save his Prophet's grandsons when they were martyred at Karbala and didn't Prophet Muhammad pray for their safety?"
>
> The Maulana answered, "God cried and said I couldn't even save my own son, how can I save your grandsons?"[10]

Finally, here is an example of non-Christian non-abusive humor aimed at non-Christians, in this case Jewish-on-Jewish. Yossel orders a pair of pants from Rabinovitch on the condition that the tailor delivers the pants tomorrow. Rabinovitch forgets, but remembers two years later, makes the pants, and delivers them to Yossel. Yossel complains that it took Rabinovitch two years to make a pair of pants when God created the world in six days. Rabinovitch responds with indignation, "Yossel, please, don't compare me to God: take a look at the world and just look at these pants!"[11]

Before moving to humor within religion, note that a common source of humor about religion is the funny papers. Their treatment of religion is also the topic of much scholarship. This humor may be abuse or non-abusive, Christian or non-Christian. It may also aim at telling a truth or simply at making someone laugh. We will not take time to discuss this further here, but one might find the scholarship interesting.[12]

---

9. "Children of Israel," http://www.christian-jokes.org/jokes54.html.

10. "A Little Islam-Christian Humor," http://www.beliefnet.com/faiths/islam/2002/07/a-little-islam-christian-humor.aspx.

11. Raskin, "God versus Man," 39–40.

12. Examples of scholarship on religion in the funny papers include: Collum, "What Would Dilbert Do?," 48; Greenspoon, "Bible in the Funny Papers," 30–33, 41; Greenspoon, "New Testament in the Comics," 40; Haverluck, "When God Was Flesh and Wild," 27–32; Lindsay and Heeren, "Where the Sacred Meets the Profane," 63–77; Mattingly, "Doug Marlette," 631–32; Short, "Peanuts at 35," 1022.

Part I: A Call to Joy

HUMOR WITHIN RELIGION

Much religious humor is *about* a religious practice, organization, or principle. We may also find humor *within* a religious practice, organization, or principle. For some people, the distinction between humor *about* and humor *within* may be too fine to be useful. Nevertheless, we can find such a distinction, both implicitly and explicitly, in our observations and in writings about religious humor. Thus, it is worth taking a few moments to note the category of humor within religion and the two subcategories: humor turned outward—engaging the world with a sense of humor—and humor turned inward—practicing one's faith with a sense of humor.

Humor Turned Outward

Two examples of Christian humor turned outward come from *Sojourners* magazine. One, Jep Hostetler's article, posits the value of such humor: "In my international travels, I have observed that peace workers often become so involved with the pain in our world that humor gets lost. People who are active in peacemaking and in justice work need a sense of humor. People with a healthy sense of humor are often much more comfortable with change, unusual circumstances, and alteration of plans, attributes that are especially important when tackling some of the most difficult tasks, such as walking in solidarity with the oppressed, speaking the truth to power, and standing between angry enemies."[13]

The other example, expressing such humor, is the many essays by Ed Spivey, *Sojourners* magazine's art director and humor columnist. For example, Spivey starts one column with this:

> "This Is Not About the Economy." Made you look. Anyway, the world economy continues to spin downward despite my previous column on the subject, which was intended to bring needed comic relief to struggling world markets. Unfortunately, their dour assessments of the future prevented them from just tossing back their heads and letting go with a hearty chuckle. So I say, "Why so glum, overly leveraged world markets?" or, alternately, "Laugh, economy clown, laugh." There, that should do the trick.[14]

---

13. Hostetler, "Is Laughter Really the Best Medicine?," 37.
14. Spivey, "This Is Not About the Economy," 50.

Humor Turned Inward

Examples of humor turned inward include humor in preaching and celebration, which we have already considered, and the ubiquitous church sign.[15] For example, from Smyrna Wesleyan Church: "Tithe if you love Jesus! Anyone can honk."[16] From St. Joseph Parish Service Center: "I don't know why some people change churches. What difference does it make which one you stay home from?"[17]

A novel example of humor turned inward is the efforts of Jana Reiss to reduce each Bible chapter to a twitter feed, that is, no longer than 140 characters. Religion journalist Cathy Lynn Grossman discusses Reiss, offering the following as an example: "G's Top Ten List: No gods, idols, or blasphemy. Keep the Sabbath holy and love mom. Don't kill, cheat, steal, lie or look at Xmas catalogs. (Exod 20:1–17)"[18]

Grossman describes a spectrum of critical responses to Reiss's efforts, ranging from strongly supportive to highly offended. These comments map nicely to more general attitudes about humor in Christianity and its sacred text.

Famous Writers and Humor about Religion

In addition to everyday examples of humor *about* religion and humor *within* religion, students of the subject might find worthwhile essays by or about famous writers and thinkers. A quick review of the literature identifies relevant essays about Peter DeVries, Erik Erikson, Søren Kierkegaard, Flannery O'Connor, Edith Stein, and Mark Twain.[19] Each of these scholars

---

15. A worthwhile collection of such signs is Paulson and Paulson, *Church Signs across America*.

16. Ibid., 34.

17. Ibid., 70.

18. Grossman, "Twible Delivers Holy Writ," 14–15.

19. Regarding DeVries, see: DeVries, "Vale of Laughter"; Wood, "Marooned in Mercy"; Wood, "Community of Laughter." Regarding Erikson, see: Capps, "Mother, Melancholia, and Humor." Regarding Kierkegaard, see: Evans, "Kierkegaard's View of Humor"; Langston, "Comical Kierkegaard"; Lippit, "Funny Thing"; Lippitt, *Humor and Irony*; Oden, *Humor of Kierkegaard*; Parrill, "Concept of Humor." Regarding O'Connor, see: Park, "Crippled Laughter"; Wood, "Talent Increased." Regarding Stein, see: Berkman, *Contemplating Edith Stein*; Sullivan, "Edith Stein's Humor"; Sullivan, "Some Instances of Edith Stein's Humor." Regarding Twain, see: Bush, "Mark Twain's American Adam"; Portaro, "Holiness and Hilarity."

Part I: A Call to Joy

has made important contributions to the world of humor in religion. You may find that their writings and essays about their writing add a lot to your understanding of the topic.

From the next chapter to the end of this book, we focus on Christian humor and its Jewish roots. Before heading that way, let us acknowledge the wealth of scholarship on religious humor outside Christianity. A quick review of the literature finds relevant scholarship by and about writers from Africa, American Indians, Buddhism, Egypt, Hinduism, Islam, Japan, Judaism, South Asia, and Taoism.[20]

---

20. Regarding Africa, see: Estepa, "Drinking from Comic Wells of Cultural Others." Regarding American Indian, see: Page, "Spider Coming Down"; Ware, "Will Rogers's Radio." Regarding Buddhism, see: Clarke, "Locating Humor in Indian Buddhist Konastic Law Codes"; Morrison, "Did the Buddha Have a Sense of Humor"; Olson, "Zen Clown Ikkyu"; Pieris, "Prophetic Humor and the Exposure of Demons"; Repp, "Buddhism and Cartoons in Japan"; Schopen, "Learned Monk as a Comic Figure"; Walters, "God's Play and the Buddha's Way." Regarding Egyptian, see: Morris, "Sacred and Obscene Laughter"; Schneider and Szpakowska, *Egyptian Stories*. Regarding Hindu/Indian, see: Alexander, "Banana Republics"; Dempsey and Durayappah, "Artificial Trick"; Harman, "Laughing Until It Hurts"; Hiltebeitel, "Recontextualizing Satire"; Jenkins, "Sacred Laughter"; John, "Joke and the 'Punch Line'"; Lindtner, "*Madhyamaka*"; McDermott, "Playing with Durga in Bengal"; Pintchman, "Friendship, Humor, Levity"; Sanford, "Don't Take It Badly"; Valpey, "Reflections on Ludic Dimensions"; West and Pokharel, "Questioning Caste." Regarding Islam/Arab/Persian, see: Amarasingam, "Laughter the Best Medicine"; Bard, "Turning Karbala Inside Out"; Cohen, "La Langue du Silence"; Djalili and Garrison, "Laughing with the Infidel"; George, "Ninurta-paqidat's Dog Bite"; Guppy, *Secret of Laughter*; Maghen, "Merry Men of Medina"; Márkus-Takeshita, "Secret of Laughter"; McDonough, "Canadian Muslims"; Mir, "Humor in the Qur'an"; Ozgur, "Cafcaf"; Pickthall, "Of Suleymân the Dragoman"; Rizvi, "Sayyid Ni'mat Allāh al-Jazā'irī"; Szombathy, "On Wit and Elegance"; Toorawa, "Play in the Qur'an"; Alster, "Two Sumerian Short Tales Reconsidered." Regarding Japanese, see: Suzuki, "Making of Tōjin." Regarding Judaism, see: Ben-Amos, "Jewish Folklore Studies"; Berkey-Gerard, "Woody Allen"; Biro, *Two Jews on a Train*; Chan, "Ira Regis"; Commins, "Woody Allen's Theological Imagination"; Efron, "From Łódź to Tel Aviv"; Freeman, "Humor, Healing and Holiness"; Goldsmith, "Divine Humor of Sholom Aleicheim"; Guesnet, "Tuml in the Shtetl"; Halkin, "Why Jews Laugh at Themselves"; Harap, "Jews in American Drama"; Krasney et al., "Badkhn"; Lapidus, "Poetry of Hayyim Lensky"; Lauder, "Woody Allen"; Mazor, "Badkhn"; Miller, "Prophecy in the Fast Lane"; Nissan, "On Joshua in Pseudo-Sirach"; Portnoy, "Exploiting Tradition"; Rommer, "Hypothetical Letter"; Roskies, "Major Trends in Yiddish Parody"; Vinokurov, "On the Brink"; Whitfield, "Distinctiveness of American Jewish Humor"; Wolski, "Secret of Yiddish." Regarding South Asian, see: Raj et al., *Sacred Play*. Regarding Taoism, see: Galvany, "Distorting the Rule"; Lee, "Chuang Tzu's Wit and Wisdom."

PART II

A Theology of Laughter

Part 1 laid a foundation for pondering the Christian call to joy. This next part considers the second proposition toward the argument against worshipping too somber a God—the appropriateness of a theology of laughter and its concomitants—and contrasts that with a theology of tears. Because these theological attempts rely on appeals to reason, we will consider several arguments for and against humor in religion. Chapter 4 offers a primer on logic in preparation for evaluation of arguments for and against the presence and value of humor in Christianity. Chapter 5 examines specific arguments for the value and presence of humor in Christianity and gathers these up in a discussion of a theology of laughter. Chapter 6 examines specific arguments against the value and presence of humor in Christianity and gathers these up in discussion of a theology of tears.

4

A Little Logic

Having looked at a summary inventory of concepts and categories regarding humor in religion, we turn to a more critical look at arguments for and against humor in Christianity. This involves more careful logical analysis and evaluation than we have engaged in so far. This in turn, requires us to have some logical tools at the ready. To that end, this chapter looks at logic as a tool we will use from time to time throughout the text.

Concerning logic, we should be clear about some basic definitions of logical elements; the basic nature of fallacies and some of the specific types; and three basic questions for logical analysis and evaluation.

BASIC DEFINITIONS

Here are some definitions to get us started, definitions of logic and argument; sentence; premise and conclusion; validity and soundness; and induction and deduction.

Logic is the study of good and bad reasoning or *arguments*. An *argument* in logic is any set of *sentences* in which one sentence, the *conclusion*, is claimed to be proven by the other sentences, the *premises*.

A *sentence* in logic is any statement that is capable of being true or false. This includes declarative sentences (e.g., "Jesus laughed"), but not imperatives ("Do not laugh in church!"), interrogatives ("Is *Jonah* a political cartoon?"), or interjections ("Hallelujah!").

Part II: A Theology of Laughter

A *premise* is any sentence in an argument that is offered as proof. In the ancient and famous example, *Socrates is a man, and all men are mortal, so Socrates is mortal*, the first two clauses are premises: that Socrates is a man and all men are mortal is offered as proof that Socrates is mortal.

A *conclusion* is the sentence in an argument that is claimed to be proven. In our example, "Socrates is mortal" is the conclusion.

VALIDITY AND SOUNDNESS

A good argument is *valid* and *sound*. A bad argument is either invalid or unsound. An argument is *valid* when the truth of its premises guarantees the truth of its conclusion, that is, if the premises are true, then the conclusion must be true. An argument is *sound* when it is valid and all of its premises are true. An argument is *unsound* when it is valid, but at least one of its premises is false. And an argument is *invalid* if it is logically possible for its premises to be true and its conclusion to be false at the same time. Note that soundness applies only to valid arguments; an invalid argument is neither sound nor unsound.

Here is an example of a valid and sound argument: *Benedictine monks should follow the Rule of St. Benedict. The Rule of St. Benedict says that monks should not be ready or quick to laugh* (ch. 7, 10th humility). *Therefore, Benedictine monks should not be ready or quick to laugh*. If the premises are true, the conclusion must be true, so it is valid. And the premises are true, so it is sound.

Here is an example of a valid but unsound argument: *All priests are comedians. My cousin Lou is a priest. Therefore, my cousin Lou is a comedian.* If the premises were true, the conclusion would have to be true, so the argument is valid. But the first sentence is false, so the argument is unsound.

Here is an example of an invalid argument: *If John is a Benedictine monk, then John rarely laughs. And John rarely laughs. Therefore, John is a Benedictine monk.* Assume that John is not a Benedictine, but that he rarely laughs because he is generally despondent. If so, then the premises—the first two sentences—are true, but the conclusion is false. Thus, this argument is invalid.

Any effort to prove one's position regarding humor in Christianity should include an attempt at a sound argument. As we examine these arguments we will ask first whether it is valid—if it is not then we need go no further with it. If it is valid, then our next question will be whether it is sound, that is, whether all of its premises are true.

A Sidebar on Truth

Much of the debate about humor's proper role in Christianity turns on different ideas about what constitutes truth. Consider five examples of propositions that exemplify five theories of truth:

1. The Dead Sea is 1,000 feet deep.
2. The consecrated host is the body of Jesus Christ.
3. Prayer can heal physical illness.
4. Red wine tastes better than white wine.
5. Jesus was a gate for the sheep.

Proposition 1 is true or false depending on a certain fact: the depth of the Dead Sea. Hence, the *correspondence* theory of truth that a sentence is true if it corresponds to the facts and false if it is contrary or contradictory to the facts. In the absence of a fact that verifies or falsifies the sentence, one must suspend judgment. For example, "On July 20, 25 CE, Jesus was in Jerusalem," may or may not be true. But unless we can find a relevant fact, we remain unsure.

The correspondence theory applies where people can agree on the alleged fact, but often unanimous agreement is not to be. Proposition 2 is true to a devout Roman Catholic and false to an observant Orthodox Jew. It would be incoherent for the former to deny it and for the latter to affirm it. And superficially at least, there is no empirical evidence to settle the matter either way. Hence, the *coherence* theory of truth that a sentence is true if it is coherent within one's system of belief and false otherwise. This relieves the proposer of having to present an objective fact on which all can agree, but it offers no help in solving disagreements between adherents of different belief systems. Moreover, it is common for people to be inconsistent regarding their own professed belief systems. How many Christians, for example, question one or more elements of the Nicene Creed, even as their belief system affirms all of it?

In some cases, neither empirical objectivity nor logical coherence is necessary for someone to accept a proposition as true. Sometimes one looks only for whether the proposition "works." Thus, for people who shortly after praying for healing no longer suffer the offending ailment, they may decide that the prayer worked and, thus, proposition 3 is true. For people who have failed to receive healing after praying for it, this proposition may be false, because the prayer did not work. This represents the *pragmatic* theory of truth, which holds that a sentence is true if it works to believe that it is true, and false if it is harmful to believe that it is true. To work in this case means that acting on the belief that the sentence is true will result in some benefit. If believing in the sentence will have no practical consequent, good or bad, then the sentence is neither true nor false, but simply nonsense.

Note that matters have become more subjective as we have worked through the list. The correspondence theory is wholly objective, depending on empirical fact. One's choice of a belief system may be subjective, but once that choice is made, consistency requires accepting certain propositions. So, the coherence theory is partly subjective and partly objective. Since what works for one may not work for another, it would appear that the pragmatic theory is wholly subjective, but a bit of objectivity remains, since someone may be mistaken about whether something is working or not. The person who believes that prayer alone is curing his cancer, while the cancer continues to grow, is wrong to propose that the prayer is working.

We come now to a wholly subjective theory of truth, with the example of proposition 4. There is no way objectively to verify or falsify the proposition that red wine tastes better than white wine. It is, as the sentence suggests, a matter of taste and taste is subjective. Hence, the *performative* theory of truth, which holds that to judge a sentence as true is merely to accept it and to judge it as false is merely to deny it. The term comes from the notion of a performative utterance, which is the act of doing something by saying something, e.g., "I apologize," "I confess," "I promise," "I thee wed," or "I thank you." In this case, to say "That is true," is nothing more than to say, "I accept it as true." If truth were nothing more than this, then debate over the truth of a sentence would be meaningless. Nonetheless, we must concede that some assertions or denials are merely matters of taste.

Proposition 5 does not fit so neatly into the framework of the first four. It represents the truth of *metaphor*. The truth of a metaphor is neither wholly objective nor wholly subjective: it depends on accepted meanings within a certain language and useful comparisons between two superficially unlikely objects. Thus, metaphorical truth fits neither in the correspondence theory nor the performative theory. But it doesn't fit neatly into the coherence theory either, unless we are to regard a given language as a system of belief, which seems odd on its face. And a metaphor may be true whether it works in any pragmatic sense. Thus, metaphorical truth stands on its own over and against the four other theories.

In the history of the idea of truth many have proposed one to the exclusion of the others. But as the examples above suggest, different theories of truth lend themselves to different sorts of propositions. Thus, for our purposes, we should keep all five theories at the ready, as we encounter propositions about the presence or absence of humor in the Christian Scripture, theology, and tradition. Is the book of Jonah humorous? It is to me and to many commentators, and for reasons which go beyond mere taste: accepted elements of humor abound in the book. Is the book of Job humorous? There is less consensus on this one, depending more on what one believes humor to entail. Does joy entail humor? Many would answer yes by definition. Were the Pharisees white-washed tombs? This appears to be an apt metaphor, and a humorous one, but it is not literally true. Let's continue, being mindful of the different ways a proposition might be true or false.

DEDUCTION AND INDUCTION

Arguments are either *deductive* or *inductive*. A deductive argument claims certainty, that is, if the premises are true, then the conclusion must be true. An inductive argument claims only probability and is usually based on past observation; that is, even if the premises are true, the conclusion is only probably true.

Here's an example of a deductive argument: *All people pray. Jim is a person. So, Jim prays.* If the premises are true, the conclusion must be true. Note that at this point we are not here assessing its validity or soundness, just whether it is claiming certainty or probability.

Here's an example of an inductive argument: *John is a Quaker and has a good sense of humor; Ellen is a Quaker and has a good sense of humor. So, probably, all Quakers have a good sense of humor.* The word "probably" indicates that the argument's claim is inductive. Again, we are not assessing it for its validity or soundness, just whether it is claiming certainty or probability.

When it comes time to assess an argument for its soundness, the assessment will depend on whether the argument is deductive, in which case it must prove its conclusion with certainty, or inductive, in which case it has only to prove its conclusion with probability. In the latter case, the challenge is that people may disagree on whether something is probable. Many people believe, for example, that the universe is so well designed that an intelligent being probably designed it. Critics of this argument point out, for example, that all that has evolved could be a function of a non-intelligent cause.

FALLACIES

A fallacy is a bad argument. It can be bad formally, because of the way it is put together, or informally, because of its language. There are three sorts of deductive fallacies: inconsistency, *petitio principii* (Latin for "assuming the initial point") or circular argument, and *non sequitur* (Latin for "it does not follow"). There also are three sorts of inductive fallacies: hasty induction, slothful induction, and forgetful induction. Since we are about to assess several arguments for and against humor in religion, it will be helpful to have a list of possible fallacies at the ready. Let's take a closer look at the deductive and inductive fallacies.

Deductive Fallacies

Fallacies of Inconsistency

An argument commits a fallacy of inconsistency when it is impossible for all its premises to be true at the same time. For example, *I am an uncompromising pacifist. Joe is a war monger. The only way I know how to deal with war mongers is to beat them senseless. Thus, I was justified in beating Joe.* The first and third premises cannot be true at the same time.

Petitio Principii—Circular Argument

A *petitio principii* fallacy or circular argument assumes in the premise what it is trying to prove in the conclusion. One way this happens is when the argument begs the question. A common example: *God exists, because the Bible says so, and the Bible is the word of God.* This answers the question "How do you know God exists?" with the answer, in effect, "Because God exists (or else he would not have been able to write the Bible)!"

Another way to commit a *petitio principii* is by using a complex question as one of the premises. A complex question is formed in such a way that it does not permit all possible answers. For example, *are you still insulting Evangelicals? Whether you answer yes or no, it is obvious that you can be intolerant.* The answer might be "I've never insulted Evangelicals," but the form of the question doesn't permit this answer.

Non-Sequitur Fallacies

In a *non sequitur* fallacy, the third kind of deductive fallacy, the conclusion does not follow logically from the premises, even if the argument has an emotional appeal. There are three basic sorts of *non sequitur*: pure/formal fallacies, fallacies of ambiguity, and fallacies of irrelevance.

A *pure or formal non sequitur* has a fallacious structure. We have already encountered such a fallacy: *If John is a Benedictine monk, then John rarely laughs. And John rarely laughs. Therefore, John is a Benedictine monk.* This argument begins with a hypothetical or conditional sentence—an "If . . . then . . ." sentence. The "if" or first part is called the antecedent, because it comes first. The "then" or second part is called the consequent because it follows the antecedent. In this example, "John is a Benedictine monk" is the antecedent and "John rarely laughs" is the consequent. The second premise affirms the consequent. And the conclusion affirms the antecedent. Any argument that begins with a hypothetical sentence, affirms the consequent in the second premise, and affirms the antecedent in the conclusion is invalid, regardless of what the words say. You can see this by swapping "John is a Benedictine monk" and "John rarely laughs," with "Jack is a tenor" and "Jack is a singer." Or "Peter is Pope" and "Peter is Catholic," or any other sentences you choose. If the first premise is a hypothetical sentence, the second premise affirms the consequent, and the conclusion affirms the antecedent, then the argument commits the fallacy of affirming the consequent, a sort of pure/formal non sequitur fallacy.

There are many other types of pure/formal fallacy, but the example should suffice for our purposes.

Incidentally, the fallacy of affirming the consequent has a valid counterpart, *modus ponens* (Latin for "method of affirming"), in which the second premise affirms the antecedent (not the consequent). For example, *If John is a Benedictine monk, then John rarely laughs. And John is a Benedictine monk. Therefore, John rarely laughs.* If the premises are true, then the conclusion must be true. Of course, if John is not a Benedictine monk, then the second premise is false and the argument is unsound. But it remains formally valid, because *if* the premises were true, the conclusion would have to be true, regardless of John's actual situation and regardless of what the antecedent and consequent are.

A *fallacy of ambiguity* is a second form of *non sequitur* fallacy. It occurs when something in the language of the argument is ambiguous. For example, *Bill has a master's in English and a master's in philosophy. But Jesus said no person can have two masters. So, Bill should earn a third.* Clearly this argument uses the word "masters" ambiguously. There are many types of fallacy of ambiguity, but the list is beyond the scope of our present study.

In a *fallacy of irrelevance*, the premises are logically irrelevant to the conclusion. There are many types of such a fallacy; here are two: (1) *Kyle says God exists, but I don't believe him because he looks weird and smells funny.* This is an *argumentum ad hominem*, or argument against the person. One commits this fallacy when trying to refute an argument by attacking the arguer rather than the arguer's logic. (2) *Jesus never laughed, because I've never seen proof that he did laugh.* This is an *argumentum ad ignorantiam*, or appeal to ignorance. One commits this fallacy when arguing that because one does not know something it must not be true, or because one has not experienced something it must not exist. All such information proves is the arguer's lack of knowledge or experience.

Inductive Fallacies

Hasty Induction

Turning to the three inductive fallacies, the first, *hasty induction*, occurs when one draws a conclusion based on insufficient evidence. For example, *there are funny passages in the Bible. Therefore, the Bible must be a comedy.* Even tragedies may have funny moments. So, the mere presence of a funny passage or two does not render the work a comedy.

Forgetful Induction

Forgetful induction occurs when one draws a conclusion from a set of premises that is missing an important premise of which the arguer is—or should be—aware. For example, *I've read the Psalms many times. Several are somber. Therefore, there is no humor in the Psalms.* The arguer has forgotten the many celebratory Psalms.

Slothful Induction

Finally, *slothful induction* occurs when one fails to draw a conclusion despite sufficient evidence to prove it. For example, *although scholars have pointed out many humorous passages in the Bible, I don't believe the Bible is meant to be humorous at all.* This argument fails to acknowledge the strong evidence to the contrary.

THREE QUESTIONS

This chapter has presented a quick look at logic in order to prepare us for careful evaluation of some arguments to follow. We may sum up this chapter by drawing three questions from it, which we will ask when encountering arguments from here on. First, what is the conclusion? Second, what are the premises (there may be only one)? Third, do the premises support the conclusion?

This third question raises several possible additional questions. If the premises are true, must the conclusion be (probably or certainly) true? If so, then the argument is valid; if not, then the argument is invalid. If the argument is valid, are all the premises true? If so, then the argument is sound; if not, then the argument is unsound. If the argument is deductive, does it commit a fallacy of inconsistency? *Petitio principii*? *Non sequitur*? If so, then the argument is a bad one. If the argument is inductive, does it commit a fallacy of hasty induction? Forgetful induction? Slothful induction? If so, then the argument is a bad one.

A comprehensive study of logic is beyond the purposes of this book, but we may find the foregoing useful in our critical encounters with the arguments that follow.

5

Arguments for Humor in Christianity

> The Bible is a record of God's historical relationship with God's people [and] people are funny.
>
> —MARK E. BIDDLE, *A TIME TO LAUGH*

SO FAR, WE HAVE discussed what it might mean to talk about humor in a religious context and we have gotten a taste of several arguments for and against the proposition that there is humor in religion. We have also paused to describe several factors that go into the analysis and evaluation of arguments. We turn now to arguments for humor in Christianity, including arguments for the value of such humor, the presence of such humor, and the appropriateness of a theology of laughter. In the next chapter we will consider parallel arguments against humor in Christianity, including a theology of tears.

ARGUMENTS FOR THE VALUE OF HUMOR IN CHRISTIANITY

This section considers some arguments for the religious value of humor as a means to some other end and as an end in itself.

Arguments for Humor in Christianity

Humor as Valuable to Some Other End

In chapter 2 we considered the value of humor as a means to the truth. In this section we consider the value of humor as a means to five other ends. We do so within this logical framework:

1. X is valuable
2. Humor is a means to X.
3. *Therefore, humor is valuable.*

Assuming that X is not ambiguous, an argument of this form is valid: if the premises are true, then the conclusion must be true. And if both premises are true, then the argument is sound as well.

Five ends toward which humor might be valuable and with which we might replace X are identity, relief, spiritual maturity, building community, and redemption/connection to God. Let's take a closer look at each of these.

Conrad Hyers notes that humor enhances our sense of *identity* in at least three ways.[1] First, humor distinguishes us from other animals.[2] Second, humor is a means to self-discovery; and third, humor is a means to self-recognition.

Pet owners and other animal lovers might challenge Hyers's claim that humor distinguishes us from other animals. While they may not have a recognizable laugh, many seem capable of play and delight, which would suggest humor in some sense. Nevertheless, it is reasonable to suggest that humor enhances or can enhance our identity, for the second and third reasons that Hyers posits.

Thus, assuming enhancing our sense of identity is valuable, this argument is sound:

1. Enhancing our sense of identity is valuable.
2. Humor is a means to enhancing our sense of identity
3. *Therefore, humor is valuable.*

It is obvious that *relief* is desirable, all else being equal. Hyers notes that humor brings relief by helping us manage tension. African American studies professor Israel Durham agrees, noting that humor helped Richard

---

[1]. Hyers, *And God Created Laughter*, ch. 1.
[2]. See also Yancey, "From Carnival to Mardi Gras," 64.

Part II: A Theology of Laughter

Pryor cope with bad experiences.[3] Greg Jones, former dean at Duke University Divinity School, holds that, spiritually, humor restores a sense of grace toward others and ourselves.[4] Pointing to the laughter of Sarah, Kuschel notes the "joyful, liberating laughter of God with the doubters and the skeptics."[5]

Assuming that *spiritual maturity* is valuable, does humor contribute to it? This is two questions in one: Is humor necessary to spiritual maturity? If not necessary, can humor enhance spiritual maturity nonetheless? Psychologist Susan McFadden argues that humor is a necessary condition for spiritual maturity, although it is not sufficient, since humor can be the expression of immaturity as well.[6]

Describing Martin Luther's humor, theologian Eric Gritsch notes ways humor contributed to Luther's spiritual development. Most notably humor enhanced his witness by helping him ridicule power and mock death and the devil.[7] Concerning Luther, theologian Elizabeth Palmer adds that "Martin Luther did believe in a God who is powerful enough to sport with us. But Luther's God was also mighty enough to laugh at the power of death and the gates of hell."[8]

Theologian Philip Anderson argues that spiritual healing comes through grace and that humor can provide that grace through the laughter it provokes: "It is laughter, the rich belly laugh, that has in it the same process and the same elements that I believe are present in experiences of grace. We laugh at some incongruity and we are momentarily healed. We unexpectedly experience grace and some ultimate incongruity is resolved."[9]

By "grace," Anderson means experiences that "increase a person's love of self, neighbor, world, and God, enabling that person to become more of a center of freedom and love. . . . These grace-filled moments are often marked by forgiveness, acceptance, reconciliation, justification. The estrangement, the incongruity is overcome, at least for now. We are healed."[10]

---

3. Durham, "Richard Pryor," 132–44.
4. Jones, "Punch Lines," 33.
5. Kuschel, *Laughter*, 64.
6. McFadden, "Authentic Humor," 131–42.
7. Gritsch, "Martin Luther's Humor," 132–40.
8. Palmer, "God's Laughter," 154.
9. Anderson, "Humor as Healing and Grace," 1.
10. Ibid.

Arguments for Humor in Christianity

To the extent that *building community* is valuable, humor may well contribute to that building. As with the other elements we have discussed, it remains arguable whether humor is necessary to community building, but it is uncontroversial that humor *can* contribute to such building.

Theologians Dorothee Sölle and Fulbert Steffensky claim that "it can be shown that in all sects the mood of joy and unity prevails over guilt and fear."[11] Presumably this contributes to the voluntary association and deliberate adherence of the community members. It also contributes to reconciliation where there has been division.

Pastoral theologian Michael Koppel assumes that creative play is part of God's nature and that play "is a means of cooperative and collaborative engagement within self and between self and others that seeks to heighten enjoyment of life experience by making space for the innovative within structured patterns of behavior."[12]

Many scholars regard humor in the right context to be *redemptive*. Pastoral theologian Brad Binau makes this clear in the title of his essay, "Humor Reconsidered: The Cultivation of 'Accurate Perception' as a Contribution to the Care of Soul."[13]

In his preface to *The Screwtape Letters* C. S. Lewis declares that hell is serious and humor is an antidote to that seriousness:

> Humor involves a sense of proportion and a power of seeing yourself from the outside. Whatever else we attribute to beings who sinned through pride, we must not attribute this. . . . We must picture Hell as a state where everyone is perpetually concerned about his own dignity and advancement, where everyone has a grievance, and where everyone lives the deadly serious passions of envy, self-importance, and resentment.[14]

Conrad Hyers repeats a sentiment we have already encountered: if we must be like children to get into the kingdom of heaven, we must engage in play, laughter, and wonder. Without humor such engagement is impossible.[15]

Theologian Howard Macy, agreeing with Lewis, holds that humor can deepen our integrity:

---

11. Sölle and Steffensky, "Christianity and Joy," 118.
12. Koppel, "Pastoral Theological Reflection," 1.
13. Binau, "Humor Reconsidered," 667–80.
14. Lewis, *Screwtape Letters*, ix.
15. Hyers, *And God Created Laughter*, 18.

Part II: A Theology of Laughter

> Laughter can help us avoid pretending to be someone we're not or letting others cast us in roles that don't fit. We can take off masks and become more transparent. Sometimes being honest with ourselves can be difficult, but a loving sense of humor can keep it from being brutal.[16]

So far, the argument for the religious value of humor as a means has included a means to identity, relief, spiritual maturity, building community, and redemption. Finally, and connected to this last one, we consider humor as a means to connection with God.

Humor connects us to God, says Hyers, by fulfilling God's wish that we walk humbly with him. "Humility," Hyers notes, has the same root as "humor."[17] Recall, too, Hyers's claim that faith without humor is fanaticism.[18] Greg Jones adds, "Laughter provides perspective and humility, reminding us that even with the best strategic planning and most effective consensus building efforts, we are not in control."[19]

Theatre professor David Charles makes a good case for the position that humor combines the sacred and the profane.[20] In this vein, Stephen Dray, editor of the Christian journal *Evangel*, regards theology as the "bridge between what God says and who he wants to say it to."[21] Humor enhances this theology in ways similar to David Charles' description.

Eric Gritsch notes Luther's position that humor helps humans navigate between the two advents. According to Gritsch, "Martin Luther (1483–1546) is the only 'church father' who incorporated humor into his life and work. He did so by posing as a court jester (an advertised self-image), a quick wit, a facetious wag, and a sit-down comedian with humorous comments in more than five thousand 'table talks.'"[22]

Finally, theologian John Morreall claims that life in relationship with God energizes and empowers us. For him, there is no other way to account for the relationships between the most prominent biblical figures and Mohammed, on the one hand, and God, on the other. Thus, far from the

---

16. Macy, "Laughter on the Journey," 143.
17. Hyers, *And God Created Laughter*, 18.
18. Ibid., 27.
19. Jones, "Punch Lines," 33.
20. Charles, "Power of the Carnival Satirist," 11–28.
21. Dray, "Good Theology," 1–2.
22. Gritsch, "Martin Luther's Humor," 132.

boring religion that many portray, the religion of Judaism, Christianity, and Islam is exciting and joyful.[23]

Before looking at humor as valuable in itself, recall that humor can be a means to undesirable ends as well. For example, religion scholar Vicki Kabat tells of a minister who crossed the line between pastoral humor and sexual harassment.[24] As Kabat tells it, "A mother made a comment about a necklace her daughter had received that she was wearing that day. And the pastor joked, 'I'd like to hang around your daughter's neck like that.' The mother and daughter laughed nervously and changed the topic. No big deal? A little joke? No. Sexual harassment."[25]

Humor as Valuable in Itself

So far we have been considering arguments about the religious value of humor as means toward certain ends. Another way humor might be religiously valuable is as an end in itself. And there are arguments to that effect. The general structure of such arguments is this:

1. X is valuable.

2. Humor is X.

3. *Therefore, Humor is valuable.*

Assuming that X is not ambiguous, this argument is valid: if the premises are true, then the conclusion must be true. Whether it is sound or not depends on what X is and whether it is true that X is valuable, and humor is X. Let's consider four candidates for X:

- Part of God's nature
- A reward from God
- Play
- Delight

We can agree in faith that *God's nature* is valuable in itself, so parts of his nature must be valuable as well. Thus, if humor is part of God's nature, then this humor must be valuable in itself.

23. Morreall, "Is This Place Stuffy," 178–85.
24. Kabat, "Nothing to Joke About," 56.
25. Ibid.

Part II: A Theology of Laughter

Episcopal bishop Eugene Taylor Sutton takes for granted that humor resides in God's nature.[26] Thus, humor belongs in sermons. As evidence, Sutton cites Psalm 2:4a: God sits in the heavens and laughs.

Kuschel, as we've seen, adds God's laughter at the wicked (Ps 37); God's derisive laughter at nations (Ps 59); and God's creation of the world for sport (Ps 104).[27] We can see here a sub-argument of sorts:

1. God laughs.
2. What God does is always good.
3. *Therefore, laughter is good.*

This argument is valid: if the premises are true, then the conclusion must be true. Whether the premises are true, and the argument thus sound, is a conversation for another time.

An argument elegant in its simplicity is that humor is a *reward from God*. On this point Kuschel cites Job 5:17, 22: "Blessed is the one whom God corrects; so do not despise the discipline of the Almighty. . . . You will laugh at destruction and famine, and need not fear the wild animals" (NIV).

Kuschel also cites Ps 126:1–2a: "When the Lord restored the fortunes of Zion, we were like those who dreamed. Our mouths were filled with laughter" (NIV).

Theologian David Steere cites John 16:22: "So with you: Now is your time of grief, but I will see you again and you will rejoice, and no one will take away your joy" (NIV).[28]

To those who accept the idea of humor in religion, the foregoing may enhance the conviction that humor can be a reward from God. But we ought not to accept this uncritically as a deductive proof, since one may dispute the veracity or meaning of the scriptural passages just cited.

We have mentioned *play* several times, especially as an indication of humor and a means to connect with God. Some scholars regard play also as religiously beneficial in itself. Hyers, for example, considers the cosmos to be God at play; thus, says Hyers, "the highest order of existence is play for its own sake."[29] Earlier we found Michael Koppel claiming that creative

---

26. Sutton, "Humor for Preachers," 9.
27. Kuschel, *Laughter*, 57. Also see Hyers, *And God Created Laughter*, 20.
28. Steere, "Our Capacity for Sadness and Joy," 15.
29. Hyers, *And God Created Laughter*, 22.

play is part of God's nature.³⁰ Finally, theologian Herbert Delaney argues for play as an end in itself both for God and God's people.³¹

If these similar claims are correct, then we have yet another compelling argument for the value of humor in religion. But to a skeptic this account of play might be debatable. Humorous ends in themselves, if real, support the argument that humor is religiously valuable. We have looked at three ends that imply humor: parts of God's nature; a reward from God; and play. We close this section with a brief look at delight.

Hyers imagines that Adam and Eve laughed in *delight* at first beholding each other, much as other humans might as they face the possibility or reality of a romantic relationship with each other.³²

Herbert Delaney posits that delight is a necessary ingredient in play, along with peace, freedom, and illusion. Thus, if play is valuable as an end in itself, delight must be as well.³³

ARGUMENTS FOR THE PRESENCE OF HUMOR IN CHRISTIANITY

We have identified two general sorts of arguments for humor in religion. One argues for the *value* of humor in religion. We covered that in the previous section. The other claims the *presence* of humor in religion. That's the subject of this section.

Schematically we have in mind an argument of this form:

1. If X, then humor is present in Christianity

2. X.

3. *Therefore, humor is present in Christianity.*

Here X represents either of two general sorts of arguments. The first is an inductive argument, since it claims probability and is based on observations. The second is a deductive argument and rests on an *a priori* claim, since it does not depend on sense experience. Let's take a look at each sort.

---

30. Koppel, "Pastoral Theological Reflection," 1–12.
31. Delaney, "Immortal Diamond," 143–59.
32. Hyers, *And God Created Laughter*, 11.
33. Delaney, "Immortal Diamond," 144.

Part II: A Theology of Laughter

Inductive Arguments for the Presence of Humor

There are several ways to argue inductively. Consider three: directly, indirectly, and by appeal to authority (a particular sort of indirect appeal).

One approach to looking for *direct* evidence of humor in religion is to look for key terms in the Bible, the fundamental authority of Judaism and Christianity. It turns out that evidence of this sort is scant. The word "humor" appears once in the NRSV (in Greek Esther 1:10) and not at all in the KJV. The word "comic" does not appear in either the NRSV or the KJV. "Laugh," laughs," and "laughter" appear a total of thirty-four times in the NRSV and twenty-four times in the KJV. Thus, to conclude from these data that humor has a presence, at least a significant one, in religion, would be to commit the fallacy of hasty induction.

Another effort at demonstrating the presence of humor in religion is an effort we have encountered more than once in this book: to demonstrate the ubiquitous and inscrutable laughter of God. Many scholars make this approach central to their argument. Recall, for example, Kuschel's appeal to the Psalms, including Psalm 2, in which God laughs at the rulers, and Psalm 37, in which God laughs at the wicked.

Generally speaking there are no more references to a laughing God than there are uses of the related words that we checked in the concordance. On the other hand, to deny that the God of the Jews and the Christians laughs is to dismiss some significant passages in the Bible and thus, perhaps, to commit the fallacy of slothful induction.

What's more, we shall see that many elements of the biblical narrative lend themselves to humorous readings or interpretations. Thus, Marcian Strange feels confident that the "instances of humor in the Bible are frequent enough to be deliberate on the part of the writers."[34] Theologian Jon Morreall adds that "if the Puritans had read their Bibles carefully . . . they would have found no ban on celebration."[35]

An *indirect approach* to finding evidence of humor in religion may be more effective than a direct approach, especially in the Bible, given the few explicit references to laughter, humor, and the like. A more promising inductive approach would be to find examples that are best interpreted as humorous. While this often requires taking the narrative at more than face value, it may also provide many more examples than the concordance does.

---

34. Strange, "God and Laughter," 2.
35. Morreall, "Is This Place Stuffy," 181.

Arguments for Humor in Christianity

Trueblood lists thirty examples of what he takes to be humorous passages in the Synoptic Gospels.[36] The list is too long to recite here, but one may want to read Trueblood's book to see whether all, or any, of those are humorous.

Hyers, attempting to set the entire Bible within "comic parentheses", also offers many examples.[37] Perhaps the most obvious is the book of Jonah. It is not a stretch to regard the whole story as satirical.

In subsequent sections we will take a closer look at many of these examples. For now, suffice it to note that one approach to arguing for the presence of humor in Christianity is to posit the presence of humor in the Bible, even where the narrative does not present the humor explicitly.

Our final example, for now, of an effort to prove inductively the presence of humor in religion is an *appeal to authority*. The many citations in this book suggest that effort. But this can be logically risky, since anyone making such an appeal must be ready to defend the authority as relevant and trustworthy. An appeal to unsuitable authority is the non sequitur fallacy of *argumentum ad verecundiam*. This fallacy appears, for example, in advertising that relies on the appeal of a celebrity to sell a product about which the celebrity may know nothing.

Our study has offered and will continue to offer many candidates for suitable authority on the matter of humor in religion. A thorough bibliographic search reveals at least seven hundred entries on the topic. But the sheer number of authorities might be irrelevant, if one can show that arguments to the contrary are stronger. We will consider several counterarguments in chapter 6.

Deductive Arguments for the Presence of Humor in Religion

We have already looked at views that constitute deductive efforts at proving the presence of humor in religion. But until now we were not focusing on the deductive nature of those positions. Recall that deductive arguments claim that if one accepts the premises, one must accept the truth of the conclusion as certain. Let's look at arguments in this vein.

One is our initial argument that Christianity calls its adherents to joy and that joy is impossible without a sense of humor. Thus, humor is essential to authentic Christian practice. For example,

36. Trueblood, *Humor of Christ*, 127.
37. Hyers, *And God Created Laughter*, ch. 2.

Part II: A Theology of Laughter

1. Philippians 4:4 says, "Rejoice in the Lord always; again I will say rejoice."
2. Rejoicing is impossible without humor.
3. *Therefore, the Bible requires humor.*

Another deductive argument begins with Hyers's claim that the Gospels are "joyful tidings" and the Gospels are the bedrock of Christian teaching. Thus, humor, which is essential to joy, must be part of that bedrock.

Then there is Hyers's argument invoking the Imago Dei:[38]

1. Our likeness to God separates us from other animals.
2. Man is the laughing animal.
3. So, our likeness to God is in our laughing.
4. Laughing entails humor.
5. Therefore, humor is essential to our relationship with God.

These arguments are valid, since if the premises are true, the conclusion must be true. But one might take issue with one or more of the premises: perhaps rejoicing is possible without humor or perhaps the humans' ability to laugh does not mark their likeness to God. But given how reasonable these sound, the ball is in the opponent's court.

A THEOLOGY OF LAUGHTER

We have considered arguments for the value and presence of humor in religion. We have also been holding forth in the spirit of a theological study. But the question remains whether a *theology* of laughter makes sense. In chapter 6 we will consider views to the contrary. Let's finish this chapter by looking at a few views championing a theology of laughter, taking our cue from Kuschel.

Each view expresses a version of a generic argument of the following sort:

1. If a theology of laughter is appropriate regarding Christianity, then there is humor in religion.
2. A theology of laughter is appropriate regarding Christianity.

---

38. Hyers, *And God Created Laughter*, 16.

Arguments for Humor in Christianity

3. *Therefore, there is humor in religion.*

We will focus on five views that embrace this argument in one way or another:

- Kuschel's Theology of Laughter
- Berger's Theology of the Comic
- Metz & Jossua's Theology of Joy
- Thoennes's Theology of Humor
- Biddle's Theology of Irony

Kuschel's Theology of Laughter

Kuschel's starting point is a description of Roman Catholicism's "Wintry season" at the time of his book's publication—1994. Kuschel notes two common responses to this condition—either perseverance with no sense of humor or bidding farewell with mocking laughter. Kuschel offers a third possibility: response with laughter in Christ's spirit of joy in both God and humans. Such laughter, he claims, is an "expression of unquenchable hope" and "a therapy for amnesia of the heart: amnesia about all that is joyful in the Christian message."[39] To be sure, notes Kuschel, there are many types of laughter, not all of which reflect the good news. For example:[40]

- Joyful, comfortable, playful, contented
- Mocking, malicious, desperate, or cynical
- Laughter for sheer pleasure in life
- Laughter for sheer bitterness in life
- Affirmative, enthusiastic laughter
- Proud laughter
- Infectious laughter
- Sick laughter

---

39. Kuschel, *Laughter*, xi.
40. Ibid., xi.

Thus, Kuschel concludes, "Laughter embraces the whole spectrum of life and morality."[41]

So what would a theology of laughter look like? First, Kuschel notes the ubiquity of laughter in churches and about churches. But this, he maintains, is not the same as a theology of laughter. A theology of laughter would exhibit the following five traits:

- "A deeper level than comic phenomena"
- Giving laughter "a right to a place in the realm of God"
- "Deriv[ing] its legitimation from the 'laughter of God' about the state of his creation"
- Investigat[ing] in what spirit God laughs
- Recognizing two sides to this sort of laughter: laughter *of* Christians and laughter *at* Christians[42]

Kuschel notes the objection that laughter can, in effect, be anti-theological, especially laughter that is malicious, mocking, or cynical, but he proceeds confidently keeping this proviso in mind.

Berger's Theology of the Comic

Where Kuschel proposes a theology of laughter, Peter Berger proposes a theology of the comic.[43] For Berger this rests on the folly of redemption and the comic as a signal of transcendence. Concerning the folly of redemption, Berger claims that "folly results in the intersection between absolute and contingent reality, between the world beyond and this world."[44] In this light, Berger notes several biblical references to holy fools. For example, in the Old Testament there is David's fear of the ark (2 Sam 6); Isaiah stripped and barefoot (Isa 20); God's telling Jeremiah to "make a yoke out of straps and crossbars and put it on your neck" (Jer 27:2 NIV); and Ezekiel's lying on his side for 390 days and taking the sins of the people (Ezek 4). In the New Testament there is Jesus on the donkey (Matt 21); Pilate's impotence and the mocking of Christ (Matt 27); and Paul's confession as a fool (1 Cor 4).

---

41. Ibid., xvii.
42. Ibid., xix.
43. Berger, *Redeeming Laughter*, part 3.
44. Ibid., 197.

In addition to the folly of redemption, the second pillar of Berger's theology of the comic is the comic as a signal of transcendence.[45] This involves certain types of incongruity. First, there is incongruity between being a body and having a body (and presumably being a spirit within that body). Second, there is incongruity in being between nothing and the infinite. Third, there is the incongruity of living in the world of sense and the world of faith, which in Christianity is more real.

Every instance of the comic, says Berger, is an escape from reality, although we are left to wonder which reality.

Berger concludes that "signals of transcendence are glimpses of Him who is playing the cosmic game of hide and seek with us."[46]

Metz and Jossua's Theology of Joy

Kuschel proposes a theology of laughter; Berger proposes a theology of the comic; and Johann Metz and Jean-Pierre Jossua propose a theology of joy.[47] Metz and Jossua are moved by their belief that "our lives [are] falling more and more under the control of an apathetic, that is, an unfeeling rationality."[48] As an antidote, they propose "joy against mourning," "cheerfulness as opposed to melancholy," and humor.[49]

To this end, they have edited a collection of essays divided into three parts: perspectives, principles, and concrete examples. We have included and will include references to several essays from this book. The perspectives include both joyful and melancholy. Principles include the proper means of predicating joy and sorrow of God, and humor as a theological virtue. Concrete examples include the humor of John XXIII, and humor and ecclesiastical ministry.

---

45. Ibid., 205.
46. Ibid., 214.
47. Metz and Jossua, *Theology of Joy*.
48. Ibid., 8.
49. Ibid.

Part II: A Theology of Laughter

Thoennes's Theology of Humor

Erik Thoennes believes that a theology of humor is worthwhile if not obligatory for Christians. He rests this claim on five premises.[50] First, "humor is a unique, God-given, universal, human experience." Second, "humor is a vital part of most meaningful, healthy human relationships." Third, "humor goes bad quickly" when it becomes a worldly pleasure that draws us away from God." Fourth, "Christian maturity means developing a godly sense of humor." And, fifth, ministers "must be able to lead people in godly laughter."

Biddle's Theology of Irony

For Biddle, "irony represents the most theological form of humor because it calls for one to look deeply into the obvious for signs of a somewhat veiled but more fundamental truth."[51]

According to Biddle, irony has three basic characteristics: two layers of reality; "it hinges on incongruity between the layers"; and "it depends on someone being unaware of the layers (and by implication someone else recognizing it)."[52] Biddle offers David as an example of the heroic anti-hero: always on the make and almost always receiving favor from God in spite of David's many shortcomings. Indeed, Biddle claims, "the Vacation Bible School David is a cartoon character with little resemblance to the Biblical David."[53]

Theologically, Biddle would have us be constantly vigilant for the many instances of irony in the Bible and through the Christian narrative, recognizing how easy it is to miss that irony and its attendant humor, and thus miss the meaning of the passage or narrative.

This ends our look at arguments for humor in religion. In the next chapter we will consider arguments against humor in religion, including against the religious value of humor, against the presence of humor in religion, and for a theology of tears.

---

50. Thoennes, "Laughing through Tears," 72–83.
51. Biddle, *Time to Laugh*, 53.
52. Ibid., 33.
53. Ibid.

6

Arguments against Humor in Christianity

> A veil of melancholy covers the whole of nature, not to be lifted until Christ returns.
>
> —Friedrich Schelling

So far we have taken an inventory of humorous concepts in religion generally and Christianity in particular. We have also considered arguments for the value and presence of humor in religion. Soon we will focus on the Bible, looking for both direct and indirect evidence to support and explain the proposition that humor plays an important role in Christianity. Before we do, however, let us give opponents their day in court. We will do this in three parts: arguments against the value of humor in Christianity, arguments against the presence of humor in Christianity, and arguments for a theology of tears.

Part II: A Theology of Laughter

ARGUMENTS AGAINST THE VALUE OF HUMOR IN CHRISTIANITY

John Morreall notes that "many people conclude from their experiences that religion is *supposed to be* boring," so proponents of humor in religion may face some tough audiences.[1]

Remember that if humor is of value to Christianity, it may be as a means to some other end or as an end in itself. Thus, among the opponents, we should look for two sorts of arguments against the value of humor to Christianity: arguments against the value of humor for achieving Christian ends and arguments against the Christian value of humor as an end in itself.

Arguments against the Value of Humor as a Means

One way to schematize arguments against the value of humor for achieving Christian ends is this:

1. X is necessary to achieve Christian ends.

2. Humor is contrary to X.

3. *Therefore, humor is not valuable as a means to Christian ends.*

We can think of X in positive terms, that is, what we should pursue, or in negative terms—what we should avoid.

Among the ends we should pursue are obedience to God's law and religious authority, faithfulness, vigilance against evil and sinful distractions, and concern for the tragic human condition. Contrary to these ends, some might argue, joy can be rebellious or subversive; and laughter can express lack of faith, worldliness, sinfulness, or a religious deprecation of this world and of the human condition. For some, these might be enough to win the argument against the value of humor in religion.

Among the ends we should avoid are idle talk, trivial gossip, idleness, drunkenness, lust, and foolishness. Humor and laughter often achieve these ends or are symptomatic of them. Proverbs 14:13 says, "Even in laughter the heart is sad, and the end of joy is grief."

Ecclesiastes 7:4 warns, "The heart of the wise is in the house of mourning; but the heart of fools is in the house of mirth." Sirach 21:15 and 20, reads, "When an intelligent person hears a wise saying, he praises it and

---

1. Morreall "Is This Place Stuffy," 178.

adds to it; when a fool hears it, he laughs at it and throws it behind his back. ... A fool raises his voice when he laughs, but the wise smile quietly."

Given these ends, some might conclude that humor is of no use and may be harmful to achieving Christian ends.

Arguments against the Value of Humor in Itself

One way to schematize arguments against the Christian value of humor as an end in itself is this:

1. No ends valuable to religion contain humor as a constituent part.
2. Therefore, all religious ends are non-humorous ends.

We have already considered such ends, which may be gathered together under the general heading of seriousness. But as we have seen a few times already, seriousness and joy are not contradictories, and since joy without humor is unimaginable, humor must not contradict seriousness either. In this case, we can regard the premise as false, or at least as unproven. Thus, even if the argument were valid, it would be unsound.

ARGUMENTS AGAINST THE PRESENCE OF HUMOR IN CHRISTIANITY

If Friedrich Schelling's observation noted in the epigraph at the beginning of this chapter is correct, then maybe humor has no place in Christianity.

We can divide arguments against the presence of humor in Christianity into two broad sorts: arguments that humor simply is not there and arguments that it may be there but we do not or cannot see it. Let's look at each in turn.

Arguments That Humor Is Not Present At All in Christianity

Arguments that humor is not present have a form like the following.

1. If humor is present in Christianity, then X.
2. It is not the case that X.
3. *Therefore, humor is not present in Christianity.*

Part II: A Theology of Laughter

Here X represents either of two general sorts of arguments, similar to the arguments for the presence of humor in religion. The first is an inductive argument, which, recall, claims probability and is based on observations. The second is a deductive argument and often rests on *a priori* claims, that is, claims that do not require sense experience.

Inductive Arguments

We have seen that there are at least three ways to argue inductively: directly, indirectly, and by appeal to authority (a particular sort of indirect appeal). The *direct* inductive approach can take at least two paths. One denies that there is direct evidence in favor of humor in Christianity; the other affirms that there is evidence against such humor. Here is the first:

1. If there were humor in Christianity, there would be direct evidence to that effect.
2. There is little or no evidence to that effect.
3. *Therefore, humor is not present in Christianity.*

Here is the other:

1. If there were humor in Christianity, there would not be so much evidence to the contrary.
2. There is so much evidence to the contrary.
3. *Therefore, there is little or no humor in Christianity.*

According to some scholars, there is no evidence to support humor in Christianity. Recall the scant number of references to humorous elements in the concordance. Old Testament scholar R. P. Carroll argues that "the concept of a humorous biblical prophet is an oxymoron [and] humor as we know it today is not a feature of the Bible."[2] Peter Berger claims that "anyone surfing through the Bible (Old and New Testament alike) or the history of Christian theology in search of the comic is bound to be disappointed."[3] Most notably, perhaps, there is little direct reference to Jesus being humorous or laughing.[4] Remarking on this, several medieval church leaders,

---

2. Carroll, "Is Humor Also among the Prophets?," 169.
3. Berger, *Redeeming Laughter*, 197.
4. Ibid. Also see Martin, *Between Heaven and Mirth*, 32.

Arguments against Humor in Christianity

including for example John Chrysostom, Augustine, Bernard of Clairvaux, and Hugo of St. Victor, declared that Christ never laughed.[5] Also, as Trueblood notes, Paul's letters appear to depict him as avoiding or lacking humor.[6]

Of course the humor might be there and we just don't see it. Thus, Berger declares: "By and large, one can fairly say that the search for comic laughter in the biblical literature succeeds only if one engages in rather labored interpretations."[7]

On this last point some scholars suggest that not only is there a lack of direct affirmative evidence but there is plenty of direct negative evidence. One need not look farther than the Scriptures. Consider the many lament Psalms. Or the book of Lamentations. Or Jesus's Sermon on the Plain. Or Paul's warning in Eph 5:4: "Entirely out of place is obscene, silly, and vulgar talk; but instead, let there be thanksgiving."

The *indirect* approach to arguing against humor in Christianity takes two paths similar to the direct approach. Thus,

1. Any *indirect evidence* that supports the claim that humor is significantly present in Christianity would have to be determined by interpretation.

2. There is no strong support for such an interpretation.

3. *Therefore, humor probably is not significantly present in Christianity.*

And there is a lot of indirect evidence against the claim that humor is significantly present in Christianity.

There have been several attempts to explain this. James Martin notes, for example, that the early evangelists had to explain the passion, which was darkly serious; the heavy Greek influence on the gospel writers emphasized virtue and accomplishment over anything humorous; and the early church in its effort to combat heresy might have expunged humorous elements from the Bible.[8] Kuschel and Capps note a historical mistrust of the comic in religion, captured in Jerome's claim that "as long as we are in a vale of tears we may not laugh, but must weep."[9] An interesting side note: while Kuschel and Capps emphasize the medieval focus on seriousness, Joseph

---

5. Kuschel, *Laughter*, 43.
6. Trueblood, *Humor of Christ*, 19.
7. Berger, *Redeeming Laughter*, 198.
8. Martin, *Between Heaven and Mirth*, 33, 34, 44, 50.
9. Kuschel, *Laughter*, 45; Capps, "Religion and Humor," 426.

Part II: A Theology of Laughter

Bastien suggests that "absence of humor and satire in Christianity began after the Protestant Reformation."[10]

The *appeal to authority* on this matter is simple.

1. Many relevant and trustworthy authorities deny the presence of humor in Christianity.
2. Therefore, probably, there is little or no humor in Christianity.

James Martin lists three authorities in particular as useful examples:[11]

- St. Clement of Alexandria: avoid "humorous and unbecoming words."
- St. Ambrose: "joking should be avoided even in small talk."
- St. Basil: Christians should not "laugh nor even suffer laugh makers."

Since, as we have seen, there are many authorities who argue for humor in Christianity, one wonders how much weight we should we give to authority in settling the matter. How do we determine which authorities to trust?

Deductive Arguments

Probably all deductive arguments against the belief in humor in Christianity subscribe to some form of this argument:

1. Christianity is serious business.
2. Humor is contrary to serious business.
3. Therefore, humor is contrary to Christianity.

We have seen a few attempts to refute the second premise, most notably Stanley Hauerwas's attempt. Of course Christianity is serious business, he agrees, but humor is essential to transacting this business well. This doesn't put the matter to rest, however, as several other deductive arguments merit our attention. Let's consider two such attempts, as Capps discusses them.[12]

---

10. Bastien "Humor and Satire," 526.
11. Martin, *Between Heaven and Mirth*, 35.
12. Capps, "Religion and Humor," 413–38.

Arguments against Humor in Christianity

First, Capps notes psychologist Vassilis Saroglou's effort to support the second premise—that humor is contrary to serious business.[13] Saroglou identifies five biases on which religion and humor differ:

Religion's Bias	Humor's Bias
Search for meaning	Enjoyment of incongruity
Planning and organization	Playfulness and spontaneity
Tradition, security, conformity	Novelty and the unexpected
Self-control	Loss of self-control
Condemns hostility; aggression	Often favors hostility and aggression

In response we might agree that religion and humor have respective biases that preclude their being synonymous, but neither religion nor humor need limit themselves to the biases Saroglou posits. For example, effort at religious understanding may sometimes start with incongruity or concede it as part of a great mystery. Some attempts at humor may rely on planning and organization to set up a joke, for example, while religion may at times promote playfulness and spontaneity. Religion may encourage hostility in certain circumstances, while humor may aim at making fun of it. It would appear, therefore, that Saroglou fails in his attempt to preclude humor from religion. Thus, relying on his authority to preclude humor from religion is logically a bad move.

Capps also notes four arguments against the presence of humor in religion from Henry F. Harris, an early twentieth-century theologian.[14] The first two are based on the premises that Jesus was Jewish and Jesus was fully human. Here is the first one:

1. Jesus was Jewish

2. The "Jewish spiritual temper, which grows out of a history that has been predominantly tragic, does not readily combine with humor."[15]

3. *Therefore, Jesus neither expressed nor exhibited humor.*

Here is the second:

1. Jesus was fully human.

---

13. Saroglou, "Religion and Sense of Humor," 191–214.
14. Harris, "Absence of Humor in Jesus," 460–67.
15. Ibid., 460.

2. So, Jesus was both masculine and feminine.

3. Psychology "generally concedes... women, broadly considered without reference to special exceptions, are defective in the sense of humor."[16]

4. Therefore, Jesus neither expressed nor exhibited humor.

We not need consider whether these arguments are valid, since the second premise of the first argument and the third premise of the second argument are patently false. Thus, even if the arguments were valid, they would be unsound and, therefore, bad arguments.

Harris's other two arguments are based on the premises that Jesus was a primitive type of man and thus not suitable for humor. Here is Harris's third argument:

1. Jesus was a primitive and simple.

2. A humorous person is witty and clever.

3. One cannot be primitive and simple, on the one hand, and witty and clever, on the other hand, at the same time.

4. *Therefore, Jesus neither expressed nor exhibited humor.*

And here is Harris's fourth argument:

1. Humor treats matters out of proportion to reality.

2. If Jesus did this, he would not be divine.

3. But Jesus is divine.

4. *Therefore, Jesus neither expressed nor exhibited humor.*

It is arguably false that Jesus was primitive and that Jesus could not be divine if he treated matters disproportionately. Thus, Harris's final two arguments are unsound, even if they are valid. Thus, relying on his authority to preclude humor from religion is logically a bad move.

Arguments against the Ability to See Humor in Christianity

In addition to alleged evidence that there is no humor in Christianity, there is evidence that while humor might be present, we simply do not see it. Scholars who consider this possibility tend to distinguish between

---

16. Ibid., 462.

ARGUMENTS AGAINST HUMOR IN CHRISTIANITY

objective reasons for our failure to see such humor and subjective reasons for failing to see it. *Objective* reasons include, for example, that much biblical comedy is lost in translation, such as from the Hebrew or Greek to English; it is difficult to capture oral humor in a written account; and humor is culture-bound.[17]

Subjectively possible explanations include our tendency to read everything literally, extreme familiarity with the text, stress on the tragedy of the crucifixion, failure to understand the Jewish context in which Jesus lived, and bad logic.[18] On this last point, Trueblood gives two examples: "assertion that sadness entails a denial of humor," and the incorrect view that tragedy and comedy are mutually exclusive.

Finally, Donald Capps notes research by Vassilis Saroglou that suggests religion negatively affects the appreciation of humor.[19] Any religious people reading this might consider their own positions in deciding whether they agree or disagree with Saroglou.

A THEOLOGY OF TEARS

We ended the previous section with the suggestion that religion negatively affects the appreciation of humor. In this vein Cal Samra, author of the *Joyful Noiseletter*, notes that "it is really surprising how many Christians cannot tolerate the image of a joyful, laughing Jesus. It is almost as if they prefer to contemplate the sorrowful Jesus of the Garden of Gethsemane and the tormented Jesus of the cross."[20]

In chapter 5 we considered Kuschel's theology of laughter, Berger's theology of the comic, Metz and Jossua's theology of joy, Thoennes's Theology of Humor, and Biddle's theology of irony. Since we are looking at contrary positions in the present chapter, let us finish it by considering a theology of tears. Here's one way to schematize an argument proposing a theology of tears as proof that there is no humor in Christianity.

1. If there were humor in Christianity, a theology of laughter, joy, or the comic would be appropriate.

---

17. Hyers, *And God Created Laughter*, prologue; Martin, *Between Heaven and Mirth*, 32 Also see Van Heerden, "Why the Humour in the Bible Plays Hide & Seek," 75–96.
18. Martin, *Between Heaven and Mirth*, 32; Trueblood, *Humor of Christ*, ch. 1.
19. Capps, "Religion and Humor," 422; Saroglou, "Humor Appreciation," 144–53.
20. Samra, *Joyful Christ*, 3.

Part II: A Theology of Laughter

2. Such a theology would be contrary to a theology of tears.

3. A theology of tears is appropriate.

4. So, a theology of laughter is inappropriate.

5. *Therefore, there is no humor in Christianity.*

In this vein, Kuschel focuses on John Chrysostom's "Theology of Tears."[21] According to Kuschel, Chrysostom says that "if you also weep such tears, you have become a follower of your Lord. For he too wept, both over Lazarus and over the city."[22] Kuschel suggests that this is one example of the standard view of the church fathers, which emphasized tears and weeping, over joy and laughter. We have already encountered several church fathers in this regard. We noted James Martin's examples of St. Clement, St. Basil, and St. Ambrose. To these we may add:

- St. Jerome (347–420 AD): The age is one of tears.
- St. Augustine (354–430 AD): Human life is "full of misery, work, pain, anger, tribulation, and temptation."
- St. Benedict (480–547 AD): Only fools burst out laughing.

We end this chapter by asking which view is more compelling: Chrysostom's theology of tears or Kuschel's theology of laughter? This book assumes the latter.

---

21. Kuschel, *Laughter*, 46.
22. Ibid.

PART III

The Bible as Comedy

Having considered the first two propositions toward our argument, the call to joy, and the appropriateness of a theology of laughter, we turn to our third proposition toward the argument against worshipping too somber a God: the Bible is a comedy. Chapter 7 offers an overview of humor in the Bible, including qualities of humor in the Bible, the Bible as comedy, a theology of laughter revisited, and Jesus's use of humor as means to the truth. Chapter 8 explores humor in the Old Testament, including the Torah, the Prophets, and the Writings. Chapter 9 focuses on the book of Jonah as a comedy. Chapter 10 explores humor in the New Testament, including the Gospels, Acts, the Letters, and Revelation. Chapter 11 focuses on the parable of the talents as a humorous story.

7

Humor in the Bible
Overview

> The Scriptures are rich with humor—people acting in foolish ways, the irony of people acting differently than one would expect, the sudden twists in a story to illustrate a meaning. The Bible is about human life—all of it—how could it not contain humor?
> —Michael Rogness, "Humor in the Bible"

> Humor smiles and chuckles and sometimes laughs right out loud in virtually every book of the Bible.
> —Steven C. Walker, *Illuminating Humor of the Bible*

THE ARGUMENT BEFORE US is that there is humor in the Bible in content and in structure, and that this serves as a plausible foundation for a theology of laughter. This chapter lays out the argument in broad strokes, dividing into three parts: humorous qualities, the comedic structure of the Bible, and a theology of laughter revisited.

Part III: The Bible as Comedy
HUMOROUS QUALITIES

So far, we have encountered many descriptions and examples of humor. As we focus on humor in the Bible specifically, we should find useful a return to a list of qualities of humor in the Bible. To that end consider two thought-provoking descriptions of humor. First, Michael Rogness, a homiletics professor, says that humor constitutes situations, comments, or stories that would cause us to smile, chuckle, or laugh.[1] What's more, "it helps us to put ourselves in the place of those first listeners or participants of these stories."[2]

Second, biblical scholar Athalya Brenner claims that "biblical humor mostly assumes the literary forms of satire, parody, irony (which is not always humorous), grotesque presentations, burlesque and dark comedy."[3] She posits the absence of "light-hearted humor" in the Bible and the presence of "contentious/subversive" humor that "undermines convention and authority, a property it shares with feminist criticism."[4]

Rogness and Steven C. Walker make room for the light-hearted humor, humor that makes us smile or chuckle, that Brenner rejects. Thus, it is apparent that even if we find humor in the Bible we may not agree unanimously about what those elements are or why they are humorous. But such disagreement need not prevent us from accusing some of worshipping a God who is too somber.

In this section, we will look at several qualities of humor in the Bible, drawn together under six general categories.

- Joy/Delight
- Playfulness
- Surprise/Reversal
- Parody
- Absurdity
- Acoustical

---

1. Rogness, "Humor in the Bible," 118.
2. Ibid.
3. Brenner, "Who's Afraid of Feminist Criticism?," 41.
4. Ibid.

In subsequent sections we will take a more in-depth look at Bible passages that exhibit these and other related qualities. For now, we will include some biblical examples.

Joy/Delight

We have said a lot about the call to joy as foundational to Jewish and Christian practice. Joy itself also figures prominently in the Bible, as Mary's *Magnificat* (Luke 1:44) exemplifies. In addition to joy and the call to joy are the more general celebrations of existence as in Adam's delight over Eve (Gen 2:23);[5] and the frequently festive tone of the biblical narrative.[6] On this last point, F. Scott Spencer, professor of New Testament, suggests that the stories of Tamar (Gen 38), Rahab (Josh 2), Ruth, and Bathsheba (2 Sam 11) contain the "comic markers" of festivity, along with incongruity, spontaneity, ingenuity, inferiority, inelasticity, and imperceptibility."[7]

Playfulness

Scholarship on biblical humor often cites the quality of playfulness. For our purposes this includes banter, a child's spirit, "gotcha" moments, puns and wordplay, and wit.

Concerning *banter*, Michael Rogness invokes Mary and Jesus at the wedding in Cana:

> At the wedding in Cana, even after Jesus rebukes Mary when she tells him about the wine shortage, saying, "What does this have to do with me?" We can detect the twinkle in a mother's eye when she turns to the servants and says knowingly, "Do whatever he tells you" (John 2:1–11). Mothers do know best![8]

Concerning the *child's spirit*, Elton Trueblood claims that "Jesus manages a balance between the childlike and maturity, and humor occurs at the meeting place of the two."[9] This is possible, but not self-evident, given

---

5. See also Hyers, *And God Created Laughter*, 11.
6. Biddle, "Are We Amused?," 241. Also see Spencer, "Those Riotous Foremothers of Jesus," 26.
7. Spencer, "Those Riotous Foremothers of Jesus," 26.
8. Rogness, "Humor in the Bible," 121.
9. Trueblood, *Humor of Christ*, 37.

the many views of Jesus as always serious in a way that only adults could manage.

Rogness offers Numbers 14:13–19 as a *gotcha* moment. After God threatens to kill the wandering Israelites, Moses talks God into forgiving them on the ground that killing the Israelites would give God a bad reputation among the nations.

The Bible is filled with *puns and wordplay*, much of which is lost in translation. An example of wordplay is in Genesis 40, when Joseph interprets the dreams of the butler and baker. To the butler, Joseph says: "Within three days Pharaoh will lift up your head and restore you to your office" (v. 13a). To the baker, Joseph says, "Within three days Pharaoh will lift up your head—from you!—and hang you on a pole" (v. 19). Both dreams report that the pharaoh will lift up the head of the dreamer, but this is good news in one case and bad news in the other. Note that logically, to conclude from the premise "within three days the pharaoh will lift up your head," that one is in for a reward, is to commit a fallacy of ambiguity—specifically, a fallacy of equivocation.

One of the more famous examples of a pun is Jesus's giving Simon the new name of Peter: "And I tell you, you are Peter, and on this rock I will build my church, and the gates of Hades will not prevail against it" (Matt 16:18 NIV).

Theologian Gerald Arbuckle defines *wit* as "the talent or quality of using unexpected associations between contrasting or disparate words or ideas to make a clever humorous effect."[10] As an example, Arbuckle cites Luke 9:57–62, which includes witty responses from Jesus to three people who promise to follow him, but with strings attached.

Surprise/Reversal

Scholarship on biblical humor often points to the quality of surprise or reversal. Presbyterian minister Casey Thomson claims that "the essence of comedy, after all, is surprise, and surprise is the essence of Easter."[11]

Consider five specific examples of surprise or reversal: incongruity, incredulous laughter, role reversal, the unexpected, and paradox.

Gerald Arbuckle cites Ps 138:6 as an example of *incongruity*: "Though the Lord is exalted, he looks kindly on the lowly; though lofty, he sees them

---

10. Arbuckle, *Laughing with God*, 13.
11. Thompson, "Living by the Word," 21.

from afar" (NIV).¹² Arbuckle also insists that incongruity and paradox are co-extensive.¹³ This challenges us to find an example to the contrary, which is difficult enough to be beyond the scope of this section.

Many sources note Sarah's *incredulous laughter* in Gen 18:12: "So Sarah laughed to herself, saying, 'After I have grown old, and my husband is old, shall I have pleasure?'"

As for *role reversals*, Michael Rogness, citing Gen 18:25–32, notes that "in a scene that resembles dickering over prices at a Middle Eastern street bazaar, Abraham negotiates the rescue of righteous people from the soon-to-be-destroyed Sodom and Gomorrah, all the while acting deferential, presumably to avoid angering God."¹⁴

Among the many examples of the *unexpected* in the Bible is the father's response to the return of the prodigal son (Luke 15:11–12).

As for *paradox*, Trueblood claims that "Christ's use of paradox is dazzling," proof of which comes in the Sermon on the Mount (Matt 5–7).¹⁵

Parody

Biblical scholar Jared Ludlow defines parody as "a composition which always assumes a pre-existing text [usually serious], which it imitates and distorts, often, but not always, for satiric purposes, mostly by means of exaggeration."¹⁶ Douglas Adams claims that the parable of the mustard seed (Mark 4:30–32) is a parody of the then well-known parable of the Cedar of Lebanon (Ezek 31).¹⁷

A combination of scholarly claims and dictionary lists of synonyms allows us to gather up seven qualities of humor under the general heading of parody: burlesque, caricature, mockery, derision, irony, sarcasm, and satire.

Athalya Brenner claims that *burlesque* is among the qualities of humor found in the Bible.¹⁸ *Merriam-Webster's Dictionary* online defines

---

12. Arbuckle, *Laughing with God*, 5.
13. Ibid., 4.
14. Rogness, Humor in the Bible," 120.
15. Trueblood, *Humor of Christ*, 43.
16. Ludlow, *Abraham Meets Death*, 19.
17. Adams, *Prostitute in the Family Tree*, 26.
18. Brenner, "Who's Afraid of Feminist Criticism?," 41.

burlesque as "mockery usually by caricature." So, we may connect burlesque to caricature.

As an example of *caricature*, Arbuckle cites Matt 3:7, in which Jesus calls the Sadducees and Pharisees "a brood of vipers."[19]

The description of God's laughter in Psalm 2 serves as an example of both *mockery* and *derision*.

Michael Rogness claims that for Greeks *irony* was the highest form of comedy. Rogness describes this irony as "the dramatic twist or effect caused by events or people who act differently than one would suppose."[20] Trueblood claims that irony is the most common type of humor for Christ.[21] Many of Christ's parables exhibit this.

Trueblood also claims that Christ sometimes crosses from irony into *sarcasm*. As an example, Trueblood cites Luke 16:17, in which Christ chastises the Pharisees for putting the law ahead of the world's wellbeing: "It is easier for heaven and earth to disappear than for the least stroke of a pen to drop out of the Law" (NIV).

Douglas Adams considers the parable of the talents to be *satirical*, a point to which we will return in chapter 11.[22]

Absurdity

That Sarah should have a baby or God should sacrifice his son for us is, in Kierkegaard's terms, *absurd*. For Kierkegaard this absurdity defies reason and thus requires us to accept it on faith or not to accept it at all. For many scholars this absurdity is at the core of much biblical humor.

Among the absurd elements in the Bible we may find clowns, foolishness, the grotesque, and the preposterous.

Douglas Adams claims that "in the miracles, Jesus and his disciples appear more as *clowns* than magicians. . . . To see humor in the stories of Jesus' miracles, look for the rough edges of each story as well the wider context."[23] It may be stretching matters to regard Jesus and his disciples as clowns, but Adams's assertion invites a second look at parts of the Gospel narrative that we traditionally regard with somberness.

---

19. Arbuckle, *Laughing with God*, 9.
20. Rogness, "Humor in the Bible," 117.
21. Trueblood, *Humor of Christ*, 57.
22. Adams, *Prostitute in the Family Tree*, ch. 4.
23. Ibid., 59–60.

There are many references to *folly and foolishness*, both in the Bible and in commentary on the Bible. Douglas Adams delights at Paul's having body parts talking to each other in 1 Cor 12:15–21. Michael Rogness asks, "How foolish is it to try to build a city and a tower with its top in the heavens" (Gen 11:4)? Rogness also reminds us of the many references to the fool in the book of Proverbs: "Think of all the gentle humor in the Book of Proverbs—the fool who thinks he can buy wisdom with money (17:16); a man too lazy to lift food to his mouth (19:24); the foolishness of not hiding from danger (22:3); the futility of speaking wisdom to a fool (23:9); and many more."[24]

As an example of the *grotesque*, consider 1 Sam 18:25–27, in which Saul demands from David a dowry of a hundred Philistine foreskins, if David wants to marry Saul's daughter, Michal. This is made all the more complicated by Saul's ulterior motive—the hope that David will die in the attempt.

Of course not all biblical examples of the grotesque suggest humor. Consider, Jer 19:9, for example: "And I will make them eat the flesh of their sons and the flesh of their daughters, and all shall eat the flesh of their neighbors in the siege, and in the distress with which their enemies and those who seek their life afflict them." No humor here.

As for the *preposterous*, Trueblood states, "Of all the mistakes which we make in regard to the humor of Christ, perhaps the worst mistake is our failure, or our unwillingness to recognize that Christ used deliberately preposterous statements to get his point across."[25] Consider, for example, the rich man and the eye of the needle (Matt 19:24).

Acoustical Humor

Douglas Adams offers a view of humor in the Bible that does not get much attention—acoustical humor: "If we make the sounds described by the creatures or actions in the Bible, the humor becomes apparent, e.g., Rev 13 (the beast of the sea 'utters proud words and blasphemies'); Mark 5:3–9 (Jesus' exchange with the mad man who lives among the tombs). And a nicely thought-provoking question is 'How different might some of the

---

24. Rogness, "Humor in the Bible," 123.
25. Trueblood, *Humor of Christ*, 46–47.

biblical narrative be for [its audience], if it were on film, staged, or at least accompanied by all of the sounds that the narratives suggest?'"[26]

THE COMEDIC STRUCTURE OF THE BIBLE

We have noted the claim that from a literary point of view the Bible is more a comedy than a tragedy. Theologians Cheryl Exum and William Whedbee consider this idea worthwhile and wonder why standard biblical criticism ignores the topic.[27] After all, they claim, Christianity calls us to joy; joy necessarily leads, at least sometimes, to "merry making"; and we get the word "comedy" from the Greek *komos*, which means "merry making."

This section has four parts. First, we will revisit Hyers's idea of the comic parentheses. Second, we will take a look at the oft-discussed U-shape of biblical narrative. Third, we will consider the incorporation of some comic elements as scaffolding for the Bible's alleged comedic structure. And fourth, we will acknowledge some caveats and objections to the claim that the Bible is a comedy.

The Comic Parentheses

We have seen Hyers's argument that the Bible is a comedy rather than a tragedy. In this regard he makes two basic points: the Gospels and the whole Bible begin and end in celebration; and tragedy moves toward destruction, while comedy moves toward constructive consequences. In short, the Christian message begins in comic absurdity, moves toward tragedy, but ends up redemptive and celebratory.

For Hyers, evidence for his position includes Jesus's poking fun at pride, vanity, and hypocrisy (e.g., Matt 23); comedy as a great leveler (e.g., David and Goliath—1 Sam 17); biblical heroes who are usually ordinary or underdogs (e.g., Moses); and the Bible's collapsing of categories, such as the least versus the greatest (e.g., Zacheus—Luke 19:1–10), self-righteousness (e.g., the Good Samaritan—Luke 10:25–37), and significance (e.g., the Widow's mite—Luke 21:1–4).

---

26. Adams, *Prostitute in the Family Tree*, 67–68.
27. Exum and Whedbee, "Isaac, Samson, and Saul," 5–40.

The U-Shaped Plot

Literary theorist Northrop Frye argues that the Bible is a single text with a U-shaped plot.[28] Theologian David Robertson explains Frye's twofold premise this way: "Tragedy exemplifies the inevitable workings of law; comedy exemplifies arbitrary actions and grace."[29] For Frye, the Bible obviously exemplifies the latter and thus is a comedy in the classical sense.

Comic Elements

Many scholars make use of Frye's image in defense of the claim that the Bible is a comedy. Here are two. Theologian James Jarrard claims that "the great comedy of the gospel is . . . that it is in the very darkest moment that the very greatest redemption comes."[30] Philosopher of religion Joseph McClelland holds that the "gospel demands a cynicism about the nobility of tragic heroes," and "without the ode to joy with which faith begins, theology would have nothing to say."[31]

New Testament scholar Dan Via argues that one can find the same comic genre in Aristophanes, some Pauline texts, Deuteronomy, and Mark.[32] While this might be overstating the case, we have seen the biblical presence of many elements that are clearly or most likely comic. Consider six such observations: Conrad Hyers's comic virtues; William Whedbee's *The Bible and the Comic Vision*; Marcian Strange's "Sense of Humor in the Bible"; Norman Gottwald's "Tragedy and Comedy in the Later Prophets"; Martin Buss's "Tragedy and Comedy in Hosea"; and Edwin Good's "The Book of Daniel as Comedy." Note that this list goes from quite broad to quite specific—from the Bible generally to specific books of the Bible.

Conrad Hyers distinguishes comic virtues from tragic virtues and argues that the former are emphasized over the latter in the Bible. Comic virtues, such as those found in Matt 5:43–46, include laughter, childlikeness, flexibility, humor, playfulness, meekness, humility, moderation, magnanimity, and willingness to compromise. Tragic virtues include courage,

---

28. Frye, *Great Code*.
29. Robertson, "Tragedy, Comedy, and the Bible," 102.
30. Jarrard, "Preaching and the Comic Side of the Gospel," 28.
31. McClelland, "Doxology as Suspension of the Tragic," 114–20.
32. Via, "New Testament and the Comic Genre," 903.

Part III: The Bible as Comedy

loyalty, duty, honor, pride, obedience, exaltation of warrior virtues, stubborn determination, and passionate involvement.

Since we can find examples of both comic virtue and tragic virtue in the Bible, a question is whether the Bible favors one over the other and how much this supports or challenges the view that the Bible is a comedy.

William Whedbee sees comedy in some unlikely places. Indeed he regards the better part of the Old Testament as a comedy.[33] In the first part of Genesis (1–11) Whedbee finds puns, parodies, and "aborted projects and incomplete fulfillments."[34] In the second part of Genesis (15–20), he finds "tricksters, dupes, and innocent victims"; word plays throughout the narrative; and U-shaped plots throughout.[35] He finds similar U-shaped plots in Exodus and Esther.[36] And in Job he finds "an improbable happy ending: restoration and regeneration in a comic mode."[37]

Whedbee may be guilty of hyperbole here, since there are several books in the Old Testament that scholars omit when offering Old Testament examples of humor. These books include, for example, Leviticus, 1 and 2 Chronicles, and ten of the Minor Prophets.

Marcian Strange identifies several biblical passages that make him laugh.[38] He suggests that these examples are the rule rather than the exception. Old Testament passages include Isaac (Gen 17ff.); proverbs about nagging women and lazy men; and Jonah. New Testament passages include the many instances of Jesus's mirth and use of incongruity (e.g., Matt 7:3; 23:24; Luke 19:3–4; John 13:9); Peter's being left at the gate by an excited maid (Acts 12:14); and Paul's hope that the knife slips on those who insist on circumcising themselves (Gal 5:11–12).

Challenges to Whedbee notwithstanding, Norman Gottwold insists that the fifteen books of the latter prophets "are comedy, not tragedy, since salvation has the last word over judgment."[39] Here again we see the U-shaped plot at work, but this may not be a fair assessment of the prophets and their prophecies.

---

33. Whedbee, *Bible and the Comic Vision*.
34. Ibid., 61.
35. Ibid., 123.
36. Ibid., 187–89.
37. Ibid., 257.
38. Strange, "God and Laughter," 2–12.
39. Gottwold, "Tragedy and Comedy," 83.

Martin Buss focuses on one of the fifteen prophets, Hosea, who "derides foolishness and mocks ritual actions."[40] Toward that end, Buss identifies three comic elements. Distancing comedy involves laughing at something or someone—in this case Israel. Integrative comedy involves laughing with someone—in this case Yahweh, as Israel's husband. Ironic tension exists in the interplay between the positive and the negative as Hosea describes Yahweh's love and disappointment.[41]

Edwin Good regards the book of Daniel as a comedy for three reasons: Daniel has U-shaped visions; Daniel's accusers receive the punishment they devised; and "the entire story is a comedy of subversion from the inside."[42]

While Good's argument is compelling, there is a long tradition of commentary on Daniel that would challenge Good's up-beat interpretation.

CAVEATS/OBJECTIONS

For all of the enthusiasm the foregoing scholars express in finding the comedy in the Bible, many of their colleagues express caution or outright skepticism. Gottwald, who sees comedy in the fifteen later prophets, nevertheless posits that there is no tragedy or comedy in the precise sense, since none except Jonah, is a narrative and, presumably, only narratives can be comedies or tragedies.[43] Exum and Whedbee note the ambiguity of ascribing the comic to the plot movement versus the vision.[44] Bruce Longenecker claims that humor is in the oral structure, not the written context, thus making it difficult for readers who don't know the original languages well.[45]

Roy Branson is willing to accept a comic reading of the Bible but only if it is set within a theology of joy.[46] David Gunn is less supportive, arguing that no serious piece of literature is simply U-shaped.[47] Bruce Longenecker wonders whether the comedy ascribed to Christ is Christ's or the

---

40. Buss, "Tragedy and Comedy in Hosea," 74.
41. Ibid., 73–76.
42. Good, "Apocalyptic as Comedy," 55.
43. Gottwald, "Tragedy and Comedy," 83.
44. Exum and Whedbee, "Isaac, Samson, and Saul," 5–40.
45. Longenecker, "Humorous Jesus?," 179–204.
46. Branson, "And Now... the Theology of Joy," 233–45.
47. Gunn, "Anatomy of Divine Comedy," 115–29.

Part III: The Bible as Comedy

storyteller's.[48] David Gunn offers a similar sentiment, asking, "Happy ending from whose perspective?"[49]

Biblical scholar Francis Landy goes further in his criticism of attempts to characterize the Bible as a comedy.[50] For Landy, a fatal objection is that comedy and tragedy refer to dramatic literature, while the Bible is universal literature; some of it may be dramatic, but it is also historical, poetic, and the like.[51] As poetry, biblical narrative contains more than comedy and tragedy: it may also be epic, lyrical, pastoral, and romantic, for example.[52] Also, the biblical vision is often "acutely tragic," with no comic relief in sight.[53] And offering a specific example, Isaac's story does not end with a U-turn.[54]

Biblical scholar Yair Zakovitch is highly critical of the effort to characterize the Bible as a comedy.[55] Focusing on the Jewish Bible, Zakovitch claims that no one in Israeli biblical studies takes the U / upside-down U distinction seriously.[56] Indeed, he insists, the concepts of comedy and tragedy, as literary models, are alien to biblical literature.[57] More specifically, each of the fifteen prophetic books is too singular and unique to lump into comedy.[58] Offering an olive branch to the other side, Zakovitch wonders whether it would not be more to the point to replace the concepts of comedy and tragedy with the characterizations of optimistic and pessimistic.[59]

All of these critics face the challenge that, as Steven C. Walker puts it, "there are too many comic situations in the Bible to be incidental."[60]

---

48. Longenecker, "Humorous Jesus?," 179.
49. Gunn, "Anatomy of Divine Comedy," 115.
50. Landy, "Are We in the Place of Averroes?," 131–48.
51. Ibid., 132.
52. Ibid., 144.
53. Ibid., 132.
54. Ibid., 136–37.
55. Zakovitch, "U and ∩ in the Bible," 107–14.
56. Ibid., 107.
57. Ibid., 109.
58. Ibid., 115.
59. Ibid., 109.
60. Walker, *Illuminating Humor of the Bible*, 5.

A THEOLOGY OF LAUGHTER REVISITED

Toward developing his theology of laughter, Kuschel cites Old Testament scholar Walter Gross: "The Abraham prostrate in worship before God and yet laughing at the same time is one of the most inscrutable images in Holy Scriptures."[61]

A provocative image, to be sure, but putting this verse in its larger context might make it less mysterious. That such an effort might be worthwhile justifies our revisiting the concept of a theology of laughter.

In returning to Kuschel's theology of laughter, let us focus on biblical examples, both Old Testament and New, saving a more detailed look at relevant Bible verses for chapters 8 through 11. Our initial focus on the Old Testament looks at human laughter and God's laughter.

Laughter in the Old Testament

Kuschel claims that there are three basic motifs of laughter in the Old Testament: the human being who laughs at or with God; the God who laughs at the rulers, the wicked, the guiltless; and "the one who laughs as the 'fool' whose laughter is simply the reflection of fatal self-deception."[62]

Humans Who Laugh At or With God

When humans laugh at or with God, says Kuschel, they laugh in unbelief, in doubt, or in delight.

We have on several occasions referred to the laughter of Abraham and Sarah. Now, consider Abraham's laughter especially as laughter of *unbelief* at the prospect of a hundred-year-old man and his ninety-year-old wife having a baby (Gen 17:15–17).

The first account of Sarah's laughter is laughter of *doubt* that she could have pleasure at her age (Gen 18:10, 12). Kuschel notes that "when Sarah laughs, she does not yet know at whom she is laughing. So Sarah is not really laughing at God.... Abraham knew from the beginning who he was dealing with."[63]

---

61. Kuschel, *Laughter*, 51.
62. Ibid., 49.
63. Ibid., 50.

Part III: The Bible as Comedy

The second account of Sarah's laughter has her laughing in *delight* (Gen 21:6). She names her son Isaac, which in Hebrew means "he laughs." At this point, Kuschel notes, "a shift can be recognized in this story of Abraham and Sarah: from skeptical laughter at God to the liberating laughter of everyone with God."[64]

God's Laughter

Kuschel moves from Bible verses in which people laugh at and with God to Bible verses depicting God's laughter. Kuschel identifies three specific instances: God laughs at the rulers, God laughs at the wicked, and God laughs at the guiltless.

According to Kuschel, God's laughter at the rulers may be threatening (e.g., Ps 2:2–6, 12) or it may be laughter of superiority. For Kuschel, "the theological point of which this Psalm seeks to make to those who use it is thus clear: no people, no nation on earth can shake the power of the God of Israel and his anointed."[65]

God's laughter in Psalm 2 is also laughter of superiority, including derisive and mocking laughter. On this point, Kuschel claims that there is a "radical change of perspective" from the story of Abraham and Sarah to the laughter of Psalm 2: "Here the talk is no longer of human beings who laugh at God, nor of a God who laughs happily with human beings. Here is talk of a God who laughs at people and nations and gets angry with them.... With this laughter God's mocking doubt on all human attempts to impose their domination against his will is revealed."[66]

God laughs menacingly not only at the rulers but all who mock and scoff at him. As an example, consider Ps 37:13, which has God laughing at the wicked, "for he sees that their day is coming." Or Ps 59:8, which has the Lord laughing at all the nations and holding them "in derision."

Note that the examples are not limited to the Psalms. Consider Wisdom 4:17–18, which finds the unrighteous having contempt for the wise and the Lord laughing the unrighteous "to scorn."

At this point Kuschel notes that "the perspective shift from the story of Sarah and Abraham could hardly be greater. Here we are far removed

---

64. Ibid., 52.
65. Ibid., 54.
66. Ibid., 55.

from a liberating laughter of human beings with God as from a laughter of skepticism and unbelief."[67]

We might find unsettling the first time we focus on God's laughter at the rulers and the wicked. What's more unsettling is God's apparent laughter at the guiltless. Consider, for example, Job's complaint that God "mocks at the calamity of the innocent" (9:23).

Kuschel notes, "God laughs at the anxiety of the innocent! With this experience of God of the man from Uz, described in chapter 9 of the book of Job, one of the boldest chapters of Old Testament theology, the image of God in the Hebrew Bible becomes completely uncanny."[68] Kuschel suggests further that "the whole of the book of Job seems to have been written against chapter 9."[69]

We must not assume that Kuschel has exhausted the list of possible ways in which God laughs. For example, Don Friedman et al. argue that the variety of situations in which God laughs suggests that God can be argued with and can change his mind: "God is omniscient, but enjoys good, playful argumentation, broadening the possibilities for reasoning and reasonability."[70]

The Laughing Fool

From people who laugh at and with God; to God laughing at rulers, the wicked, and the guiltless; to the person who laughs as a fool. Here, says Kuschel, we find one "whose laughter is simply the reflection of fatal self-deception."[71] A specific example is the sinner as mocker, whom Kuschel identifies in Ps 1:1: "Happy are those who do not follow the advice of the wicked, or take the path that sinners tread, or sit in the seat of scoffers." Kuschel would have us note that this passage reads "like a warning notice": "here the wicked person is portrayed as a mocker, as one who laughs. The wicked man does not laugh in doubt about God like Abraham and Sarah, still less rejoicing with God, but in mockery against God."[72]

---

67. Ibid., 59.
68. Ibid., 61.
69. Ibid.
70. Friedman et al., "What's So Funny," 57.
71. Kuschel, *Laughter*, 56.
72. Ibid.

For Kuschel, laughter is a character of the fool: "His laughter is the sign of frivolity and lack of thought."[73] Consider Sirach 21:14, 15: "The mind of a fool is like a broken jar; it can hold no knowledge. When an intelligent person hears a wise saying, he praises it and adds to it; when a fool hears it, he laughs at it and throws it behind his back." Or Sirach 27:12–13: "Among stupid people limit your time, but among thoughtful people linger on. The talk of fools is offensive, and their laughter is wantonly sinful."

For the better part of this study we have been regarding humor as something to celebrate. But much of the humor in Kuschel's biblical examples so far seems contentious or unsavory. One may wonder whether these examples hurt Kuschel's effort to promote a theology of laughter. Kuschel's response is to remind us of the many sorts of laughter in the Old Testament: the laughter of humans, which may be doubting, mocking, or joyful; and the laughter of God, which may joyful, mocking, or inscrutable.[74]

Laughter in the New Testament

Because Kuschel refers to the Gnostic Gospels at times in inferring the laughter of Jesus in the Gospels, it is worth spending a moment on Kuschel's reference to one Gnostic Gospel in particular.[75] The Coptic Gnostic Apocalypse of Peter tells of Peter's vision of Christ laughing at Jesus on the cross. Kuschel describes it this way: "What a scene! The living Christ, the risen savior, stands beside the cross intended for him and watches while another man is nailed to the wood in his place. He laughs, and his laughter is evidently all the more justified since the executioners do not know that the true Christ has long parted from his earthly body."[76]

Since the Gnostic Gospels are not canonical, we may not put much weight on them in determining Christ's humor, but the phenomenon speaks to the likelihood that humor has been present in Christianity from its beginning.

In the Gospels proper, Kuschel finds humor in the nativity and in the new creation that Jesus promises. On this point Kuschel says we do not have "a Jesus who denounced laughter and joy. Rather, through the Gospels

---

73. Ibid., 63.
74. Ibid., 64–65.
75. Ibid., 65.
76. Ibid., 66.

there runs the warm current of a joy at creation and human beings which emanates from Jesus."[77]

Kuschel singles out Luke for its many references to humor, including joy at the coming Christ child (Luke 1:41–44—Mary and Elizabeth; Luke 1:46–55—Mary's Magnificat); joy at the beginning of Jesus's ministry (Luke 4:18, 19—"The Spirit of the Lord is upon me . . ."); Messianic jubilation (Luke 19:36–38—Jesus enters Jerusalem); and joy over sinners (Luke 10:21).

There is more to say about laughter and other forms of humor in the Old and New Testaments, much of which will add support to the idea of a theology of laughter. This will develop across the next four chapters.

---

77. Ibid., 69.

8

Humor in the Old Testament

> Just as the book of Genesis holds pride of place as the fundamental story of beginnings in Western culture, so it is also a dominant generative source of comedy in Western literature.
>
> —William Whedbee, *The Bible and the Comic Vision*

IN THIS CHAPTER WE begin a deeper look at humor in the Bible, focusing on the Old Testament. We will take the organization of the Jewish Bible, the Tanakh, as our guide, dividing this chapter into three parts: humor in the Torah, humor in the prophets, and humor in the writings.

HUMOR IN THE TORAH

Regarding the Torah we will consider humor in Genesis, Exodus, and Numbers. There is little writing, if any, on humor in Leviticus or Deuteronomy, although as we noted in chapter 7, Dan Via believes that one can find a common comic genre in Aristophanes, some Pauline texts, Mark, and Deuteronomy.[1]

---

1. Via, "New Testament and the Comic Genre," 903.

Genesis

Although we have looked at several passages in Genesis already, especially concerning Abraham and Sarah, we can benefit from a further look, while trying to avoid duplicating our efforts.

Many writers find humor in Genesis. Steven Walker claims that "Genesis generates an amusing scenario . . . almost every chapter."[2] Part of the continuous humor, Walker claims, is the frequent introduction of odd pairs of characters: Adam and Eve, Cain and Abel, Jacob and Esau, Abraham and Lot, Isaac and Rebecca, Rachel and Leah, and Joseph and Judah, among others.[3] Walker sees an analogy between these pairings and modern comic pairings such as Abbott and Costello, Laurel and Hardy, Martin and Lewis, and Burns and Allen.

Hennie Kruger, while claiming that the Old Testament contains "no Hebrew term for humor as such," nevertheless believes that "the phenomenon of humor can serve as an interpretative key to understanding the idea of laughter in the Old Testament," including in Genesis.[4] Let us look at eight examples:

- The Comedy of Creation
- Noah
- The Tower of Babel
- Abimelech
- Isaac
- Esau and Jacob
- Joseph and his brothers
- Joseph and Aseneth

William Whedbee reminds us that "*the creation story* is filled with puns."[5] For example, "Adam" may come from the Hebrew *ha-adam*, "the man," or *adamah*, "earth." "Eve," *Chawwah* in Hebrew, may mean to breathe or to live.

---

2. Walker, *Illuminating Humor of the Bible*, 5.
3. Walker, *Illuminating Humor of the Bible*, 157.
4. Kruger, "Can the Phenomenon of Humor Serve," 6.
5. Whedbee, *Bible and the Comic Vision*, 59.

Part III: The Bible as Comedy

Whedbee notes that the creation story also contains "primal plots, and parodies; as well as programmatic pronouncements, aborted projects, and incomplete fulfillments."[6] While the situation may not always be funny for the actors in the story, the audience may well have taken delight in the wordplay and plot lines, and we can frequently imagine God laughing either joyfully or contentiously. Then there is the ubiquitous U-shaped plot.

Conrad Hyers adds the foolishness and playfulness of sex (Gen 2:23–24) that would surely be part of the situation in which Adam and Eve first found themselves.[7] Moreover, there could not have been a fall into seriousness if there was no humor to fall from.

Arbuckle finds humorous the fact that "*Noah* is told to build a large boat a long distance from any water" (Gen 6:11–9:29).[8] Christopher Meredith wonders where Noah put all the excreta.[9] Too scatological a topic for church, perhaps, but an interesting and potentially funny issue.

Andrew Giorgetti regards the story of the *Tower of Babel* (Gen 11:1–9) as mocking and subversive humor.[10] At the time of the story it was common for Mesopotamian leaders to build monuments to themselves and to include on those buildings inscriptions of self-praise. Giorgetti believes that the Hebrew author of the story, at odds with Mesopotamian royal ideology, "subverts the imperial hubris presented in the Mesopotamian royal building ideology by creating a 'mock' building account based on components traditional to the building-account genre."[11]

Biblical scholar Tzvi Novick finds humor in the story of *Abimelech* (Gen 20).[12] Abimelech has designs on Sarah, accepting Abraham's word that Sarah is his sister. God warns Abimelech that Sarah is Abraham's wife but decides to go easy on Abimelech given that he has not touched Sarah. After a testy exchange Abimelech and Abraham come to terms and the story ends on a happy note.

Novick argues that "the delphic brevity of [Gen] 20:2 . . . sets the comic stage."[13]

6. Ibid.
7. Hyers, *And God Created Laughter*, 10–11.
8. Arbuckle, *Laughing with God*, 24.
9. Meredith, "Big Room for Poo," 61–77.
10. Giorgetti, "Mock Building Account," 1–20.
11. Ibid., 1.
12. Novick, "Almost, at Times, the Fool," 284.
13. Ibid., 282.

Many commentators have observed that this verse explains neither why Abraham prevaricates nor why the king takes Sarah.

Second, Novick notes that this story ridicules the king "by concealing and then revealing God's affliction of Abimelech."[14] Abimelech and Abraham stand in stark contrast to each other, the former being pretentious and self-righteous, the latter acting heroically: "Abimelech, whose loud and prosaic piety undermines his majesty, gives way to and makes way for Abraham, the knight of faith."[15]

As is often the case with such interpretations, we are left to wonder whether there is as much humor in the story as the proponents suggests. But Novick has made a good case for finding at least some humor in the story of Abimelech.

We have already looked briefly at *Isaac* as a humorous character. As biblical scholar Joel Kaminsky notes, there is much scholarship on "the character of Isaac and the narratives that surround him with an eye toward uncovering elements of humor."[16] Generally, scholars have tended to refer to various Greek genres such as comedy, satire, or irony to illuminate these stories. For example, Gerald Arbuckle notes that Isaac often appears to be foolish or out of touch: "He claims that he is about to die and needs his last meal (though he does not die for another twenty years, according to Gen 31:38 and 35:29); this is an excuse to get Esau to prepare more game for him. . . . Isaac comes across as gullible, for he ignores the fact that the voice is that of Jacob (Gen 27:22–23)."[17] Mark Biddle notes that having gotten his wife Rebecca without even trying (Gen 24), "he greets Rebecca (who fell off her camel upon seeing her fiancé!) and immediately takes her into his mother's tent: a 40-year-old man living in his mother's tent—a momma's boy!"[18]

A brief side note while we are looking at Genesis 24: Biddle also notes the humor in Rebecca's watering the camels of Abraham's servants (Gen 24:17–22), when they first approach her about marrying Isaac. On its face, this story is not remarkable, nor is any humor evident. But as Biddle notes, "modern readers see no incongruity here because they do not know the

---

14. Ibid., 284.
15. Ibid.
16. Kaminsky, "Humor and the Theology of Hope," 364.
17. Arbuckle, *Laughing with God*, 25.
18. Biddle, *Time to Laugh*, 22–23.

norms."[19] Given the amount a camel can drink in a single effort (40 gallons), the number of camels the servant had (10), and the weight of a five-gallon jug filled with water (42 pounds), "Rebekah had to make almost one hundred round trips between the well and the watering trough, carrying a total of more than four hundred gallons of water weighing more than 3,330 pounds or more than two and one-half tons!"[20]

Back to Isaac: Cheryl Exum and William Whedbee claim that Isaac tends to be "a victim characteristically acquiescent to personages stronger and more clever than he."[21] For Exum and Whedbee the scene that most vividly illustrates "Isaac's role as dupe and victim who is manipulated but who nonetheless comes forth as a survivor" is the deathbed scene in Genesis 27.[22] In sum, they conclude that the story of Isaac contains "three ingredients of the comic vision": a U-shaped plot; word play and farce; and a comic "characterization of Isaac as a passive victim."[23]

Joel Kaminsky regards these as "excellent readings," but he feels they "overlook ways in which the biblical text reveals a type of humor less related to Greek literary forms and more closely linked to the character of the schlemiel, the bumbling stupidity of the Three Stooges and the slapstick antics of the Marx Brothers."[24] He posits two reasons for scholars' failure to find humor of this sort in the biblical text: they regard "the text as a classic masterpiece and presume that such an elevated work could not contain coarse forms of humor; [and these] scholars . . . are more likely to be familiar with Greek literary forms than with slapstick comedy and other crude forms of humor."[25]

Kaminsky posits a "structural affinity [and] direct connection, between humor and hope," because each denies the final word to everyday reality: "So it seems that the character most associated with comic laughter in Genesis is purposefully introduced at the point in the narrative where one's everyday beliefs are most called into question."[26]

19. Ibid., 18.
20. Ibid.
21. Exum and Whedbee, "Isaac, Samson, and Saul," 16.
22. Ibid., 17.
23. Ibid., 19.
24. Kaminsky, "Humor and the Theology of Hope," 364.
25. Ibid.
26. Ibid., 373.

Finally, Kaminsky notes that "in particular, the humor generated by the encounter between the mentally slow Isaac and the larger world in which he lives is part of a theology that hints at a God who makes fools wise and the wise foolish."[27]

The fruit doesn't fall far from the tree when it comes to the humor of Isaac's sons, *Esau and Jacob*. As biblical scholar Dean Burkey puts it, "Esau sells his birthright for a bowl of lentil stew."[28] Later, "Rebecca tells Jacob to stay with her brother Laban until Esau's anger subsides; and he forgets Jacob tricked him out of his birthright and blessing. Right. Like that's something easily forgotten" (Gen 27:43–45).[29]

Still later, says Burkey, is the world's worst first date: "Jacob meets Rachel, kisses her, and weeps. Kind of creepy and romantic at the same time. Normally guys don't do that" (Gen 29:11).[30]

Concerning *Joseph and his brothers*, Arbuckle notes the story's sarcasm: "Joseph's brothers denigrate his talents and sarcastically say of him 'Here comes this dreamer' (Gen 37:19). And, since sarcasm aims to destroy its victims, the brothers finally throw Joseph into the pit and sell him to foreign merchants (Gen 37:26–28)."[31]

We can be sure that Joseph does not find this humorous, but we may wonder whether the narrator meant it to be humorous or whether Arbuckle is seeing humor that was unintended.

For our final look at Genesis, theologian Angela Standhartinger finds comic elements in the story of *Joseph and Aseneth* (Gen 41).[32] She notes a growing consensus that the story reflects the genre of the Greek novel, especially comedy and mime. Accepting an Aristotelian definition of comedy as "an imitation of an action that is ludicrous and imperfect," Standhartinger claims that "the story of Joseph and Aseneth is colored by both, persiflage and parodist imitations of biblical accounts, and characters well known from comedy and mime."[33] If one takes the text solely on its own terms without putting it in any larger historical or literary context, one might still

---

27. Ibid., 374.
28. Burkey, *Holy Laughter*, 13.
29. Ibid.
30. Ibid., 14.
31. Arbuckle, *Laughing with God*, 11.
32. Standhartinger, "Humor in Joseph & Aseneth," 239.
33. Ibid., 242–43.

see the arrogance of Joseph and the boastfulness of Aseneth as humorous, along with the fact that no big deal is made of Joseph marrying a foreigner.

Exodus

William Whedbee believes that the book of *Exodus* is a comedy of deliverance.[34] As one of the "laughter-invoking incidents," Gerald Arbuckle notes that "Moses, who is 'slow of speech and slow of tongue' (Exod 4:10) is chosen to lead the Israelites out of slavery in Egypt."[35] Burkey adds that "Moses tries to weasel out of having to do God's will," even as God turns Moses' staff into a snake, makes Moses' hand leprous and heals it, and has Moses turn water into blood.[36] What further proof does Moses need that God has picked the right person?

Arbuckle finds divine humor in the exchange between God and Moses in Exod 34:6–7. While God insists that he "is neither vengeful nor inconstant and does not prize justice over mercy," the standard view of God at the time is of one who demands justice first.[37] The humor here appears to be in the ill-kept secret of God's true posture toward humans, even as God is claiming otherwise.

Numbers

Let's consider two allegedly funny stories in *Numbers*: Moses standing between God and the people (Num 11) and Balaam's ass (Num 22).

For many the quest for humor in the book of Numbers might look like a fool's errand. But even here scholars claim to have found humor. Concerning Numbers 11, in which God sends manna to the hungry sojourners, biblical scholar Pamela Reis claims that reading the passage as a literary work reveals "coherence, humor, and integrity in a single complete story from a single source. Narrative continuity as well as puns, wordplay, and an ingenious man/quail metaphor unite all verses of this chapter in a story that shows but one view of Moses."[38]

---

34. Whedbee, *Bible and the Comic Vision*, 129.
35. Arbuckle, *Laughing with God*, 24.
36. Burkey, *Holy Laughter*, 16.
37. Arbuckle, *Laughing with God*, 20.
38. Reis, "Numbers XI," 208.

Reis praises Moses for successfully striking a deal with God to spare the children of Israel, thus establishing "Moses' side of the covenant (vv. 21–22)."[39] Reis also posits the presence of "multiple examples of puns and wordplay" throughout chapter 11.[40] This may be one time among many where knowledge of biblical Hebrew is necessary to appreciating all of the humor that the passage intends.

The story of *Balaam's ass* (Num 22:22–35) has caught the eye of many scholars looking for biblical humor. Arbuckle says that while "Balaam, a non-Israelite prophet . . . is believed to have wide knowledge of many things, [he] finally discovers the most memorable lesson in life from, of all things, an ass."[41]

Burkey thinks it is especially funny that Balaam carries "on a conversation with this animal without credulity."[42]

HUMOR IN THE PROPHETS

Concerning humor in the prophets, Norman Gottwald says that biblical prophecy reveals "a sustained ironic abrasion between the tragedy Israel's leaders are repeatedly arranging when they think they are making comedy and the comedy which God through many agencies, including other Israelites and the nations, is steadily building on the tragic shambles."[43]

Relative to our purposes, Gottwald makes two comments about humor in the prophets in general. First, he cautions us not to look too precisely for comedy in the prophets, because tragedy and comedy usually refer to "narrative literary form," while the prophetic books are not narrative.[44] Instead, we should look in the prophecies for "the presence and interplay of tragic or comic views of life, what the literary critics tend to call 'visions.'"[45]

Second, lack of narrative notwithstanding, every prophetic book follows the U-shape of comedic development.[46]

---

39. Ibid., 231.
40. Ibid.
41. Arbuckle, *Laughing with God*, 24.
42. Burkey, *Holy Laughter*, 23.
43. Gottwald, "Tragedy and Comedy," 93.
44. Ibid., 83.
45. Ibid.
46. Ibid., 84.

Part III: The Bible as Comedy

In this section we will look for humor in the following prophetic books:

- Judges
- 1 and 2 Samuel
- 1 and 2 Kings
- Isaiah
- Jeremiah
- Hosea
- Amos
- Ezekiel
- Micah
- Nahum

Note that by one traditional typology, this list includes all of the former prophets (Judges, Samuel, Kings), but Joshua; the three latter prophets (Isaiah, Jeremiah, and Ezekiel); and four of the minor prophets (Hosea, Amos, Micah, and Nahum). We will devote a whole chapter to a fifth minor prophet, Jonah, and we will briefly consider the remaining seven minor prophets (Joel, Obadiah, Habakkuk, Zephaniah, Haggai, Zechariah, and Malachi), in the concluding chapter.

Judges

By some accounts the book of Judges contains a lot of humorous stories. We will consider five:

- Ehud and Eglon
- Jael and Sisera
- Gideon
- Samson
- Micah-Danite

On first read there is something potentially funny, if darkly so, about *Ehud's* assassination of Eglon, king of the Moabites (Judg 3:12–30). Eglon is apparently sitting on the toilet when Ehud enters and stabs him. Eglon's fat swallows Ehud's dagger. At that moment the Israelites become free from eighteen years of slavery under the Moabites. This is the typical English version of the story and as biblical scholar Lowell Handy notes, it depicts a canny Ehud and a stupid Eglon.[47]

But Lawson Stone, professor of Old Testament, would have us consider the Hebrew carefully.[48] If we do, he argues, we will find Eglon to be of robust health, thus contemporary readers should be careful about not projecting their own wishes and ideologies on the original text.[49]

For Stone, this doesn't remove the humor from the story, but it removes much of the coarseness from it, in favor of a more sophisticated story of Israel's putting one over on the Moabites.

According to Pamela Reis, "*Jael's* assassination of Sisera, narrated in Judges 4:7–22 and sung in Judges 5:24–31, smolders with sex. . . . This understanding highlights the bawdy ridicule of Israel's enemy, Sisera."[50] For Reis, careful exegesis of the Hebrew text reveals that the story is "about a woman's use of sexuality to overmaster a man."[51] History also supports this interpretation. At the time of the story the audience "understood that Jael is loose and brazen to come out and meet Sisera and that when she entices him into her tent, dismissing his fear, she is offering a sexual liaison. Sisera also understood."[52]

After the second "covering," which Reis says is a second act of intercourse in a relatively short time, Sisera says, "Stand in the doorway of the tent, and it shall be if a man comes and inquires of you and says, 'Is a man here?' you will say 'No'" (Judg 4:20, Reis's translation). According to Reis, "To the first readers . . . Sisera›s addressing Jael as though she were a man is funny and appropriate, considering that she has twice usurped the male position in their coupling. It is as though Sisera himself admits Jael has become the man, and he, by contrast, has become effeminate."[53]

Gerald Arbuckle considers the story of *Gideon* to be a laughter-evoking incident.[54] Arbuckle finds funny that "when Gideon goes into battle

---

47. Handy, "Uneasy Laughter," 233–46.
48. Stone, "Eglon's Belly," 649–63.
49. Ibid., 654.
50. Reis, "Uncovering Jael and Sisera," 24.
51. Ibid.
52. Ibid., 27.
53. Ibid.
54. Arbuckle, *Laughing with God*, 24.

against the Midianites he has no weapons and his soldiers have only clay pots, horns, and burning torches, but he succeeds in placing trust in God" (Judg 7:1–23).[55]

Hyers reminds us that Gideon started with a force of thirty-two thousand men, but God insisted on reducing the threat, "lest Israel vaunt themselves against me, saying, 'My own hand has delivered me'" (Judg 7:2).[56] Eventually Gideon's force is reduced to three hundred. But they are able to surprise the sleeping Midianite horde, making enough noise to throw the Midianites into confusion and causing them to kill each other or run away. Hyers interprets this as a comic act on God's part for the underdog, even though the underdog status of Gideon was contrived.

Exum and Whedbee identify "stock elements of comedy" in the story of *Samson* (Judg 13–16), including "wit and humor, bawdy riddles and amorous escapades, a rapid pace, an episodic structure, and a hero of incredible vitality."[57]

Professor of Old Testament Dale Davis argues that the *Micah-Danite* story (Judg 17–18) is the writer's attack on false religion.[58] "It speaks of judgment on false religion; it suggests an antidote for false religion; it underscores the stupidity of false religion; and it describes the tragedy of false religion."[59] For example:

> Engaging in overt sarcasm, the writer reports Micah's complaint in 18:24: "My god(s) which I have made you have taken." Here the theological polemic reaches its climax. Is the narrator not using Micah's words as a vehicle for teaching orthodox theology? Were it not so tragic would not any convinced Yahwist find Micah's words utterly hilarious? A god who can be made is surely a contradiction in terms; and a god who cannot avoid being pilfered must be a non-god indeed (cf. 6:31)! Thus the narrator artlessly permits Micah himself to emphasize the insanity of the whole affair.[60]

---

55. Ibid.
56. Hyers, *And God Created Laughter*, 44.
57. Exum and Whedbee, "Isaac, Samson, and Saul," 20.
58. Davis, "Comic Literature," 156–63.
59. Ibid., 156.
60. Ibid., 161.

1 AND 2 SAMUEL

In the books of Samuel the stories of Saul and of David appear to contain humor. Exum and Whedbee claim that "the *Saul* story has its moments of comic incongruity such as the unsuspecting lad who seeks lost asses and finds a kingdom (1 Sam 9–10) and the future king who hides among the baggage when he is chosen by lot (1 Sam 11:20–24)."[61]

Hyers notes that "later, when the people clamor for a king in order to be 'like all the nations,' the reluctant prophet Samuel anoints the young Saul, whose principal distinction seems to be that he is tall and handsome."[62] Saul's response, however, is to point out that he is "from the least of the tribes of Israel" and his family "is the humblest of all of the families of the tribe of Benjamin" (1 Sam 9:21). Furthermore, as Exum and Whedbee note, "When the tribes are assembled for the selection of the king, Saul is so reluctant that he hides himself among the baggage."[63]

As for David, Steven Walker claims that through the David narrative, "David wears an angelically white hat at the same time he rides a devilishly dark horse and he manages both magnificently."[64] Walker claims that David is both a hero and an antihero, and exhibits ten classic characteristics of a prankster or trickster: underdog, outsider, rebel, border crosser, situation twister, taboo breaker, shape shifter, deceiver, friends of the gods, and comic.[65] In brief, "David's central narrative function is disrupting social normality."[66]

Mark Biddle focuses on the incongruities of David's life, suggesting that they reveal two truths: "The Vacation Bible School David is a cartoon character with little resemblance to the biblical David [and] we misread the Bible if we assume that everything in it expresses the will of God."[67]

One running theme that does appear to express the will of God, Biddle notes, is David's ability to escape Saul's many attempts to kill him.[68] As David plays the lyre, Saul throws a spear at him—three times (1 Sam

---

61. Exum and Whedbee, "Isaac, Samson, and Saul," 21.
62. Hyers, *And God Created Laughter*, 44.
63. Exum and Whedbee, "Isaac, Samson, and Saul," 21.
64. Walker, *Illuminating Humor of the Bible*, 128.
65. Ibid., 129.
66. Ibid., 130.
67. Biddle, *Time to Laugh*, 55.
68. Ibid., 40–49.

18:10–11; 19:9). David ducks and keeps on playing. Saul sends David to fight the Philistines, telling David not to come back without at least one hundred Philistine foreskins (1 Sam 18:27). Saul does not expect David to survive. David survives. Saul sends a group to ambush David in his bed, but his wife Michal and Michal's brother Jonathan put a dummy in David's bed, dressed to look like David, and David flees to Samuel at Naioth (1 Sam 19:13). On three separate occasions, Saul sends groups to Naioth to retrieve David, but each time the group is overcome by a spirit of prophecy that renders them useless as kidnappers. Then Saul tries the scheme himself only to be struck by the prophetic spirit that "left him lying naked for a day and a night and that brought him infamy in Israel: 'Is Saul also among the prophets?'" (1 Sam 19:24).[69]

For Hyers, the story of David and Goliath (1 Sam 17:43–44) is "the quintessential example" of one for the underdog: with a single stone, the shepherd boy David kills the ten-foot-tall giant.[70]

Arbuckle sees a joking pattern in the story of David's becoming king. As he laments the loss of Jonathan (2 Sam 1:25–26) and turns to God for comfort, God "calls David to an unexpected new leadership role (2 Sam 2:1–4)."[71] Arbuckle concludes that "God loves us so much that goodness can emerge from the chaos in surprising ways."[72]

1 and 2 Kings

At least four allegedly humorous accounts appear in the books of Kings. First, Hyers notes that "Elijah had ridiculed the priests of Baal who wailed and slashed themselves in the frenzied hope that Baal would send fire from heaven. 'Shout louder! . . . Perhaps he is deep in thought or busy, or traveling; or perhaps he is sleeping and must be awakened!'" (1 Kgs 18:27 NIV).[73]

Second, Arbuckle, noting the manipulation by Bathsheba and Jezebel (1 Kgs 1 and 1 Kgs 21), posits that the original audience of this story would have found such manipulation shockingly funny.[74]

---

69. Ibid., 44.
70. Hyers, *And God Created Laughter*, 45.
71. Arbuckle, *Laughing with God*, 57.
72. Ibid.
73. Hyers, *And God Created Laughter*, 7.
74. Arbuckle, *Laughing with God*, 25.

Third, an account which is horrific and funny at the same time has forty-two teenagers teasing and being cursed by Elisha, and subsequently being eaten by she-bears (2 Kgs 2:23–24).[75]

Fourth, Michael Press argues that the Rabshakeh's speech (2 Kgs 18:34; Isa 36:19) is not masterful rhetoric, but "superficial bluster, taking part in the larger Deuteronomic (and prophetic) ridicule of false gods and divine statues."[76]

While it is easy to imagine original audiences laughing at these, perhaps at times in some discomfort, may we conclude that it remains proper to regard these accounts as funny?

Isaiah

Many of us might not immediately associate Isaiah with humor, yet some scholars find much humor in the prophecies and in the stories about the prophet. For example, Arbuckle notes that "in the lives of the prophets we often see rather comic actions, and bystanders must have been amused by what they saw. Isaiah strolls about naked for three years" (Isa 20:2–3).[77]

Hyers notes that "Isaiah made fun of the idol-makers of Babylon who would cut down a tree, carve a god out of one-half of the tree and roast meat over the other" (44:14–17).[78] Arbuckle agrees, claiming that "the prophets were given to both sarcasm and satire. They mocked the belief in idols (Isa 44:9–20; Hos 13:2) and the ostentatious display of feminine jewelry" (Isa 3:16–23).[79]

Gottwald takes a broader look at Isaiah, suggesting that chapters 40–55 are "exceptional in specifying some of the historical agencies of comic salvation."[80]

---

75. See Burkey, *Holy Laughter*, 53.
76. Press, "Where Are the Gods of Hamath?," 201.
77. Arbuckle, *Laughing with God*, 25.
78. Hyers, *And God Created Laughter*, 7.
79. Arbuckle, *Laughing with God*, 11.
80. Gottwald, "Tragedy and Comedy," 85.

Part III: The Bible as Comedy

Jeremiah

Arbuckle finds humor in Jeremiah, where others may miss or deny that humor. For example, Arbuckle notes "the negative laughter of the scoffer who responds to the word of God with ridicule" (Jer 20:7–8).[81]

Arbuckle regards Jeremiah's breaking of the pots (19:1–13) and wearing the yoke (28:10–16) as comic actions that would have amused witnesses.[82]

Arbuckle notes Yahweh's condemnation of Israel at Jer 30:12, 14; and Yahweh's surprisingly quick about-face in Jer 30:17, 22. The last word, says Arbuckle, is clemency: "For I will restore health to you, and your wounds I will heal. . . . And you shall be my people, and I will be your God" (Jer 30:17, 22).[83] Thus, Jeremiah ends on an up note, which, as we have seen, many scholars regard as a sign of the comic.

Ezekiel

Arbuckle finds humor in Ezekiel, and assumes the original audience would have readily seen that humor, in two passages: Ezekiel's preparing food at a fire fueled by human manure (4:12), and Ezekiel's consuming God's word, written on a scroll, for a meal (3:1–3).[84]

Amos

William Domeris considers Amos to be an ironic use of "anti-language."[85] Amos was a member of the Yahweh-only party, a minority party at a time when a majority accepted the possibility of many gods. Describing anti-language as the language of anti-society, Domeris claims that "the rhetoric of Amos includes a wonderful mixture of humor, threat, sarcasm, irony, hyperbole, and prediction."[86]

Amos's audience includes both those whom God will punish and those whom God will reward. Punishment awaits those who abuse their

---

81. Arbuckle, *Laughing with God*, 23.
82. Ibid., 25.
83. Ibid.
84. Ibid.
85. Domeris, "Shades of Irony," 1–8.
86. Ibid., 1.

political power and those who are willing to compromise with pagans.[87] An example of Amos's "biting sarcasm" is his "skewing his audience with a prophetic lament": "Go to Bethel and sin; go to Gilgal and sin yet more. Bring your sacrifices every morning, your tithes every three years" (Amos 4:4 NIV).[88]

An example of caricature is at 6:4–5: "You lie on beds adorned with ivory and lounge on your couches. You dine on choice lambs and fattened calves. You strum away on your harps like David and improvise on musical instruments" (NIV).

Domeris sums up his treatment of Amos by declaring that "the singular critique of the wealthy class and their oppression of the poor and the weak is the most memorable aspect of Amos."[89]

Hosea

Gerald Arbuckle and Martin Buss find both distancing and integrative humor in Hosea. Buss explains the distinction in terms of laughing *at* someone, which is distancing, versus laughing *with* someone, which is integrative: "Distancing humor exposes foolishness or expresses glee over an enemy's fall, supporting a sense of one's own superiority over the other. Like integrative humor it expresses joy, but one's own advantage is at another's expense."[90]

In terms of distancing humor, Arbuckle notes Hosea's mockery of belief in idols (Hos 13:2) and Buss claims that "the foolishness derided by Hosea involves the pursuit of superficial values and limited powers in preference to a relation with the real God."[91]

---

87. Ibid., 3.
88. Ibid., 5.
89. Ibid.
90. Buss, "Tragedy and Comedy in Hosea," 73.
91. Arbuckle, *Laughing with God*, 21; Buss, Tragedy and Comedy in Hosea," 74.

Part III: The Bible as Comedy

Micah

Dean Burkey regards Micah as the "Punster Prophet."[92] According to Burkey, Micah contains a lot of wordplay that gets lost in translation. For example,

> In 1:10, [Micah] tells the people who live in Beth Aphrah (which means "House of Dust") to roll themselves in the dust. In 1:11 (NKJV): "the inhabitant of Zaanan ('Going Out') does not go out." In 1:14 (NKJV): "The houses of Achzib ('Lie') shall be a lie to the kings of Israel." 1:15 (NKJV): "I will yet bring an heir to you, O inhabitant of Mareshah ('Inheritance')."[93]

Nahum

Burkey also finds ironic that Nahum means "comforter," yet Nahum's "idea of comforting is to warn about the forthcoming wrath of God."[94]

HUMOR IN THE WRITINGS

We are working our way through the Old Testament. We have looked at humor in the Torah and humor in the prophets. Our last step in this chapter is to consider eight books from the writings:

- Psalms
- Proverbs
- Ecclesiastes
- Job
- Song of Solomon
- Lamentations
- Esther
- Daniel

---

92. Burkey, *Holy Laughter*, 106–7.
93. Ibid.
94. Ibid., 109.

Psalms

We have said a good deal already about humor in the Psalms. For example, we have noted, with Hyers and Kuschel, the various types of God's laughter, including laughter for sport, mocking laughter, and laughter of superiority.[95]

We have also noted, with Kuschel, that laughter can be a reward for the tormented.[96] Arbuckle adds that in some psalms: "God prepares for himself praise from the mouths of children and very young ones" (Ps 8:2).[97]

Even in the lament psalms, Arbuckle notes, "the petitioners, while intensely suffering, experience a surprising inner energy, a newness of joy, a gift from a loving God."[98]

Arbuckle notes in Psalm 8 a "vivid paradoxical contrast" between the creator God and the created humankind, which is "further intensified when humankind is called to collaborate with God in additionally enhancing creation."[99]

Arbuckle turns to Psalm 88, claiming that, in spite of its note of despair, "three types of humor are identifiable: negative humor, laughter of the heart, and divine humor."[100]

Finally, Old Testament scholar Rebecca Hancock notes that every psalm but Psalm 137 ends on an up note.[101]

Proverbs

We opened chapter 1 with Prov 17:22: "A cheerful heart is good medicine, but a downcast spirit dries up the bones." In chapter 7 we noted Michael Rogness's reminder of "the gentle humor in the Book of Proverbs—the fool who thinks he can buy wisdom with money (17:16); a man too lazy to lift food to his mouth (19:24); the foolishness of not hiding form danger (22:3); the futility of speaking wisdom to a fool (23:9); and many more."[102]

---

95. Hyers, *And God Created Laughter*, 20; Kuschel, *Laughter*, 53, 55.
96. Kuschel, *Laughter*, 60.
97. Arbuckle, *Laughing with God*, 14.
98. Ibid., 28.
99. Ibid.
100. Ibid., 29.
101. Hancock, "Psalms."
102. Rogness, "Humor in the Bible," 121.

Less gently, Hennie Kruger notes God's (in the form of Wisdom's) mocking laughter in Prov 1:20–26.[103]

Ecclesiastes

Ecclesiastes 7:4 warns that "the heart of the wise is in the house of mourning, but the heart of fools is in the house of pleasure." But Benjamin Morse argues that Qoheleth is like Dadaist Marcel Duchamp, "For what is the Book of Qoheleth but a collection of observations that have been assembled with a witty irreverence for conventional wisdom."[104]

Job

We have had occasion to wonder whether there is humor in Job. Here let's consider four premises on which some scholars have made the case for that humor.

The first premise concerns the distinction between a happy spirit and a happy ending. William Whedbee regards the book of Job as a comedy based on "two central ingredients . . . : (1) its perception of incongruity and irony; and (2) its basic plot line that leads ultimately to the happiness of the hero and his restoration to a harmonious society."[105] Whedbee holds that, viewed from this perspective, Job is a "great reservoir of comedy [containing] such comic elements as caricature and parody in the depictions of Job's friends, young Elihu, God, and even Job himself."[106] Whedbee also considers the happy ending of Job as an element that brings up the curve of the U-shaped comedic plot.

Hyers agrees that Job is ultimately a comedy, but for Hyers, it is because of Job's *spirit*, not because of the ending.[107] We see this spirit from the beginning when Job says, "The Lord gave, and the Lord has taken away; blessed be the name of the Lord" (1:21).[108]

---

103. Kruger, "Can the Phenomenon of Humor Serve," 4.
104. Morse, "Introduction to a Dandy," 235.
105. Whedbee, "Comedy of Job," 1.
106. Ibid.
107. Hyers, *And God Created Laughter*, 37.
108. Ibid.

The second premise for regarding Job as a comedy comes from Dean Burkey's imagining a *movie trailer* for Job:

> One man caught in a game between the forces of good and evil. His patience will be tested. His faith will be tried. His wife will be nagging. His comforting friends will offer no comfort at all. But if he remains true to the end, he'll double his profits and wind up with his own book in the Bible. So good job, Job![109]

The third premise for regarding Job as a comedy comes from Old Testament scholar Abigail Pelham's argument that Elihu, "an obvious buffoon," is a comic figure. Until Elihu appears, Job has been regarding himself as "a tragic hero." Then, Elihu appears and babbles about how urgent it is that he speak, which he delays by continuing to speak!

> This introduction reaches its comic apex when Elihu splutters, "My heart is indeed like wine that has no vent, like new wineskins, it is ready to burst. I must speak, so that I may find relief" (32.19–20a). He portrays his need to speak as a bodily function over which he has no control. He really has to *go. Now.* And yet, even after this proclamation, he does not get to the substance of his message until nine verses later, and even then he only quotes Job. His own words come twelve verses after he has claimed that he will explode if he is not able to reveal his thoughts.[110]

Pelham concludes that Elihu's inability to keep silent is "funny in its own right," but also a caricature of Job's discussion with his other friends: "They, too, have been unable to keep silent. They, too, have had important things to say—but did it look like this? Suddenly, the discussion between Job and his friends looks not noble and important, but like a tendency to run off at the mouth."[111]

The fourth premise for regarding Job as a comedy concerns the *whirlwind speech* (Job 38). Old Testament professor Kathryn Schifferdecker pictures God describing, "with obvious pride and delight, the wild things and the wild places that make up God's magnificent world."[112] She notes that "Job responds to the whirlwind speeches by choosing to live with the same freedom God grants all of God's creatures."[113]

109. Burkey, *Holy Laughter*, 62.
110. Pelham, "Job as Comedy, Revisited," 97–98.
111. Ibid.
112. Schifferdecker, "Of Stars and Sea Monsters," 361.
113. Ibid., 357.

Part III: The Bible as Comedy

Song of Solomon

Old Testament scholar W. J. Kynes, citing Athalaya Brenner, and William Whedbee, finds humorous parody and paradox in the Song of Solomon, especially in its "humorous parody of the *wasf*, or descriptive love poem, a genre evident in several ancient Near Eastern texts (7:1–10)."[114] Kynes notes Brenner's suggestion that "the poet here, draws a comic picture of a 'mixed bag' with fat belly, jumpy breasts, long neck, turbid eyes, and outsized nose. In this way, the parody of the *wasf* serves satirically as a 'protest against conventional, idolized, idealized images of love and of the female love object.'"[115]

Whedbee claims that social roles in the song involve reversals and that it revels in love-making; the bodies are beautiful in playful parody; the union and reunion of love occurs in comic play; and the song is sung in a comic key.[116]

Kynes and Whedbee invite us to consider whether they are reading qualities into the song that are not in the song itself.

Lamentations

It is hard to imagine finding humor in the book of Lamentations, but Arbuckle reminds us that humor, in the form of laughter, is not always positive.[117] In Lamentations we find the enemies of Jerusalem laughing at its collapse. Humor for the enemies; tragedy for Jerusalem.

Esther

Dean Burkey regards the book of Esther as "a textbook on how to write a great comedy." It makes Haman, the villain, pompous, and Mordecai, "the righteous rival."[118] Showing pride to be a fatal flaw, the book deflates Haman's pomposity—"a key element in many forms of humor."[119]

---

114. Kynes, "Beat your Parodies into Swords," 295.
115. Ibid., 296.
116. Whedbee, *Bible and the Comic Vision*, 265, 268, 273, 275.
117. Arbuckle, *Laughing with God*, 23.
118. Burkey, *Holy Laughter*, 60.
119. Ibid.

When Haman is hanged on the gallows he had prepared for Mordecai (Esth 7:10a), we have, says Burkey, the "perfect ending: The villain gets caught in his trap. Kind of like Wiley E. Coyote."[120]

Arbuckle considers this and other examples of manipulation by a woman to be inherently funny and certainly funny to its original audience.[121]

Mark Biddle claims that "the book of Esther may be the only book in the Bible . . . that can be classified, start to finish, as a comedy."[122] Contrary to Biddle, one might also make the case that Jonah is a comedy from start to finish, a point to which we devote the next chapter. But there is little doubt that Esther contains hyperbole and ridicule and, in Steven Walker's words, is "a narrative that seeks to lampoon the pretensions of the Persian government."[123] While Biddle argues persuasively that there are no Persian records of any of the characters in Esther, this only enhances the likelihood that the book means to make fun of the Persian government, while disguising itself a bit.[124]

Rabbi Josiah Derby does Burkey's hyperbole one better by declaring Esther to be the "funniest book in the Bible."[125] However, this is lost on the public, Derby maintains, "because it is read with such speed (and by many worshipers in English), so the nuances in the Hebrew text are lost."[126]

Within the funniest book, says Derby, is the funniest word. In chapter 7, Esther indicts Haman, which causes the King to angrily go out to his garden. When he returns, he finds Haman on Esther's couch begging her for mercy. The King newly enraged shouts, "Will he even assault the Queen . . . in my own house?" The Hebrew words for "in my own house" are *imi babayit*. Derby claims that this is especially funny since the king's wrath appears not to be about the assault so much as it is about the assault taking place under his nose.

We may not be convinced that this is the funniest word in the Bible; we may not be convinced that is the funniest book in the Bible. Indeed, Jonah may be much funnier than most, if not all, of the other books. We will

---

120. Ibid.

121. Arbuckle, *Laughing with God*, 25.

122. Biddle, *Time to Laugh*, 72.

123. Walker, *Illuminating Humor of the Bible*, 54. Also see Kissling, "Self-Defense and Identity Formation," 105–19.

124. Biddle, *Time to Laugh*, 72.

125. Derby, "Funniest Word in the Bible," 116.

126. Ibid.

PART III: THE BIBLE AS COMEDY

devote the next chapter to Jonah. In the meantime, we are left to consider whether the scholars just noted have made their case.

Daniel

Edwin Good regards Daniel as a comedy in the ancient Greek sense, not only because it ends on a high note, but because it has the detailed structure of a classical Greek comedy.[127] The key is that the apparently inferior character brings down the apparently superior character, and the inferior character is promoted to a higher position in the end. That said, Good warns us not to look for laughter in Daniel.[128]

Good concludes with the argument that "with Daniel in the lion's den [Dan 6], we come to the cap of the comedy. . . . His survival demonstrates his innocence by ordeal, and, as in Esther, the accusers receive the punishment they had devised. . . . The entire story, then, is a comedy of subversion from the inside."[129]

This ends this chapter in which we have looked for examples of humor throughout the Old Testament. The next chapter looks at one Old Testament book in particular, Jonah, which one might regard as clear proof that there is at least some humor in the Old Testament.

---

127. Good, "Apocalyptic as Comedy," 47.
128. Ibid., 41.
129. Ibid., 54–55.

9

Jonah as Comedy

> The book of Jonah is a satire. In purpose and method it belongs to the same general type of literature as *Don Quixote* and *Gulliver's Travels*.
>
> —Millar Burrows, "The Literary Category of the Book of Jonah"

It is common for writers to regard Jonah as a comedy. Steven Walker calls it "the funniest book in the Bible . . . funny in format, funny in content, funny even in its rapid fire delivery."[1] To be sure, this view is not unanimous. As we saw in the previous chapter, Rabbi Josiah Derby considers Esther to be the funniest book in the Bible.[2] Kenneth Craig claims that the story of Jonah "is too earnest for laughter."[3]

The evidence for Jonah's being a comedy is much greater than evidence to the contrary, but even scholars who agree on this disagree on what sort of comedy it is. Juliana Claassens believes that Jonah is meant to be read as a tragedy turned into a comedy, thus evoking tragic laughter.[4] Claassens believes that "tragic laughter emerges out of a context of trauma and its purpose is to interrupt a system of oppression, thus serving as a form

---

1. Walker, *Illuminating Humor of the Bible*, 28, 32.
2. Derby, "Funniest Word in the Bible," 116.
3. Craig, *Poetic Jonah*, 143.
4. Claassens, "Rethinking Humour in the Book of Jonah," 655.

of resistance or protest."[5] The oppression in this case is the "devastating violence caused by empires . . . [and] by transferring tragedy into comedy this plays an important role in fostering hope, thus enabling the survival of the human spirit."[6]

The greatest consensus about Jonah appears to be that it is a satire. If so, then what are the satirical elements and what is the purpose of the satire? Further, if Jonah is a comedy, but not a satire, then what sort of comedy is it?

The following examines Conrad Hyers's view that Jonah is a satire; two other views that treat Jonah as a satire, the views of John C. Holbert, and Lance Wilcox; and Judson Mather's and Yvonne Sherwood's views that Jonah is a comedy, but not primarily a satire.

JONAH AS SATIRE—HYER'S VIEW

There are six parts to Hyers's treatment of Jonah:

- The improbable
- Unprophetic prophet
- Jonah as comic satire
- Playing with words
- Comic exaggeration and understatement
- The punch line

The Improbable

Concerning the improbable, Hyers highlights God's choosing Jonah as a messenger—improbable in its own right, given Jonah's lack of qualifications or interest—and the success that Jonah unhappily has in spite of himself. Jonah's success at warning Nineveh was for him a failure.

Steven Walker agrees that the improbable is a key component in Jonah: "What may be the shortest and certainly reigns as the crankiest sermon on religious record . . . results in the most amazing missionary success

---

5. Ibid.
6. Ibid.

in history and this among people about as likely to humble themselves as a modern New Yorker."[7]

The Unprophetic Prophet

A question among commentators on Jonah is who is the prophet? Hyers concludes that the writer of the story, not Jonah, is the prophet, and Jonah is a device in the prophecy. As evidence, Hyers offers three premises. First, there is no explicit prophetic message in the text except "yet forty days and Nineveh will be overthrown." Second, Jonah neither resembles nor is referred to as a Hebrew prophet. And third, Nineveh was so hated that it provided an "ideal test case" for God's grace.[8]

Jonah as Comic Satire

Hyers identifies four major features of Jonah as comic satire. First are the satirized aspects of Jonah. In Jonah's relationship with God, these aspects include Jonah's pride and stubbornness, with which he attempts to disobey God's order; and Jonah's hypocrisy concerning the well-being of the plant over the well-being of the Ninevites. Concerning Jonah's attitude toward the Ninevites, the satirized aspects include Jonah's prejudice, exclusivism, selfishness, and animosity. As Hyers puts it, Jonah would rather swallow the whale than go to Nineveh.[9]

The second major feature of Jonah as comic satire, Hyers claims, is the emphasis on human wisdom and divine foolishness. On this point, Hyers notes Jonah's worry that God will change his mind, Jonah's tragic view of human relationships, the writer's ridicule of Jonah's view, and Jonah's stubbornness which makes him, not God, the fool.

The third major feature is the set of eight comedic devices—"The stock-in-trade of comedy—that appear obviously in Jonah and appear in different combinations in many books of the Bible: "overstatement, understatement, surprise, opposite reaction, inconsistency, inappropriate response, ludicrous behavior, absurdity."[10]

---

7. Walker, *Illuminating Humor of the Bible*, 35.
8. Hyers, *And God Created Laughter*, ch. 7.
9. Ibid., 92.
10. Ibid., 96.

The fourth major feature is a set of four comic plot elements unique to the book of Jonah. One is Jonah's reaction to God's command: no sooner does God command Jonah to go to Nineveh than Jonah silently runs in the opposite direction. A second element is Jonah's fear that Nineveh will repent and be saved. A third element is the gaggle of compassionate sailors who strike us as more virtuous and exemplary than Jonah, the alleged prophet. And a fourth is the whale's vomiting Jonah where Jonah first left shore. This would have struck the original audience as funny on two counts: the gross bodily function and Jonah's landing right back where he started.

Word Play

Hyers notes other comic features of Jonah that may not necessarily suggest satire. One of these is word play. For example, "Jonah, son of Abittai" literally means, "Dove, son of faithfulness"—an ironic description of the faithless Jonah. There is the frequent image of rising and falling—in Jonah's movements, in the sea, and in the protective plant, for example. Jonah's prayer comes across as "fish-belly" or "fox-hole" religion. And Jonah's deliverance by being *vomited* is: "the most humiliating and undignified example of salvation in the Bible."[11]

Comic Exaggeration and Understatement

Another comic feature of Jonah is frequent exaggeration and understatement. For example, the exaggeration of Nineveh's size and the few steps Jonah takes before quickly and quietly issuing the warning; the rapid conversion of the entire city; Jonah's uncontrolled frustration at Nineveh's repenting; Jonah's mood swings under the plant; and Jonah's anger at the death of the plant while failing to understand God's pity for Nineveh.

The Punch Line

Having identified satirical and other comical elements in Jonah, Hyers offers a three-part punch line: there is no explicit resolution or moralizing;

---

11. Ibid., 103.

Jonah represents the audience, whose beliefs and attitudes are reduced to absurdity; and "if even Nineveh can be spared, who cannot be forgiven?"[12]

JONAH AS SATIRE: HOLBERT'S AND WILCOX'S VIEWS

Homiletics professor John C. Holbert and literature professor Lance Wilcox agree with Hyers that Jonah is a satire, but Holbert and Wilcox offer different reasons than Hyers offers, thus strengthening the argument that Jonah is a satire.

Holbert's View

In arguing that Jonah is a satire, Holbert rejects the view held by some that Jonah is a history. Holbert also rejects the view that Jonah is a novella, holding instead that it is a short story with satiric elements.[13]

Holbert begins helpfully by positing five basic characteristics of satire.[14] First, it includes humor based on "the fantastic, the grotesque, [or] the absurd." Second, it "has a definite target which must be familiar enough to make the assault meaningful and memorable." Third, satire "is characterized by indirection of attack. The charge comes from the flanks rather than head-on." Fourth, satire "pillories inferior excesses; hypocrisy is one classic and familiar example." And fifth, satire "is usually external in viewpoint. The psychology of the actor is less important."

With these characteristics in mind, Holbert turns his focus to Jonah. First, Holbert notes the ironic meaning of "Jonah, son of Abittai" ("Dove, the son of faithfulness") and then notes that Jonah is the object of the satirical attack.

Next Holbert notes the description of Jonah's movements: God says "Go east!" and Jonah immediately and silently goes west. Note that, in Holbert's words: "The wordless flight of the prophet is unique."[15] God says "arise!" but Jonah goes down to Joppa and goes down in the hold of the ship. The ship itself thinks that it will break up. God hurls a great wind; and the sailors hurl the ship's cargo. Holbert notes further that Jonah has gone

---

12. Ibid., 109.
13. Holbert, "Deliverance Belongs to Yahweh," 59–81.
14. Ibid., 62.
15. Ibid., 64.

down as far as he can in the ship. Finally, Jonah is now as far as possible from where God wanted him to be. Jonah thinks he has gotten away with it.

Next, Holbert notes that the captain of the storm-tossed ship thinks to call God, but Jonah does not. In Holbert's view, the Captain's command mimics God's command and it accomplishes three things: It "reiterates the huge gulf between the active, praying pagan sailors, and the sleeping, disobedient, so-called prophet of Yahweh"; "it tells the reader immediately that Jonah has not escaped God"; and "the pagan ends up commanding Jonah to do his duty."[16] What's more, the sailors become obedient to Yahweh in contrast to Jonah's disobedience. In Holbert's words, "they are Yahweh's men now."[17]

In summing up Holbert's account of the satiric elements of Jonah, Holbert notes three key satirical elements: the fantastic (storms and instant calming); the grotesque (pagans worship Yahweh, while Yahweh's prophet seeks escape); and the absurd (sleeping prophets and "worthy pagans").[18]

Having identified key characteristics of satire in general and examples of those in Jonah, Holbert turns to Jonah's psalm in the belly of the fish.[19] Here again is the grotesque—this time the great fish. Jonah's cry is about himself, not about Nineveh or the sailors. With Hyers, Holbert notes that Jonah seems to have embraced fox-hole or fish-belly religion: he promises to sacrifice and make vows, although he never does either. And the psalm ends with what turns out to be at least a double-segue: "Deliverance belongs to Yahweh": Yahweh delivers Jonah from the fish by having the fish vomit up Jonah right where Jonah set out to sea to escape Yahweh. And Yahweh delivers Nineveh.[20]

Holbert ends with two notes. First, Jonah "goes to Nineveh . . . enters the massive city part-way, and utters a five-word sermon of doom. Mark Biddle translates this from the Hebrew as, "Within forty days, Nineveh turns!"[21] "Fantastically, the entire city is seized with a fever of repentance

---

16. Ibid., 67.
17. Ibid., 69.
18. Ibid.
19. Ibid., 70.
20. Ibid.
21. Biddle, *Time to Laugh*, 57.

from the king to the cows" (3:5–9).[22] Second, Jonah is the only Hebrew and the only one who is unrepentant.[23]

Wilcox's View

Keeping in mind Holbert's claim that Jonah is the only Hebrew and the only one who is unrepentant, we find common ground in Lance Wilcox's position that the book of Jonah is a satirical attack on the Jewish purity movement.[24] To this end, Wilcox suggests, we see the silliness of Jonah's attempt to flee "the 'Eye of Omniscience'"; the ship captain's command as "pathetic and hard-boiled at once"; and the sailors' compassionate attempt to help Jonah to land.[25]

In addition, Wilcox highlights the funny speediness in turns of events; the funny matter-of-factness, e.g., "But the Lord provided a large fish to swallow up Jonah"; and the undignified rescue: "for Elijah, a flaming chariot; for Jonah, a slimy fish."[26]

The great satirical moment comes, says Wilcox, when the Ninevites repent and God forgives them. At this point "Yahweh treats Jonah much as the Prodigal Son's father treats the older brother, the good brother and Jonah react like the famously grumpy sibling" (Luke 15:29–30).[27]

Wilcox wonders how Jonah might end, if there were an ending. Wilcox imagines an ending in which "Jonah is told that if he kills Sargon, the King of Assyria, Nineveh will be destroyed. But Jonah refuses."[28]

At this point one might ask oneself, "If I were staging Jonah, whom would I cast?" The late actor in westerns, Gabby Hayes, would be an interesting possibility, if we could choose a character living or dead.

---

22. Holbert, "Deliverance Belongs to Yahweh," 74.
23. Ibid.
24. Wilcox, "Staging Jonah," 20–28.
25. Ibid., 22.
26. Ibid., 25.
27. Ibid., 27.
28. Ibid.

Part III: The Bible as Comedy

JONAH AS NON-SATIRICAL COMEDY

Humanities professor Judson Mather and religious studies professor Yvonne Sherwood regard Jonah as a non-satirical comedy. Let's consider each of these views in turn.

MATHER'S VIEW

Mather is interested in the aesthetic form of the book of Jonah, especially its emphasis on iconoclasm and mercy, and on the interplay between story and reader.[29]

In terms of its aesthetic form, Mather regards it as a situation comedy, not a satire. He bases this on two stylistic features: the frequency and audacity of burlesque and parody (especially of piety), and the artistic use of farce. On this later point, Mather highlights the relationship between Jonah and God. Mather notes that Jonah is discredited when he disobeys God and when he obeys God. Moreover, Mather asserts, Jonah is not a sinner in the hands of an angry God, but "a foil in the hand of a puckish one."[30]

Mather does regard Jonah's psalm as satirical, since it comes from the belly of a fish and Jonah appropriates "pious stock phrases."

Mather insists that the book's aesthetic form shapes its content, especially with respect to iconoclasm and mercy. The basic iconoclastic theme is Jonah, not the writer, as God's prophet. Moreover, the writer is burlesquing his own tradition for trying to idealize the incomprehensible. There is, for example, the tradition's tendency to project onto God "the consistency of idealized human rationality."[31] This consistency, in turn, comes at the expense of God's freedom. But farce, such as the story of Jonah, "provides a counter-analogy to the analogies of idealization," reminding us that "God does not have to worry about dignity."[32]

For Mather God's mercy and iconoclasm are two sides of the same theme, and eight points indicate this complexity:[33]

- God appears only to Jonah

---

29. Mather, "Comic Art of the Book of Jonah," 280–91.
30. Ibid., 283.
31. Ibid., 287.
32. Ibid.
33. Ibid., 288.

- God is Jonah's troubler
- Jonah is to the world as God is to Jonah: a "trouble bringer"
- God is merciful to Jonah and to the world
- But God waits for Jonah to be merciful first
- Jonah's appreciation of God's mercy is qualified
- Jonah's virtue of resilience and durability
- The divine character's resilience and durability

For Mather, the reader can experience Jonah's comic seduction on three levels: the reader's sense of being privy to the author's real purpose; "as an audacious, almost blasphemous satire of conventional piety"; and the intertwining of Jonah and God. At this point, Mather suggests, the reader's comic distance collapses because "The reader has been taken in by the author as Jonah has been taken in by God."[34]

Sherwood's View

Yvonne Sherwood agrees that Jonah is a comedy, but regards it as a comic dialogue and a Midrash. She claims that a comic dialogue between Jonah and God is contained in a biblical cartoon or theatre of the absurd. As cartoon it has God hurling and the worm smiting, rather than God merely sending or the worm merely nibbling. What is more, inanimate objects come alive, such as the ship who fears that it will soon break apart. As theatre of the absurd it includes scenes such as the animals donning sackcloth and mourning their sins.

At this point, Sherwood asks a thought-provoking question: who is the object of ridicule in this story? She acknowledges the consensus that Jonah is the object, but she insists that the text is ambiguous enough to invite wonder "about whether God succeeds in handling Jonah at all."[35]

Sherwood concludes that "the book of Jonah is (or is like) a Midrash, an exercise in inner biblical aggada, that does within the canon the same thing that the rabbis do to canonical texts, and that shows all of the

---

34. Ibid.
35. Sherwood, "Cross-Currents in the Book of Jonah," 56.

problematising, subverting, aggrandising, dialogising qualities of the midrashic tradition."[36]

This chapter has argued that Jonah is a comedy, whether satirical or non-satirical. This is proof that there is humor in the Old Testament. We turn next to the New Testament to see whether we can find evidence of humor there.

---

36. Ibid., 68.

10

Humor in the New Testament

> Set against the solemn humorless narrative of the gospel author are the literally repeated words of Jesus, and often they are quite out of key with the gospel author's sobrieties.
>
> —L. M. Hussey, "The Wit of the Carpenter"

> Paradox is the language of the incalculable. We are doomed to live by paradox, by the hope that rises from the tomb of Christ.
>
> —David Power, *Love without Calculation*

> One can achieve more with a smile than a frown. I think it is only natural to assume that Paul knew this also and used it in order to get his points across. There is nothing wrong in reading Paul and, for that matter, other parts of the New Testament, including Jesus' teachings, with an eye open to incongruity, sarcasm, and humor
>
> —Wilhelm Linss, "The Hidden Humor of Paul"

Part III: The Bible as Comedy

We have seen many examples of humor from the New Testament, but we have not taken a systematic look at the New Testament. Rather we have selected specific sorts of humor and then looked for those types throughout the texts. This chapter takes a more systematic look at the New Testament in three parts:

- Humor in the Gospels
- Humor in Acts and the Epistles
- Humor in Revelation

HUMOR IN THE GOSPELS

We have seen many examples of humor in the Gospels, focusing especially on the Gospels as joyful news. This section looks at humor in the Gospels in general and then at each of the four Gospels in closer detail.

Humor in the Gospels in General

Recall three aspects of New Testament humor that we have discussed already: failure to recognize Christ's humor, joy, and Christ's humor as means to the truth.

Noting that many commentaries ignore or reject the idea of humor in the New Testament, Trueblood regards these as *failures to recognize Christ's humor* and offers three possible reasons for such failure: extreme familiarity with the text; stress on the tragedy of the crucifixion; and bad logic—the false assumption that "an assertion of sadness entails a denial of humor."[1]

If Trueblood is correct, then we do well to rectify the error by looking carefully for humor in the Gospels.

The Gospels, says Hyers, are *joyful* tidings, and as we have remarked before, joy without humor is a contradiction. In addition, the Gospels often describe or point to joy. Three examples are Mary's Magnificat (Luke 1:46–55); Jesus's command to receive the kingdom of God like children (Mark 16:15); and Jesus's greeting to the two Marys after his resurrection (Matt 28:9). In this third example, while English often translates the Greek greeting simply as "Greetings!" the Greek word is *chairete*, which literally means "Rejoice!"

---

1. Trueblood, *Humor of Christ*, 21.

Other than joy, the most significant aspect of New Testament humor is Jesus's use of it to *reveal the truth*. Early on we considered humor as a means to the truth. We have talked about qualities of religious humor in general and touched on Jesus's humor more particularly. But there is more to say about Jesus's humor in general, before focusing on key parts of each Gospel. First, we should acknowledge the possible criticism that ours is a fool's errand, since Jesus never laughs in any of the Gospel narratives. That is, Jesus is "anti-gelastic," from the Greek *gelos*—laughter.[2] He even warns those who do laugh that they will weep (Luke 6:25b). But this does not preclude his having a sense of humor. Indeed, as theologian Karl Hand notes, "Many of the sayings of Jesus, which have traditionally been taken 'seriously', might be better understood as humorous subversions of oppressive discourses by a Galilean peasant with a wicked sense of humor."[3] Mark Biddle cites many instances in which Jesus appears to be winning a battle of wits, using "the riposte, the retort, and the snappy comeback."[4] Therefore, before turning to the Gospels themselves, let's look more closely at Jesus's use of humor as a means to the truth.

Different writers organize Jesus's humor in different ways. Doug Adams suggests four broad categories of Jesus's humor. Gerald Arbuckle offers several examples of Jesus's "transformative joking." Several writers offer lists of humorous elements in Jesus's life and teaching. Each of these approaches is useful and gives us a framework for seeking the humor in the Gospels.

Adams' Four Categories

Doug Adams identifies four sorts of humor that Jesus displays at one time or another.[5] First is the "Wounded-Healing Humor of Jesus" in parables such as the Prodigal Son (Luke 15:11–32). As seriously as some might tell or read the story, there is humor in the father's joy and in the older son's indignation. There also is the central theme of a healing of the relationship between the father and the wayward son. There is, in other words, the humor of joy, whether one finds anything else funny about the story.

---

2. Nel, "He Who Laughs Last," 1.
3. Hand, "Wicked Sense of Humor," 119.
4. Biddle, *Time to Laugh*, 95.
5. Adams, *Prostitute in the Family Tree*, chs. 2–5.

Second is the "Mind-Boggling Humor of Jesus' Parables" such as the mustard seed (Mark 4:30–32). Here Adams posits a humorousness besides joy: Jesus is cracking wise, using exaggeration and preposterousness.

Third is the "Cutting-Edge Satire of Jesus" in parables such as the unjust judge (Luke 18:2–5). Again, the humor is other than joy, especially using irony and paradox.

Fourth is the "Clowning Humor of Jesus' Miracles" as at the wedding of Cana (John 2:1–11). This category differs from Adams's other three in that this one describes a humorous story about Jesus in which Jesus does not seem to be acting with humor. One senses petulance on Jesus's part when his mother tells him to perform the miracle. Perhaps Jesus did delight in pulling this off, but for our purposes the point is that we may find humor in the Gospels where Jesus himself did not intend it but where the gospel writer is writing with a sense of amusement.

Arbuckle's "Transformative Joking"

Gerald Arbuckle argues that there is a joking pattern that appears throughout the Bible, including the New Testament.[6] This pattern has three stages. First, the separation from the ordinary course of things gives a cue that a joke is about to take place. Second, in the liminal stage, "the incongruity is presented and a resolution called for."[7] Third, reaggregation is "the stage in which the invigorating experience of the joke or comic incident is to be carried through into daily life."[8] Arbuckle seems to hold that any time Jesus uses humor or the gospel writer is offering a humorous narrative, the reader can find this pattern. Consider a couple of Arbuckle's examples: the Annunciation (Luke 1:26–45) and the Transfiguration (Matt 17).[9]

In Luke 1:26–39, the separation stage for Mary is from ordinary young woman to the mother of God. The liminal stage occurs with the angel's greeting. And the reaggregation stage occurs when Mary visits Elizabeth and Mary takes on full responsibility for her role. The joke appears to be that someone as socially insignificant as Mary will be the mother of God and that she will conceive without losing her virginity. Moreover, for being so humble she assumes the responsibility with courage and determination.

6. Arbuckle, *Laughing with God*, 7.
7. Ibid.
8. Ibid.
9. Ibid., 71, 72.

It is easy to see Arbuckle's three stages in this narrative; it is more difficult to determine whether there is a joke of the sort Arbuckle imagines.

Something similar happens with Arbuckle's analysis of the transfiguration. The separation stage "is the ascent of the mountain (Matt 17:1); this is to remind the disciples that something extraordinarily important is about to happen."[10] The liminal stage begins with God's speaking (17:5) and includes the comic elements of Jesus as the suffering servant (not a political revolutionary); Peter's loss for what to do and his offer to build three shelters; and Jesus's concern to calm the fears of the witnesses. The reaggregation is marked by the discovery that "Jesus is now alone, back to his normal physical self."[11] Again, the three stages in the narrative may be more obvious than the humor, especially if the humor was intentional.

Eight Types of Humor in Jesus's Preaching and Practice

Eight types of humor stand out in Jesus's ministry even as one might identify many more:

- Irony
- Paradox
- The Preposterous
- Banter
- Exaggeration
- The Unexpected
- Repetition
- Justice

Trueblood singles out the first four of these; Earl Palmer discusses the other four while adding seven others (misunderstanding, healing, argument, saltiness, love and joy). Let's take a closer look at each of the eight.

---

10. Ibid., 77.
11. Ibid., 78.

Part III: The Bible as Comedy

Irony

Elton Trueblood notes three ways Jesus uses irony in conveying the truth: controversy, parable, and short dialogue.[12] We will consider short dialogue under the heading of banter.

Regarding *controversy*, Trueblood claims that "Christ's major weapon against the Pharisaic attack was laughter and He used it fully," as in Matt 23:1–12, when Jesus tells the crowds and his disciples to do as the Pharisees teach, but not as they do, "for they do not practice what they teach" (v. 3b). They foist their burdens on others and they live ostentatiously. To their detriment, "The greatest among you will be your servant. All who exalt themselves will be humbled, and all who humble themselves will be exalted" (vv. 11, 12).

As for a humorous *parable*, Trueblood cites Mark 2:21–22, "the finest example of humor in the parables of Christ."[13] In this passage, Jesus notes that no one puts a new patch on old cloth or new wine in old wineskins. Trueblood claims that "the point of the double parable is transparently clear ... the change in order to be effective, must be a radical change."[14]

Presbyterian minister Earl Palmer cites the *short dialogue* among Philip, Nathaniel, and Jesus as a sophisticated example of Jesus's irony (John 1:45–51).[15] The key is Jesus's remark about Nathaniel: "When Jesus saw Nathanael coming toward him, he said of him, 'Here is truly an Israelite in whom there is no deceit!'" (v. 47). Palmer explains that "what is ironically funny here is that the name Israel in the Hebrew language actually means 'guile, deception.' It was Jacob's deception of his brother Esau that had given Jacob his less than heroic name 'Israel,' which means 'deceiver.' Jesus has told an ironic joke about the very name of God's beloved people and in the heart of the humor Jesus has honored Nathaniel."[16]

Paradox

Two obvious examples of Jesus's use of paradox are Luke 6:39 and Matt 5:3–5. Luke writes, "He also told them a parable: 'Can a blind person guide

---

12. Trueblood, *Humor of Christ*, 10.
13. Ibid., 98.
14. Ibid., 10.
15. Palmer, *Humor of Jesus*, 77.
16. Ibid.

a blind person? Will not both fall into a pit?'" Matthew has Jesus saying, "Blessed are the poor in spirit, for theirs is the kingdom of heaven; Blessed are those who mourn, for they will be comforted; Blessed are the meek, for they will inherit the earth."

Gerald Arbuckle notes that "to live the paradox of Christ's detachment and exaltation we need to follow the ritual joking pattern established by him."[17]

Trueblood adds, "What is bound to occur to one who is familiar with the Gospels is that the humor of Christ is based on connections which are genuine, but which ordinary men do not recognize without help."[18]

The Preposterous

Trueblood describes the *preposterous* as the coming together of surprise opposites.[19] He cites two biblical examples, noting that they both have in common a preposterous invoking of a camel. Mark 10:25 reads: "It is easier for a camel to go through the eye of a needle than for someone who is rich to enter the kingdom of God." Matthew 23:24 reads: "You blind guides! You strain out a gnat but swallow a camel!" Trueblood notes that "Christ made sure that it was memorable, whereas a prosy, qualified statement would certainly have been forgotten."[20]

Banter

As an example of Jesus's *banter*, Trueblood cites the encounter with the Syrophoenician woman in Mark 7:24-30:[21] The woman asks Jesus to cast a demon out of her daughter. Jesus rebuffs her initially, "Let the children be fed first, for it is not fair to take the children's food and throw it to the dogs" (v. 27). But the woman persists, "Sir, even the dogs under the table eat the children's crumbs" (v. 28). Because she said that, Jesus changes his mind and heals the daughter.

---

17. Arbuckle, *Laughing with God*, 70.
18. Trueblood, *Humor of Christ*, 42.
19. Ibid., 46.
20. Ibid., 47.
21. Ibid., 79.

Part III: The Bible as Comedy

Trueblood makes two points concerning this passage. First, "the clue to Christ's spirit in the entire encounter is His immediate affirmative and friendly response to the woman's wit."[22] Second, "there is a more widespread recognition of this encounter as humorous than of any other particular part of the Gospel record."[23]

Exaggeration

An obvious example of Jesus's *exaggeration* is his chastising the hypocrite in Matt 7:3–5 for presuming to remove the speck from his neighbor's eye without noticing or removing the log from his own eye. This also serves as an example of the preposterous.

Earl Palmer regards as "hyperbole at its most extreme," the exchange between Jesus and Peter in which Jesus says, "Get behind me, Satan! You are a stumbling block to me; for you are setting your mind not on divine things but on human things" (Matt 16:23).[24] As Palmer notes, Peter is not Satan or any sort of angel—fallen or unfallen: "The disciples would be able to laugh about this shocking rejoinder of Jesus, but this word to Peter and the other disciples is clearly heard through the exaggeration. They must not, indeed they *cannot* finally stand in the way of the journey that Jesus knows is his and his alone."[25]

The Unexpected

According to Palmer, the parable of the vineyard workers (Matt 20:1–16) offers an example of the humor of the *unexpected*: "The laughter belongs to the one-hour workers who could not imagine such a windfall of good fortune after they had spent most of a day worried about how they could earn enough money to feed their families and then by surprise near the end of the day they are employed and paid as if that had worked all day."[26]

---

22. Ibid., 122.
23. Ibid., 116.
24. Palmer, *Humor of Jesus*, 67.
25. Ibid.
26. Ibid., 42.

Repetition

Palmer claims that Jesus's parables exhibit masterful "use of repetitious humor and pathos."[27] Palmer offers two examples: the three parables in Luke 15 and Jesus's exchange with Peter in John 21:15–17. The parables in Luke 15 include the Lost Sheep, the Lost Coin, and the Prodigal Son. For Palmer, these parables are "whimsical and exciting.... Each story is the same; each builds in intensity, and each story is humorous at different levels."[28]

In Jesus's exchange with Peter, Jesus asks Peter three times whether he loves Jesus, and Peter answers three times, with exasperation, that he does. For Palmer, these three questions "are another example of the use of repetition that has about it a troubling aspect for Peter but at its core there is the unmistakable mark of humor too."[29]

Justice

Rounding out our list of examples of Jesus's use of humor as a means to the truth is his appeal to justice. As an example, Palmer cites the story of the adulteress in John 8. The scribes and Pharisees have brought this woman before Jesus and noted her offense and the Mosaic law that calls for her being stoned to death. What, they ask Jesus, does he say? He answers, "Let anyone among you who is without sin be the first to throw a stone at her" (v. 7). When no one condemns her, Jesus sends her on her way, telling her not to sin again.

For Palmer, this is an example of Jesus as a righteous judge, using "the humor of justice to clear the air and to encourage us to see into ourselves and our motives and to look closely at our freedoms and at our captivities."[30] Palmer regards this as "righteous humor because it connects the listener to his or her own obedience to the law of God."[31]

Having taken a look at humor in the Gospels in general, let's look more closely for humor in each of the four Gospels in turn.

---

27. Ibid., 49.
28. Ibid.
29. Ibid., 50.
30. Ibid., 56.
31. Ibid., 58.

PART III: THE BIBLE AS COMEDY
Humor in Matthew

For our purposes it is useful to divide the Gospel of Matthew into seven parts:

- Jesus's birth and childhood: Matt 1:1—2:23
- Jesus's preparation for ministry: Matt 3:1—4:11
- Jesus's ministry in Galilee: Matt 4:12—18:35
- Jesus's ministry in Judea: Matt 19:1—20:34
- Jesus's ministry in Jerusalem: Matt 21:1—25:46
- Jesus's suffering: Matt 26:1—27:66
- Jesus's resurrection: Matt 28:1-20

In all but part 6—Jesus's suffering—we may identify some elements of humor.

Matthew, describing *Jesus's birth and childhood*, opens with a genealogy that includes women of questionable repute (Tamar [Gen 28] and Rahab [Josh 2 & 6]). Some have found this funny, including Douglas Adams who entitled his book *The Prostitute in the Family Tree*. There is also the joy of Jesus's birth.

Arbuckle argues that Jesus's *preparation for ministry* turns on his initiation as the anointed prophet.[32] This initiation follows the three-part joke pattern of separation (removal to the river Jordan and then the dessert); liminality (the temptation of Jesus and his resistance); and reaggregation (the arrival of the angels and Jesus's taking up his role as prophet and son of God).

By most accounts the section of Matthew most full of humorous elements is the section describing *Jesus's ministry in Galilee* (4:12—18:35). It contains, for example, the irony in the Sermon on the Mount (5-7) and several digs at the Pharisees, including the preposterousness of presuming to remove the speck from one's neighbor's eye while failing to remove the log from one's own eye (7:34). It describes the blind leading the blind (15:14), "Peter" as Simon's nickname (16:18), and Jesus's banter with the Canaanite woman (15:21-28).

Matthew's account of *Jesus's ministry in Judea* (19:1—20:34) includes exaggeration and paradox. The account of *Jesus's ministry in Jerusalem*

---

32. Arbuckle, *Laughing with God*, 73.

includes Jesus's biting and sustained roasting of the scribes and Pharisees, invoking the image of the camel through the eye of the needle (19:24) and warning that the first shall be last (19:30). The account of Jesus's resurrection has him hailing the Marys with *"chairete"*—Rejoice!

Humor in Mark

It's useful for our purposes to divide Mark into four sections:

- The Beginnings of Jesus's Ministry: Mark 1:1–13
- Jesus's Ministry up to the Passion: Mark 1:14–10
- The Passion of Jesus: Mark 11–15
- The Resurrection of Jesus: Mark 16

Biblical scholar Kelly Iverson claims that "in Mark, humor is a natural byproduct of performance and is a powerful means of communicating a central theme of the Gospel."[33] Much of what we find in Matthew either in spirit or in content, we find also in Mark and generally in the same parts of the narrative. Thus, during Jesus's ministry, there is the banter with the Canaanite woman (7:24–30) and the quip about the camel through the eye of the needle (10:25). Iverson finds the third sea crossing (Mark 8:14–21) to be humorous because of the absurdity of the disciples and whether they had bread.[34] As in Matthew (18:3) there is Jesus's call to receive the kingdom of heaven like children (10:15). Note especially Mark's observation, as the Passion approaches, that as Jesus's jousts with the scribes and the Pharisees, "the large crowd was listening to him with delight" (12:37). As Lee Van Rensburg notes, this speaks volumes about the humor with which Jesus presented himself.[35]

Humor in Luke

As the third of the Synoptic Gospels, Luke's narrative is similar to Matthew's and Mark's, but Michael Potella claims that Luke's version of the

---

33. Iverson, "Incongruity, Humor, and Mark," 2.
34. Ibid., 11.
35. Van Rensburg, *Sense of Humor*, 25.

resurrection "rewrites the whole story of biblical laughter."[36] For our purposes, we may divide Luke into eight parts:

- Introduction: Luke 1:1–4
- Jesus's birth and childhood: Luke 1:5—2:52
- Jesus's preparation for ministry: Luke 3:1—4:13
- Jesus's ministry in Galilee: Luke 4:14—9:50
- Jesus's journey to Jerusalem: Luke 9:51—19:48
- Jesus's preaching and teaching in Jerusalem: Luke 20:1—21:38
- Jesus's suffering and death: Luke 21:1—23:56
- Jesus's resurrection: Luke 24:1–53

Luke contains many of the humorous qualities of Matthew and Mark, but it is arguable that Luke emphasizes joy more. Thus presaging Jesus's birth, we find John the Baptist leaping in the womb for joy at Mary's greeting to Elizabeth (1:44). Most notable is Mary's *Magnificat* (1:46-55). Arbuckle notes that the song proclaims three revolutions: the moral revolution of scattering the proud; the social revolution of lifting up the lowly; and the economic revolution of filling the hungry with good things and sending the rich away empty.[37] Note too the shepherds receiving the joyful news of Jesus's birth (2:10).

During Jesus's ministry in Galilee, Luke reports, Jesus used paradox, as in the reference of the blind leading the blind (6:39). Luke notes the joyful return of seventy evangelists during Jesus's journey to Jerusalem (10:17). And Jesus offers many parables, often humorous. There is the Good Samaritan (10:29–37), which Earl Palmer says is an example of the humor of love and Van Rensburg calls a comic reversal.[38] Bruce Longenecker claims that while listeners to the parable might have laughed, Jesus didn't mean it to be funny.[39]

There is the parable of the dinner (14:15–24), which Longenecker calls the "only truly jocular tale in the New Testament" and Van Rensburg considers another example of the comedy of reversal.[40]

---

36. Potella, "And God Created Laughter," 160.
37. Arbuckle, *Laughing with God*, 31.
38. Palmer, *Humor of Jesus*, 104; Van Rensburg, *Sense of Humor*, 26.
39. Longenecker, "Humorous Jesus?," 183.
40. Longenecker, "Humorous Jesus?," 183; Van Rensburg, *Sense of Humor*, 26.

Then there are the three parables in Luke 15, which Palmer claims reflects the humor of repetition.[41]

Palmer regards as salty humor Jesus's call to render unto Caesar what is Caesar's, during his teaching in Jerusalem (20:21–26).[42] Palmer does not explain in detail what it means to call this humor "salty."

Van Rensburg notes Jesus's continued use of paradox even as he nears the end of his earthly ministry, when Jesus tells his disciples that the greatest must serve the least (22:26).[43] And we may note that as in the other Gospels, Luke has the U-shaped plot that ends on a happy note with Jesus's resurrection (24:1–53)—the plot device that several commentators regard as the essence of classical comedy.

Humor in John

It's useful for our purposes to divide the Gospel of John in to five parts.

- Prologue: Jesus as the incarnate word: John 1:1–18
- Four witnesses: John 1:19–51
- Jesus's works, words, and signs: John 2–12
- Jesus's witness to his disciples: John 13–17
- The Trial, Death, and Resurrection: John 18–21

The humor comes especially in the middle three parts, with irony being paramount. And as usual the Gospel ends on the up-note of the U-shaped plot that we have seen identified with classical comedy.

Through the witness of Nathaniel, we see the humor of irony when he asks, "Can anything good come out of Nazareth?" (1:46). Among the many stories of Jesus's works, we find the humor of the unexpected, as at the Wedding at Cana (2); the humor of banter in Jesus's conversation with the Samaritan woman at the well (4:7–26); and the humor of justice when Jesus saves the woman who is about to be stoned to death (8).[44]

---

41. Palmer, *Humor of Jesus*, 15.
42. Ibid., 104.
43. Van Rensburg, *Sense of Humor*, 26.
44. Palmer, *Humor of Jesus*, 58.

Part III: The Bible as Comedy

While irony is the key humorous element in John, John also calls us to joy, as is evident in Jesus's promise to his disciples that their grief will turn to joy and no one will take that away (13–17).

Where joy is the key humorous ingredient in the Gospel of Luke, scholars tend to identify irony as the main humorous ingredient in John. As an example, theologian Paul Duke offers

> the interesting interplay on the theme of the weak and the strong. Who gives the most direct witness to Christ? An outsider, a Samaritan woman. Who claims the body of Christ after crucifixion? The strong disciples? No, two weak ones—Nicodemus, who comes off quite badly earlier in the Gospel, and Joseph of Arimathea. Who is indisputable victor in the Gospel?[45]

Lutheran pastor Frank Honeycutt has a novel take on the humorous Jesus in the Gospel of John.[46] Honeycutt regards Jesus as a theological tease. For example, he tricks Mary into thinking he is the gardener (John 20:15). Also, he teases Philip about what to feed the people, already knowing what he, Jesus, is going to do (John 6:5). Honeycutt believes that Jesus is doing this to teach.

HUMOR IN ACTS AND THE LETTERS

In this section we look at humor in the book of Acts, Paul's letters, and non-Pauline letters.

Humor in Acts

Steven Walker claims that "Acts may have proven to be, after a closer look, the funniest book in the New Testament."[47]

The book of Acts has four major parts:

- The beginning of the church: Acts 1
- The church in Jerusalem: Acts 2—8:3
- The church spreads into Palestine and Syria: Acts 8:4—12:25 (including Paul's conversion: Acts 9:1–9)

---

45. Duke, *Irony in the Fourth Gospel*, 32.
46. Honeycutt, "Jester and Tester," 33.
47. Walker, *Illuminating Humor of the Bible*, 121.

- The church spreads further: Acts 13–28

Biblical scholar John Goldingay finds a lot of humor in the second through fourth parts of Acts, while acknowledging that few people have made such an effort. The humor is threefold: "humor at the expense of outsiders (unbelieving Jews, pagans, and imperial authorities); . . . humor at the expense of insiders (great leaders and ordinary believers) . . . and humor to mediate doom and gloom."[48]

Concerning humor at the *expense of outsiders*, Luke aims to draw a stark contrast between Caesar's power and God's power.[49] The Jewish leaders mistakenly think that people have been drinking too much (2:13); and while the leaders see Peter and John healing, the leaders cannot acknowledge their implications or stop their activity (4:13–22). Also, angels subvert the Sadducees' attempt to imprison the apostles—opening the prison doors, sending the apostles back to the temples, and "evidently also locking the doors again behind them (5:17–26), with the comic speed of an old Keystone Cops movie."[50]

Jewish unbelievers in Damascus conspire to catch the converted Paul, but he escapes in a basket (9:24–25). Later similar folks in Antioch and Iconium "think they've stoned Paul to death, but he gets up and goes back into their city" (14:19–20).[51]

Also, Sceva's sons—exorcists possessed by evil spirits—"ask of unbelievers exorcising in Jesus' name, 'We know Jesus and Paul, but who are you?' [but are] are overcome and flee naked (19.13–16)."[52]

As for the pagans, they feel compelled to worship Paul and Barnabas, the latter's protest notwithstanding (14:18), and "the Maltese regard Paul as a murderer, but then as a god (28:1–6)."[53] The presence of Paul also affects Felix, who is frightened by Paul's preaching (24:25); Festus, who "thinks Paul is mad (26.24)"; and Agrippa who "nearly gets converted (26.28–29)."[54] Also, "the authorities become the means of Paul's reaching Rome itself with his gospel (28.31)."[55]

48. Goldingay, "Are They Comic Acts?," 102–6.
49. Ibid., 104.
50. Ibid., 102.
51. Ibid., 103.
52. Ibid.
53. Ibid., 104.
54. Ibid.
55. Ibid.

Part III: The Bible as Comedy

Concerning humor at the *expense of insiders*, Goldingay believes that some passages in Acts are gently mocking in order to show that we should not take the apostles too seriously and to show God's freedom.[56] For example, at Pentecost when some suggest the apostles are drunk, "Peter produces as contrary evidence the consideration that it is only nine o'clock in the morning (2.15), which seems a feeble argument."[57] Also, when people ask Stephen about his preaching, he "delivers a gargantuan summary of Old Testament history which must have left his audience puzzled over its relevance (7.1–53)."[58] And once Paul has achieved prominence, he "becomes open to being a fool for Christ," escaping Damascus in a basket (9:24–25), and later preaching so long a sermon that Eutychus falls asleep listening to it and falls out of a window (20:9).[59]

Acts also contains humor *to mediate joy and gloom*:

> Humour can buttress the message by suggesting a happy incongruity between what one might have expected and what actually, happens. It can mirror the joy of the events that are related or ... it can mediate or convey or engender that joy, as metaphor facilitates understanding rather than merely communicating it.[60]

Two examples are the disabled beggar who gets healing and joy instead of alms (3:2–8), and "the puzzled Ethiopian who gets good news and joy instead of merely the solution to an exegetical problem" (8:26–40).[61]

In spite of the foregoing, Goldingay claims that the humor in Acts tends to be "macabre or black humour, another form of incongruity."[62] Examples include the death of Judas by falling over so his bowels gush out (1:18); Ananias and Sapphira collapsing dead after trying to deceive the church (5:1–11); the execution of Peter's prison guards for failing to prevent the angel from freeing Peter (12:19); and Herod's death from being eaten by worms (12:23). According to Goldingay, the grotesqueness of the humor puts distance between the awful events in Acts and us: "In this form, at least, what happens could not happen to me."[63]

56. Ibid.
57. Ibid., 105.
58. Ibid.
59. Ibid.
60. Ibid., 106.
61. Ibid.
62. Ibid.
63. Ibid.

Humor in Paul's Letters

We turn to Paul and his letters. First, we consider some remarks about Paul's humor in general. Then we look at some examples of his humor in six of his letters:

- Romans
- 1 and 2 Corinthians
- Galatians
- 1 Thessalonians
- Philemon

Wilhelm Linss holds that "Paul uses humor, irony, and sarcasm," although it is difficult to find any scholarship that acknowledges this.[64]

Douglas Adams claims that Paul writes "grandmother letters" rather than parental letters in that they "avoid bragging in favor of more realism."[65] These are "grandmother letters," says Adams because they include Paul's failings and the failings of the early church, where "a parental letter would have mentioned only the successes."[66] Adams would have us look for Paul's parody of prideful autobiographies; his boasting of weakness through parody and sarcasm; and his "mind boggling" humorous digressions.[67]

Arbuckle makes three points concerning Paul's humor. First, Paul's oppression does nothing to dampen his joy now that he lives in Christ (Gal 2:20).[68] Second, Paul preaches "the need to build a peaceful community, but [acts] in ways that prevent this happening."[69] Third, in spite of the somber language of Paul's letters, "he uses ironical language to contrast the gaps between Christ's teachings and those of worldly people."[70]

Wilhelm Linss claims that Paul's letter to the *Romans* contains several sarcastic and ironic remarks. For example, in Romans 9:20, Paul chastises people for asking questions of God, as if they were pots asking the potter

---

64. Linss, "Hidden Humor of Paul," 195.
65. Adams, "Paul as Humorist," 85.
66. Adams, *Prostitute in the Family Tree*, 78.
67. Adams, "Paul as Humorist," 86–87.
68. Arbuckle, *Laughing with God*, 31.
69. Ibid., 32.
70. Ibid.

why he made them: "It points out the ridiculousness of people who argue with God."[71]

More generally, Douglas Adams says that central to the humor he sees in Romans is the inhabitant's sense of superiority and Paul's refusal to play to it: "Paul writes to the Romans at length about issues that are not central to their concerns (like writing to someone in New York and going on and on about Iowa corn prices)."[72]

If we look for humor in *1 Corinthians* we will find Paul acting as a fool for Christ, using irony, digression, sarcasm, and mockery.

Recognizing the foolishness of the cross to those who don't get it, Paul admits in that vein to being a fool for Christ (1:18). It is no surprise, then, to find him directing humor at himself. Van Rensburg offers three examples of this: Paul can't remember whether he has baptized anyone else (1:16); Paul regards himself as the dregs of all things (4:13); and Paul regards himself as untimely born (15:8).[73]

Positing a lot of irony in 1 Corinthians, Van Rensburg offers three examples of this. First, Paul acknowledges the irony of his ministry as the least of the apostles being given so grand a mission (1 Cor 15:8–9). As Van Rensburg puts it, "It is the least of the Apostles that gives us the majority of our New Testament!"[74] Second, Paul anticipates the irony of his being rejected after having preached to others (1 Cor 9:27).[75] Third, Paul preaches the irony of the gospel in God's making fools of the "wise" and choosing the "weak things of the world, that he might put to shame the things that are strong" (1 Cor 1:27–28).[76]

Regarding Paul's use of digression, Douglas Adams notes that Paul ignores the questions the Corinthians have written to him until the beginning of chapter 7, where he says, "Now concerning the matters about which you wrote."[77] Adams continues,

> By ignoring the Corinthians' questions, Paul punctures the inflated importance they have attached to them. When he finally deals with them (1 Cor 7:3–4), Paul gives both/and rather than either/

---

71. Linss, "Hidden Humor of Paul," 197.
72. Adams, "Paul as Humorist," 87.
73. Van Rensburg, *Sense of Humor*, 5.
74. Ibid.
75. Ibid.
76. Ibid.
77. Adams, "Paul as Humorist," 83.

or answers: that is, he affirms both contending parties rather than siding with one or the other. . . . The humor comes in part from piling, one on top of the last, a whole string of such both/and responses in chapter 7, much as he piles up a whole string of complex questions in chapter 6. The effect is to boggle the mind.[78]

Regarding Paul's sarcasm and mockery, Arbuckle notes that Paul uses "stinging and mocking" humor to distinguish loyal from disloyal followers of Christ.[79] He does this by naming himself foolish while his opponents are "wise" and "strong," held in "honor" but he is in "disrepute" (1 Cor 4:10). Adams agrees, noting also Paul's cruel sarcastic laughter (1 Cor 1:18).[80]

Concerning 2 *Corinthians*, Douglas Adams regards Paul's references to himself as "anti-autobiography," which in turn parodies traditional autobiographies.[81] The latter tend to celebrate the author—why write an autobiography if you're not a celebrity? But Paul writes about being an unworthy fool.

Arbuckle adds that "the same wry humor is evident in Paul's self-assessment of his apostolic zeal in the face of personal suffering, as recorded in" 2 Corinthians.[82] He is as fragile as a clay pot (2 Cor 4:7), but because he has God's power, "he is not crushed or destroyed."[83]

Although scholarly treatment of Paul's humor emphasizes the letters to the Corinthians, scholars find humor in other letters as well. Adams notes that some of Paul's humorous expressions may seem unfunny when taken out of context. For example, in Gal 1:8–9, "Paul appears to be harsh when saying that an unnamed person should be 'accursed,' but he goes on in the first three chapters to include himself and then Peter and finally all the Galatians in the same boat as the one who is accursed and then adds that Christ has redeemed us from the curse"[84] Several scholars have noted the humor of Gal 5:1–12 in which Paul ridicules the argument that circumcision is necessary to salvation. If minor surgery is good than radical surgery must be better!

---

78. Ibid.
79. Arbuckle, *Laughing with God*, 89.
80. Adams, "Paul as Humorist," 83.
81. Ibid., 80–81.
82. Arbuckle, *Laughing with God*, 35.
83. Ibid.
84. Adams, *Prostitute in the Family Tree*, 95.

Part III: The Bible as Comedy

James Martin notes that in *1 Thessalonians*, "Paul isn't responding to heated theological debate nor is he scolding," unlike in other letters.[85] Thus, there is an unusual lightheartedness, which Paul punctuates with his comment toward the end of the letter: "Rejoice always, pray without ceasing, give thanks in all circumstances; for this is the will of God in Christ Jesus for you" (1 Thess 5:16–18).

Concerning *Philemon*, Adams notes that Paul uses "a different style of humor... praises instead of curses to lead Philemon to do as Paul wishes."[86] Linss notes that "the name Onesimus in the letter to Philemon means 'useful.' So it is a humorous statement when Paul says about him in v. 11, 'Formerly he was useless to you, but now he is indeed useful both to you and to me.'"[87]

Humor in Hebrews and James

Given the lenses we have encountered in this inquiry, we might well find humor in every biblical letter. For now, let's close with a brief look at the letter to the Hebrews and the letter of James. In both cases the emphasis for those seeking humor is joy. Recalling the many times we have noted that joy without a sense of humor seems impossible, we can conclude that both of these letters have enough humor to undergird the call to joy. Hebrews 12:2 calls us to look to Jesus "who for the sake of the joy that was set before him endured the cross."

James 1:2–4 reads, "My brothers and sisters, whenever you face trials of any kind, consider it nothing but joy, because you know that the testing of your faith produces endurance; and let endurance have its full effect, so that you may be mature and complete, lacking in nothing."

HUMOR IN REVELATION

Revelation might be one of the last biblical books we think of when we think of humor in the Bible, but it ends on an up-note, the ubiquitous U-shape of the biblical narrative, according to many scholars. And it promises endless joy to people. Beyond that it might be difficult to locate specific examples

---

85. Martin, *Between Heaven and Mirth*, 213.
86. Adams, *Prostitute in the Family Tree*, 96.
87. Linss, "Hidden Humor of Paul," 196.

of humor in the text. Nonetheless biblical scholar Stephan Witetschek has made a convincing attempt at this in his essay "The Dragon Spitting Frogs: On the Imagery of Revelation 16:13–24,"[88] Witetschek regards this passage as "a short intermezzo of comic relief within the apocalyptic drama."[89] To make his point Witetschek means to show that to Greeks and Jews, frogs imply "silliness and loquaciousness ... therefore, frog-like demons constitute John's strategy of reassuring his audiences by ridiculing the dragon and the beast of the powers they represent."[90] To demonstrate this Witetschek develops his essay in five steps: the "diabolic bestiary" of Revelation; the selection in context; frogs in contemporary Greek literature; frogs in the Old Testament and early Jewish literature; and the function of imagery in Rev 16:13–14.

Regarding the diabolic bestiary, Witetschek notes that "John uses a highly developed animal imagery, drawn from previous apocalyptic traditions, to depict the enemies of God and of the Christians as graphically as possible."[91] In this case, Witetschek notes, "three unclean spirits like frogs come from the mouths of the satanic triad: the dragon, the beast, and the fake prophet."[92]

According to Witetschek, frogs are a common literary device in the Greek literature that was contemporaneous with Revelation. This was true in earlier Greek authors as well. One finds frogs in Aesop, Aristophanes, Artemidorus's dream book, Plutarch, Chrysostom, and medical writers. The common purpose, Witetschek suggests, is to display the "unintelligible but intrusive croaking and silliness."[93]

Frogs make up the second of ten plagues that God brings upon Egypt for not letting the Israelites go (Exod 7:26–8:11). For Witetschek, "one can hardly deny an intention to entertain the audience and to make fun of mighty Egypt in these verses."

Witetschek describes in detail the Book of Wisdom's reception of Exodus, including the plague of frogs (Wis 16:1–4; 15:18–19; 19:10). But he believes that Wisdom treats frogs differently than Exodus does: in the Exodus, frogs are "just elements of comic; Wisdom in its reception of the

88. Witetschek, "Dragon Spitting Frogs," 557–72.
89. Ibid., 572.
90. Ibid., 557.
91. Ibid.
92. Ibid.
93. Ibid., 559.

Exodus story gives the frogs a clearly negative meaning of themselves: they are ugly and silly."[94]

According to Witetschek, Philo of Alexandria, in his *On the Sacrifices of Abel and Cain*, "allegorises the frogs with their loud and senseless croaking as the 'soulless opinions' that blind the eyes of Pharaoh's soul."[95] And Flavius Joseph "particularly stresses the abominable appearance of frogs—especially when they come into contact with food—and the disgust caused by dead and rotting frogs."[96]

Witetschek notes that many scholars see frequent references to Exodus in Revelation, thus it is possible that the frogs in Revelation are meant to invoke the frogs of Exodus. The problem with this hypothesis, Witetschek concedes, is that the frogs in Revelation are not unclean animals although the spirits they contain are unclean. Nevertheless they may symbolize inane croaking and silliness in a similar way.

Witetschek reminds us that John speaks of unclean spirits *like* frogs. Witetschek asks, why frogs and not some other animal that could also contain unclean spirits? He rejects the possible answer that it has to do with frogs' possible similarity to dragons and snakes. John is too creative for this, thus, "it should be assumed that the simply frog-like appearance of these unclean spirits is not without a specific purpose."[97]

Often when John invokes beasts (as in Rev 13, for example), he does so in "polemical parallelism" to Christ. Thus, we might benefit from figuring out what corresponds to the frogs on the right side."[98] It could be the three angels of Rev 14:6–13, although Witetschek decides that the parallelism is between the frogs on the one hand and the many Christ visions on the other. As Witetschek puts it, 'polemical parallelism' means that "all impressive displays of the ungodly powers are in fact nothing but poor imitations of God's genuine power and glory."[99]

Another purpose of the frogs, says, Witetschek, is to deceive, but John makes it clear that they will ultimately fail. The frogs are, in other words, foolish deceivers.

---

94. Ibid., 563.
95. Ibid., 564.
96. Ibid.
97. Ibid., 566.
98. Ibid., 567.
99. Ibid.

Witetschek concludes that the frogs represent a satanic triad, talk of which is "ultimately nothing better than silly, senseless, even grotesque croaking."[100] Therefore, John is using the frog imagery "to ridicule the demonic powers." And, therefore, the frog image is a deliberate joke.

We have come to the end of this chapter in which we looked for humor throughout the New Testament. In the next chapter we will focus on one small, but important piece of the New Testament—the parable of the talents.

---

100. Ibid., 569.

11

Humor in the Parable of the Talents

> The parable [of the talents] appears at first sight to be straightforward and simple, but it is one of the most difficult parables of Jesus to interpret.
> —George O. Folarin, "The Parable of the Talents in the African Context"

This chapter focuses on one parable, the parable of the talents, in Matthew, and, where useful, its Lukan counterpart, the parable of the pounds. The many possible and posited interpretations of the parable make it possible, if not likely, that the original audience would have regarded the parable as humorous. This chapter has three parts: comparison and contrast of the texts of the two parables; a look at several interpretations of the parables, other than those that ascribe humor to them; and a look at several interpretations which agree that the parable of the talents is humorous.

PARABLE OF THE TALENTS/ POUNDS

This section compares the texts in Matthew and Luke, identifies the common and different elements in each text, and considers whether the two parables are making the same point.

Humor in the Parable of the Talents

The Two Texts

Matthew 25:14–30

Before leaving on a journey a master distributes his talents among three slaves: five talents to one slave, two talents to another slave, and one talent to the third slave. The first two slaves manage to double their holdings in successful business deals; the third slave hides the one talent to keep it safe.

When the master returns and learns of his slaves' handling of the money, he rewards the first two for their trustworthiness and invites them to "enter into the joy of your master" (vv. 21, 23). The third slave, admitting his fear of the master as someone who is "a harsh man, reaping where you did not sow, and gathering where you did not scatter seed" (v. 24), hands the one carefully hidden talent back to his master. Enraged, the master calls this third slave "wicked and lazy," notes that he should have invested wisely as his two counterparts did, demands that the one talent be given to the slave with ten talents, and concludes,

> For to all those who have, more will be given, and they will have an abundance; but from those who have nothing, even what they have will be taken away. As for this worthless slave, throw him into the outer darkness, where there will be weeping and gnashing of teeth. (vv. 29–30)

Luke 19:12–27

Before leaving on a journey "to get royal power for himself and then return" (v. 12), a nobleman gives a pound each to ten of his slaves and tells them to "do business with them until I get back" (v. 13). At this point the narrative takes an odd turn: "But the citizens of his country hated him and sent a delegation after him, saying, 'We do not want this man to rule over us'" (v. 14).

When the nobleman returns, "having received his royal power," he gathers his slaves to see how well they have done with his money. One slave returns ten pounds for the one he had received. Another slave returns five pounds for the one he had received. And the third, admitting his fear of the nobleman as "a harsh man" who takes what he does not deposit and reaps what he does not sow (v. 21), returns the once carefully hidden pound back to the nobleman. Enraged, the nobleman tells the bystanders to take the one talent and give it to the slave with ten talents. The bystanders seem to think this unfair—(and they said to him, "Lord, he has ten pounds!") (v.25)—but the nobleman persists, concluding,

> I tell you, to all those who have, more will be given; but from those who have nothing, even what they have will be taken away. But as for these enemies of mine who did not want me to be king over them—bring them here and slaughter them in my presence. (vv. 26–27)

Common Elements

Both parables have a similar basic plot and both express similar attitudes among the central characters. The plot of each has four parts in common: the master/nobleman gives slaves money; all but one of the slaves invest the money successfully, while the remaining slave hides the money for safekeeping; the master returns and learns what each did with the money; and the master rewards all but the cautious slave and punishes that slave.

Each parable also expresses similar attitudes among its key characters: the thriftiness of the slaves who invest; the caution/fear of the slave who does not invest; the master's delight at the successful investors; and the master's anger at the cautious slave

Different Elements

Among some of the obviously different elements in each parable are these seven. First, Matthew describes a master with business aspirations; Luke describes a nobleman who would be king.

Second, Matthew mentions three slaves; Luke mentions 10.

Third, in Matthew each slave receives talents; in Luke each slave receives a pound. A talent was worth 6,000 denarii, or about $1,000 according to Trueblood.[1] A day-laborer earned about a denarius per day, so a talent was worth six thousand-days' pay. If the laborer worked every day of the year, he would earn one talent in about sixteen years. A pound was worth 100 drachma or about $20 according to Trueblood.[2] A day-laborer earned about one drachma per day, so it would take the laborer about one hundred days to earn a pound.

---

1. Trueblood, *Humor of Christ*, 110.
2. Ibid.

Fourth, the three slaves in Matthew each received a different amount of talents, 5, 2, and 1, respectively. The slaves in Luke each received the same amount: 1 pound.

Fifth, Matthew includes more development of the story than Luke does.

Sixth, the punishment is greater in Matthew than in Luke.

Seventh, as New Testament scholar Lane McCaughey notes, many of the key words in each parable differ in Greek where they are rendered more similarly in English.[3]

Are They Making the Same Point?

Despite the differences in the two parables, there is disagreement among scholars about whether both parables make essentially the same point. In the next part we will consider different theories about what the point is or the points are, for now let us consider a few answers to the more basic question.

We have already noted the number of elements the two parables have in common. In addition, biblical studies professor Brian Schultz claims that a common view is that Luke rewrites the parable from Matthew "albeit augmented with a second motif based on the life of Herod Archelaus."[4] Schultz, however, disagrees with this view, arguing that "the presence of the throne pretender in Luke" makes it likely that this was a different parable from the one in Matthew.[5]

McCaughey suggests that the many differences between the two versions suggest that "although both Matthew and Luke understand the parable in light of the delay of the parousia, Luke has reworked the parable far more extensively than Matthew to make it consistently reflect his eschatological views."[6]

N. T. Wright claims that Jesus probably used this parable on several occasions for different audiences and that there is no evidence that one is derived from the other, or that both are derived "from a single original."[7]

---

3. McCaughey, "Fear of Yahweh," 235–45.
4. Schultz, "Jesus as Archelaus," 105.
5. Ibid., 108; also see Braun, "Reframing the Parable of the Pounds," 443.
6. McCaughey, "Fear of Yahweh," 238.
7. Wright, *Jesus and the Victory of God*; cited in Schultz, "Jesus as Archelaus," 107.

Part III: The Bible as Comedy

INTERPRETATION OF THE PARABLES

As Christian ethicist Carolyn Dipboye notes, how we interpret these parables today may be vastly different from "the radical moment of confrontation and call to discipleship that the parables posed for hearers of the first century."[8]

There is an impressive number of interpretations of the parable of the talents and the parable of the pounds. They differ on the meanings of the specific elements and they differ on whether we should take the story at face value or treat it as an allegory. This section divides along those lines. First, we will consider several views about what the specific elements represent; then we'll consider several views about the overall meaning of the parable.

Five Elements

If the parable is an allegory, then any or all of its elements may stand for something other than its literal presentation. There are many competing suggestions for what that something is. Let's look at five elements in the parable along with some suggestions of the meanings of those elements:

- The Master
- The Talent
- The Slaves
- The Third Slave: Hero or Coward?
- The Audience

The Master

Whom does the master represent? It's tempting to answer God or Jesus and many scholars have given into this temptation. Theologian Ben Chenoweth, for example, argues that the Master is the Son of Man and that the proof lies in the surrounding parables.[9] Carolyn Dipboye disagrees, noting that Jesus never associates himself with the "harsh taskmaster."[10]

---

8. Dipboye, "Matthew 25:14–30," 507.
9. Chenoweth, "Identifying the Talents," 61.
10. Dipboye, "Matthew 25:14–30," 508.

Religious studies professor Mary Ann Beavis cites affirmatively theologian Elizabeth Dowling's claim that the nobleman in Luke is neither God nor Jesus, "but simply an oppressive master whom, as the parable states, was hated by his citizens, who sent an embassy to complain about his rule (v. 14)."[11] The description of the master as "a severe man" supports this description, adding that he "took up what he did not lay down, and reaped what he did not sow (vv. 21, 22), and . . . had his 'enemies' executed in his presence (v. 27)."[12] There simply is no parallel to Jesus.

The Talent

On its face, the parable is about money—a lot of it. Recall that a talent equals almost sixteen-years' pay for a day laborer. Pastor John Carpenter agrees, saying that we should not allegorize the parable, "unless the context calls for it," in keeping with an Evangelical hermeneutical rule.[13]

Religion professor Bruce Chilton disagrees, claiming that the talent represents "the divine endowment which has been bestowed on us" and which Jesus wants us to expand.[14]

Biblical literature professor Brad H. Young says that the talents constitute "everything that a person has whether it be goods or abilities."[15] In a similar vein biblical scholar I. H. Jones claims that the talent is "whatever endowment a Christian may have received, although gifts of 'hearing' and 'understanding' are emphasized."[16]

That the word "talent" should be taken in its modern form is a common element in sermons, as is the claim that the talents represent faith and the more faith we have the more we should spread it around. On this latter point New Testament scholar C. H. Dodd regards the talent as "Spiritual Capacity."[17]

---

11. Beavis, "Like Yeast that a Woman Took," 226.
12. Ibid.
13. Carpenter, "Parable of the Talents," 166.
14. Chilton, "Talents and the Art of the Parable," 19.
15. Young, *Jesus and His Jewish Parables*, 37; cited in Chenoweth, "Identifying the Talents," 63.
16. Jones, *Matthean Parables*, 478, 471; cited in Chenoweth, "Identifying the Talents," 65;
17. Dodd, *Parables of the Kingdom*; cited in Carpenter, "Parable of the Talents," 167.

As for the possibility that the talent represents a divine message or gift, consider the following six views. Chenoweth claims that the talents represent knowledge of the secrets of the kingdom of heaven.[18] John Calvin believed that the talents are the gifts of the Holy Spirit.[19]

Professor of New Testament Craig Blomberg regards the talents as a portion of God's resources: "The principle applies in a preliminary fashion already in this life. . . . The principle will be applied more consistently in a once-for-all fashion on Judgment Day."[20] Professor of New Testament Simon Kistemaker sees the talent as "the sacred trust of God's revelation."[21] Theologian Joachim Jeremias regards the talents simply as the word of God.[22] And New Testament scholar G. R. Beasley-Murray regards the talent as a "symbol for the saving sovereignty of God."[23]

The point for us is not to settle on one interpretation or the other but to recognize the many interpretations in preparation for the next section in which we consider some humorous interpretations.

The Slaves

Whom do the slaves represent? The obvious answer is the laborers, but since the parable appears to make more than an economic point, many scholars offer other interpretations.[24] Chenoweth claims that the slaves represent the disciples whom Christ expects to run the show while he is away.[25] Dipboye believes that each servant represents "any or all of Israel's religious leaders" who erratically executed their duty to spread God's word.[26] Similarly, the slave might represent any Jew, not just the leaders.

---

18. Chenoweth, "Identifying the Talents," 61.

19. Calvin, *Commentary on a Harmony of the Evangelist*, 444; cited in Chenoweth, "Identifying the Talents," 64;

20. Blomberg, *Matthew*, 374; cited in Chenoweth, "Identifying the Talents," 65.

21. Kistemaker, *Parables of Jesus*; cited in Carpenter, "Parable of the Talents," 167.

22. Jeremías, *Rediscovering the Parables*; cited in Carpenter, "Parable of the Talents," 167.

23. Beasley-Murray, *Jesus and the Kingdom of God*; cited in Carpenter, "Parable of the Talents," 167.

24. Cadwallader, "Building of Awareness of Hermeneutics," 8.

25. Chenoweth, "Identifying the Talents," 69.

26. Dipboye, "Matthew 25:14–30," 509.

Humor in the Parable of the Talents

The Third Slave

The third slave in Matthew and in Luke appears at first blush to be overly cautious, if not a coward. Professor of biblical languages E. Carson Brisson agrees: while it may appear that the third slave was "derelict" it is fairer to regard him as cautious, since the law at the time supported protecting money by burying it—so much so, that to bury it upon receipt was to absolve oneself of liability if it were stolen.[27]

Mary Ann Beavis cites favorably Elizabeth Dowling's view that the third slave is a hero because "he refuses to imitate his master's unscrupulous dealings and make windfall profits, [which keeps the third slave from being] lavishly rewarded with political power (vv. 17, 19)."[28]

For Dowling, the sympathy of the audience is with the resistant slave, rather than with the tyrannical master or his accomplices.

The Audience

Who is the audience for the parable of the talents? Let's consider three possibilities.

1. Jesus's Immediate Audience—Crowds vs. Disciples; All Jews vs. Jewish Leaders

How one interprets the elements of the narrative and Jesus's purpose for telling it may depend on who one thinks the audience is. The most obvious answer is the crowd to whom Jesus has been preaching all along.[29] This crowd would consist mainly of poor Jewish people to whom the sort of money that the parable describes is well out of reach.[30]

If this is the audience, it would seem unlikely that Jesus means for the people to take literally a message about investing money wisely. It is possible, consistent with some modern interpretations, that Jesus is warning the people to make wise use of whatever God gives them, lest they be punished for unwise use of those gifts. But it is more likely that Jesus is making fun of

---

27. Brisson, "Matthew 25:14–30," 307–10.
28. Beavis, "Like Yeast," 226.
29. Braun, "Reframing the Parable," 448; Dipboye, "Matthew 25:14–30," 508; McCaughey, "Fear of Yahweh," 244.
30. Folarin, "Parable of the Talents," 94; Chilton, "Talents and the Art of the Parable," 118.

an image that is contrary to the well being of the people, such as the image of a greedy tyrant. This depends in part on whom the master is supposed to be—God, Jesus, or a caricature of the God the Pharisees worship—one who rewards the rich and punishes the poor.

If the crowd is the immediate audience, Jesus may still intend the message for someone else. For example, the Pharisees have been paying close attention to Jesus and his ministry, and Jesus may mean this parable as a warning to them, that, for example, they have lost or should lose the trust of their people.[31]

If we broaden the context of the parable from the narrative itself, we see that Matthew appears to be describing the disciples as the audience. The most recent setting for Jesus's ministering is to disciples on the Mount of Olives (Matt 24). Chenoweth notes that the disciples

> have been given inside information about the kingdom—they were given the interpretation of Jesus' parables unlike the crowds who only heard the parables—and therefore, they must make use of this knowledge to bring about a profit for Jesus. Those who do will be rewarded; failure to do so will result in punishment.[32]

2. Matthew's and Luke's Readers: Early Christians

It is not Jesus describing the telling of the parable but Matthew (and Luke). Therefore, the intended audience may be the Jewish Christian audience to whom Matthew was writing (or the Gentiles to whom Luke was writing).[33] As Brisson puts it, for Matthew, the audience is his community. By his teaching, "the community knows what to remember and how to wait. Tucked in the middle of Ch. 25 of this manual is Matthew's parable of the talents (vv. 14–30). The parable tells the community a story about what three servants did in their master's absence. Two know how to wait, one did not."[34]

3. All Receivers of the Gospel, Believers and Non-believers Alike

It is commonplace to regard the Bible's message as relevant to us no matter the year or day. Thus, it is plausible to regard the parable's audience as us. This does not preclude the other possibilities, but it puts the relevance of the message on our lives. Dipboye describes the message as promoting

---

31. Folarin, "Parable of the Talents," 9.5.
32. Chenoweth, "Identifying the Talents," 61, 63.
33. Schultz, "Jesus as Archelaus," 117.
34. Brisson, "Matthew 25:14–30," 307.

stewardship for the twenty-first century.[35] Carpenter agrees.[36] Chenoweth claims that what Jesus says to and about his disciples "applies just as much to the readers of Matthew's Gospel. Support for this view is found in 1 Corinthians 4:1–5."[37]

The point here is not to determine with certainty who the audience is, but to round out our examination of the possible interpretations of the parable in order to show that conventionally stuffy or somber interpretations need not be the final word. Indeed, many of the interpretations that posit humor in the parable appear to offer better explanations of its meaning than those who omit or deny such humor.

Allegory? Apocalyptic?

There are many ways we might organize the various interpretations of the parable. One way is to acknowledge two basic disagreements among scholars: whether the parable is allegorical and whether it is apocalyptic. For our purposes we may combine apocalyptic with eschatological. This yields four possible general categories of interpretation of the parable:

- Allegorical and Apocalyptic
- Allegorical but Non-apocalyptic
- Non-allegorical and Non-apocalyptic
- Non-allegorical but Apocalyptic: No examples

We will take a closer look at three of the four, while noting the lack of attempts to interpret the parable as non-allegorical, but apocalyptic.

Allegorical and Apocalyptic

It is common to regard the parable as allegorical, which *Merriam-Webster's Dictionary* defines as "having hidden spiritual meaning that transcends the literal sense of a sacred text." Some scholars who believe this also believe that the hidden meaning refers to the end times and thus is apocalyptic or eschatological.

---

35. Dipboye, "Matthew 25:14–30," 510.
36. Carpenter, "Parable of the Talents," 166.
37. Chenoweth, "Identifying the Talents," 61.

Part III: The Bible as Comedy

New Testament scholar Adam Braun says,

> In the context of Jesus' prediction of the destruction of the temple (Matt 24:2), his discussion of the signs of his coming (Matt 24:3–28), his apocalyptic description of the Son of Man's coming (Matt 24:29–35), and the revelation that no one knows the day or the hour of these events (Matt 24:36–44), Jesus tells four parables in succession, including the parable of the talents. . . . In this narrative sequence, we see the apocalyptic conclusion of the Old Age and the rising of a New Age, and the question Matthew's Jesus is keen on answering is, "How does a faithful and wise slave remain vigilant until the New Age is here?"[38]

Matthew scholar R. V. G. Tasker claims that the parable aims at the disciples who, until the Second Coming, "must make continuous, practical use by the effort of their wills of those *gifts of the Spirit* with which they are endowed" or lose those gifts.[39]

Biblical studies scholar Alan Cadwallader believes that the peasants were the parable's first audience and that they would have seen the message as an indictment of the wealthy—a common theme for Jesus—and the encouragement to stand fast in anticipation of the Lord's coming again.[40]

Luke Timothy Johnson, speaking of the parable of the pounds, holds that the parable "must refer allegorically to the ascension of Jesus and his return at the parousia for judgment."[41] Luke has Jesus tell the story here "to counter any misunderstanding about the entry of Jesus as a messianic enthronement, and, for his Christian readers, to show that Jesus himself predicted the delay of the parousia."[42]

Lane McCaughey argues that Matthew and Luke both regard the parable as "an apocalyptic warning about the conduct of the faithful during the delay of the Parousia."[43] Thus, the servants are the Christians.

---

38. Braun, "Reframing the Parable," 443.
39. Tasker, *Matthew* 236, emphasis added; cited Carpenter, "Parable of the Talents," 167.
40. Cadwallader, "Building of Awareness," 13.
41. Johnson, "Lukan Kingship Parable," 140.
42. Ibid.
43. McCaughey, "Fear of Yahweh," 237–38.

Humor in the Parable of the Talents

Allegorical but Non-apocalyptic

The most common view among commentaries on the parable of the talents is that it is allegorical but not apocalyptic or eschatological. Cadwallader, noting different sorts of interpretation in different periods of history, holds that contemporary interpretation of the talent or pound tends to be "taken to mean gifts which are opportunities for service. The slide to the notion of talent as ability, God-given or otherwise, is clear here."[44] During the Patristic and Medieval period, "the three servants were readily equated with the three-fold office of the Church: bishop, priest and deacon."[45]

Ben Chenoweth believes that unlike the crowds, the disciples have received "inside information about the kingdom . . . and therefore they must make use of this knowledge to bring about a profit for Jesus. Those who do will be rewarded; failure to do so will result in punishment. Furthermore, this applies just as much to the readers of Matthew›s gospel."[46]

Carolyn Dipboye holds that the parable is not simply about money but is "a powerful indictment of the sin of presumption and holds a timely message for churches approaching the twenty-first century, tempted to substitute a fearful fortress-protectionist-exclusionist mentality for risk-taking, inclusive discipleship."[47]

George Folarin, looking at the parable in an African context, argues that the parable encourages the audience to "promote God's kingdom on earth," and in spite of the consequent persecution, to "resist exploitation in a nonviolent way and to be ready to suffer for such action."[48] What's more the audience should rejoice in the suffering (Matt 5:21).[49]

Professor of New Testament Daniel Harrington holds that "the hermeneutical framework in which Matthew placed" the parable should be seen primarily as "part of Matthew's polemic against the so-called 'synagogue across the street,' [rather than] as primarily for advice for Christians within Matthew's church."[50]

---

44. Cadwallader, "Building of the Awareness," 5.
45. Ibid., 8.
46. Chenoweth, "Identifying the Talents," 61.
47. Dipboye, "Matthew 25:14–30," 507.
48. Folarin, "Parable of the Talents," 106.
49. Ibid.
50. Harrington, "Polemical Parables," 287.

The challenge for Matthew, says Harrington, is to help Christians navigate through the Judaism of AD 70.

Regarding the third slave, Pastor James Howell suggests that Jesus is claiming that the church does not know how to handle his "astonishingly ravishing gift," and is referring not to "our individual abilities, but [is soliciting the] rather the frank, embarrassing admission of our corporate inability."[51]

Theologian Ernest Van Eck claims that in the parable Jesus, in condemning the master's viewpoint, "criticizes the use of honor to enhance power and privilege, class, status and wealth and the economic exploitation of the peasantry by the ruling elite."[52]

Non-allegorical and Non-apocalyptic

Recall Elizabeth Dowling's view that the third slave is the hero of the story for standing up against an oppressive master. Dowling and Beavis see this as a straightforward attack on economic exploitation.

Theologian Carol Thysell offers a non-allegorical, non-apocalyptic interpretation of the parables, citing Calvin's rejection of the distinction between Matthew's "talent" and Luke's "pound." According to Thysell, Calvin "focuses on the parable's criticism of those who hide their gifts, describing such 'slothful' people as those who are 'privately devoted to themselves and to their own advantage, avoid all the duties of charity, and have no regard to the general edification.'"[53]

Characteristically employing the Protestant reformers' more literal reading of Scripture, Calvin in effect returns to the earliest, economic sense of the term *talent* while retaining the church fathers' emphasis on social responsibility.

---

51. Howell, "Trojan Horse," 19.
52. Van Eck, "Do Not Question My Honour," 1.
53. Thysell, "Unearthing the Treasure," 12.

HUMOR IN THE PARABLE OF THE TALENTS

Concerning the parable of the talents, Bruce Longenecker claims that "Jesus' audience would have laughed at the third servant for missing out on such an apparently glorious opportunity."[54]

We have looked at many interpretations of the parable of the talents and its constituent parts. In the examples so far there has been no humor. Yet, we should not be afraid to look for humor in the parable, given the aim of this book. In this spirit, James Martin notes that "many parables delight in the use of hyperbole," including the parable of the talents, which preachers may use to "illustrate the need to use our 'talents' in life to the full."[55]

Elton Trueblood and Douglas Adams spend notable time explaining the humor they find in the parable. Let's look at each effort in turn.

Trueblood admits that humor may or may not be present in the parable, but "a humorless interpretation is intolerable," presumably since such an interpretation favors an image of an unloving God and condemnation of cautious stewardship.[56]

The usual interpretation of both parables, Trueblood suggests, is "Work hard!" But he sees three problems with this interpretation. First, the master does not represent the God that Jesus usually describes, as in, for example, the parable of the Prodigal Son or the parable of the Lost Sheep. Second, the rewards are preposterous. And third, the punishment seems especially cruel.

The solution, Trueblood believes, is that Jesus is lampooning the popular/conventional conception of God as one who is possessive and plays favorites. And the master is the villain.[57]

Douglas Adams tries to examine the parable from the context of its original time and audience. This audience of peasants and laborers would have regarded the slaves' doubling the money to be unethical and preposterous.[58] Note too that Matthew says the slaves doubled their money "at once," but the master returned "after a long time." What did the slaves do to earn so much money so fast, and why didn't they continue to earn money while the master was away?

---

54. Longenecker, "Humorous Jesus?," 182.
55. Martin, *Between Heaven and Mirth*, 52–53.
56. Trueblood, *Humor of Christ*, 114.
57. Ibid., 113.
58. Adams, *Prostitute in the Family Tree*, 43.

Adams regards the treatment of the master as satirical as well. He accepts the first two slaves' money without questioning their methods and he is described as a "rip-off artist."[59]

Not only did the slaves probably engage in unethical behavior to double their money so quickly, but they must also have acted to earn interest. As Adams notes, "Earning any interest on money was viewed as usury and is one of the most frequently damned sins in scripture, for it made the rich richer and the poor poorer and so undermined society."[60] Yet the master berated the third servant for not earning interest on the money the master had left with him.

Where is the good news for the poor in this parable? Adam's answer is in four parts.[61] First, "the one who got ahead was unethical and the master who blesses him is unscrupulous and perhaps unethical himself; so that master is not God." Second, "in the Near East, the common people cheer the behavior of the one who buries the coin in the ground; they feel an affinity for him and not for the trader or master, who may be seen as belonging to the merchant class that exploits them." Third, Jesus's parables often undercut the conventional wisdom, which associates wealth, health, and wisdom with salvation. So, for example, in Luke 16:19–31 the rich man goes to hell while the poor sick man goes to heaven. Fourth, and finally, "it is significant that Matthew does not introduce this parable of the talents by saying, 'The kingdom of God is like . . .' as he usually does when introducing parables."

We end this chapter by acknowledging that, at best, a plausible inductive argument exists for regarding the parable of the talents as humorous, and acknowledging the traditional and critical challenges to this interpretation. That it is possible, if not probable, invites us to look for humor in the Christian narrative where many have failed to look, and thus to avoid worshipping too somber a God. The next chapter sums up our efforts so far and offers a look forward.

---

59. Ibid., 44.
60. Ibid.
61. Ibid., 45.

12

Conclusion

> My happy childhood was a gift my parents and the world offered to God.
> —Charles Hartshorne[1]

A GROUP OF FELLOW philosophy majors and I had dinner with philosopher and theologian Charles Hartshorne at Hamline University in 1975. One of my colleagues gently chastised the cheerful Hartshorne for not taking the troubles of the world or his own shortcomings (as an inheritor of original sin) seriously enough in his constant delight in his life and in God's handiwork. Hartshorne paused for a moment, stroking his chin, and responded with a friendly laugh, "Well, if I were God and I had gone through all this trouble, I would rather have you say 'God, I'm not sure why you have done all this for me, but thanks! This is great!' and dance merrily before me than to beat your chest and say 'God, I stand before you a horrible wretch fully aware of my shortcomings and those of my fellow humans!'"

Given the imperative to rejoice in the good news of Jesus Christ, Hartshorne offers the better alternative. The image he rejects is those whose God is too somber.

In this light, let's sum up the work we have done so far and consider what might come next

---

1. Cited in Easterbrook, "Hundred Years of Thinking about God," 61.

Part III: The Bible as Comedy
SO FAR: YOUR GOD IS TOO SOMBER

Your God is too somber if your posture before God lacks a spirit of joy and commitment to rejoicing as much as possible. This is not to deny the sadness, tragedy, and horror that one can experience, often in fearsome amounts. But the good news of Jesus Christ is that he is on the throne; God's kingdom has won; and while we may face suffering for a time, that time is far shorter than the endless delight that God promises through Christ's sacrificial love. So, "rejoice in the Lord always; again I will say, Rejoice!" (Phil 4:4)

Any moment of humor may be a means toward some other end, such as the truth, or it may be an end in itself. The humor may be aimed within or without. The humor may be aimed at Christians or non-Christians. Your God is too somber if you lack non-contentious humor necessary and sufficient to rejoice in the good news.

Your God is too somber if you embrace a theology of tears, rather than a theology of laughter. Anyone who has thoughts about God has a theology, whether embedded or deliberate. Theology is logical thinking about God, recognizing that the logic may be good or bad. It is good when the premises one offers for the conclusion one draws are true premises and sufficiently relevant to the conclusion to prove it. The logic is bad when the premises fail to support the conclusion, either because the premises are false or because they are irrelevant.

Embedded theology is theology of which we may not be aware, but is reflected in our thinking and our practice. Deliberative theology is theology that one exposes to the light of critical thinking, hoping that one is thinking well rather than poorly. As the son of a Methodist minister, I spent many years going to church and thinking and talking about God, without once considering where my views were coming from or whether there were more reasonable alternatives to my views. I enjoyed church a great deal and took comfort in its community and its teaching. In time, I began to question my faith and the views of my church and all these years later, as an Episcopal priest, I continue to ask tough questions about God, my faith, and my church. I pursue these questions with faith, hope, and love, trusting that the truth and goodness of the news are far greater than my limited understanding or than the worldly news of despair, hopelessness, and hatred suggest. My theology has become more deliberate.

Through Scripture, tradition, reason, and experience, Christianity provides rich ingredients for deep thinking about God—for doing theology

Conclusion

deliberately. In doing theology we may veer toward tears and despair or toward joy. A major aspiration of this book has been to make a case for the latter.

But a word of caution: we should not overstate the case and end up worshipping a God who is too frivolous. Salvation of the world and sacrifice of one's Son to that effect are serious business. Even as Christianity calls us to joy, it calls for moments of penitential reflection, confession, and atonement. But all of this so we can shake off the shackles of our shortcomings and celebrate fully and joyfully the gift of salvation.

Your God is too somber if you fail to see the humor in the Bible—the word of God. In addition to calls to joy, humor abounds scripturally in paradox, irony, burlesque, play, and wordplay. God laughs, sometimes with us, sometimes against us—at least some of the more tyrannical and self-righteous of us. Jesus may not be described as laughing outright, but his humor is evident in many of his parables and sayings, all with the goal of helping us see and hear the truth. What's more, it is hard to imagine Jesus attracting the crowd he attracted, especially the children, if he lacked a robust sense of humor. Then there is the U-shaped structure of the Bible itself and of the many stories within it. The text is comedy in the classical sense, rather than a tragedy—an inverted U—even if there are tragic elements within it.

Our argument for Christians, therefore, is this:

1. You should engage in orthodoxy and orthopraxis.
2. Orthodoxy and orthopraxis require proper devotion.
3. Proper devotion entails rejoicing, embracing a theology of laughter, and recognizing the Bible as a comedy rather than a tragedy.
4. To fail to rejoice, embrace a theology of laughter, and/or regard the Bible as a comedy rather than a tragedy is to worship a God who is too somber.
5. To worship a God who is too somber is to engage in improper devotion.
6. To engage in improper devotion is to fail at orthodoxy or orthopraxis or both.
7. Therefore, you should worship a God who is not too somber.

This is a deductive argument, in its claim that if the premises (1–6) are true, then the conclusion (7) must be true. Thus, the argument is sound if all of the premises are true. Premises 1 and 2 are axiomatic. Most of this book has been dedicated to proving premise 3. Premises 4–6 follow from the preceding premises.

Thus, this argument rises or falls primarily on premise 3 and thus the most vulnerable to criticism. It is the conclusion of an argument of the form "A is true," "B is true," and "C is true," therefore "A + B + C is true." In particular, "proper devotion entails rejoicing"; "proper devotion entails a theology of laughter"; "proper devotion entails regarding the Bible as a comedy rather than a tragedy"; therefore, premise 3 above. That rejoicing entails humor is taken to be true by definition. But the propriety of a theology of laughter and of regarding the Bible as a comedy is based on observation and, hence, open to debate.

SOME POSSIBLE CRITICISM

In addition to challenging assertion of the propriety of a theology of laughter and regarding the Bible as a comedy, critics might offer at least three other challenges. First, as noted above, we have not offered an argument for when a Christian's God might be too frivolous. Is it possible that the God premise 3 points to is already more frivolous than is proper? Our response has appeared throughout the book, as we grant their day in court to proponents of a theology of tears and of regarding the Bible as a tragedy. The reader is left to decide which side has the stronger argument.

Second, while the argument offers the three elements of premise 3 as *necessary* to proper devotion, the question remains whether these elements are *sufficient* to proper devotion. To respond, while proper devotion may entail more than the three elements in premise 3, to omit one of these elements is to worship a God who is too somber. In other words, these three elements are necessary to proper devotion, but they may not be sufficient.

Third, in our argument for the regarding the Bible as a comedy, we left out many books of the Bible. Can one apply the method proponents of a comedic Bible use when referring to several books of the Bible to the books these proponents have omitted? The biblical books we did not consider include:

Conclusion

Old Testament	New Testament
Leviticus	Ephesians
1 and 2 Chronicles	Colossians
Ezra	2 Thessalonians
Nehemiah	1 Timothy
Joel	2 Timothy
Obadiah	1 Peter
Nahum	2 Peter
Habakkuk	1 John
Zephaniah	2 John
Haggai	3 John
Zechariah	Jude
Malachi	

If there is no humor in any of these books, then the argument that the Bible is either essentially a comedy or contains significant comic elements faces a big challenge. And since biblical comedy is one of three elements in the argument warning us away from worshipping too somber a God, if this element is false, then the larger argument is considerably weakened.

Given the Bible's clarion call to rejoice, which entails humor, and the compelling observation that the Bible is U-shaped and thus comic in its grand structure, we might be tempted to dismiss the list above as a minor distraction from our overall effort. But we might find more profitable an attempt to fit these outliers more snuggly into the proposed comic fabric of the Bible. Thus, for example, recall Norman Gottwald's claim that biblical prophecy reveals "a sustained ironic abrasion between the tragedy Israel's leaders are repeatedly arranging when they think they are making comedy and the comedy which God through many agencies, including other Israelites and the nations, is steadily building on the tragic shambles."[2] And while Gottwald cautions us not to look too closely for comedy in the prophets, since comedy is about narrative and the prophetic books are not narrative, he thinks we should look in the prophecies for the presence and interplay of tragic or comic views of life—"what the literary critics tend to

---

2. Gottwald, "Tragedy and Comedy," 93.

call 'visions.'"[3] Gottwald reminds us too, that every prophetic book follows the U-shape of comic development.[4]

If Gottwald is correct, then we may remove all of the prophetic books—Ezra to Malachi—from our list of outliers.

Superficially, there appears to be no humor in Leviticus, which would explain its appearing on our list above. And we might let it go, agreeing that not every element of the Bible need contain humor for the Bible's overall comic structure to stand. But consider commentator Jeffrey Stackert's observation that Leviticus's "Priestly authors claim that following the commandments in Leviticus will ensure the tangible benefits and protection of the divine presence in the Israelites' midst."[5] The offer of God's benefit is of a piece with the rest of the Pentateuch which speaks to God's covenant with his people. If the people can fulfill their end of the bargain the news will be good indeed. According to Leviticus, the Israelites are to obey God, but this does not make God so somber that the Israelites cannot celebrate and worship in good humor. At the least, then, Leviticus does not offer a counterargument to our thesis.

Given the structure and content of 1 and 2 Chronicles, it belongs on our list of outliers. But one might develop an argument for its U-shaped structure beginning with Adam and ending with Cyrus's calling the exiles to return to Judah. There also are reports of prophets that might remind us of Gottwald's comments about the comic elements of the prophetic books.

Given the question whether Paul is the author of Ephesians, Colossians, and 2 Thessalonians, we must avoid the temptation to remove them from our list of outliers on grounds we cited for regarding Paul as apt to use more humor than is obvious on first reading. In chapter 10 we noted Paul's use of humor, irony, and sarcasm. We noted Douglas Adams's description of Paul's letters as "grandmother letters," involving parody of prideful autobiographies, boasting of weakness, and humorous digressions.[6] And we noted Paul's frequent expressions of joy.

Ephesians seems to lack the humor, irony, and sarcasm that we noted in other letters. Indeed, Eph 5:4 reads, "Entirely out of place is obscene, silly, and vulgar talk; but instead, let there be thanksgiving." But this rejection of silliness is not a rejection of good humor, which is probably essential to the

---

3. Ibid.
4. Ibid., 84.
5. Stackert, "Introduction to Leviticus," 142.
6. Adams, "Paul as Humorist," 86–87.

Conclusion

thanksgiving called for. In Ephesians there is a hint of boastful weakness: "Although I am the very least of all the saints, this grace was given to me to bring to the Gentiles the news of the boundless riches of Christ" (3:8). And there is the celebratory message of Christ's gift, accompanied by a warning to live appropriately in gratitude for that gift: "Put away from you all bitterness and wrath and anger and wrangling and slander together with all malice, and be kind to one another, tenderhearted, forgiving one another as God in Christ has forgiven" (4:31–32). It is difficult to imagine living this way in the absence of good humor, although this is a far cry from the more comic elements that some have looked for and allegedly discovered in other letters.

For our purposes there are enough similarities between Ephesians and Colossians to posit that how each stands on the question of humor, so stands the other. Note especially, Paul's comment, "I am now rejoicing in my sufferings for your sake" (1:24). A couple of times in this book we have encountered the idea of rejoicing in suffering. This is a paradox, that challenges the necessary coextension of rejoicing and humor. But this opens up possibilities along the lines of our thesis, rather than closing those possibilities.

As we noted in chapter 10, James Martin posits "an unusual lightheartedness" in 1 Thessalonians.[7] This is expressed especially in Paul's exhortation to "rejoice always, pray without ceasing" (5:16–17). Indeed, God wills it! (5:18). The similarities between 1 Thessalonians and 2 Thessalonians may be enough to put them in the same category for our purposes: not an attempt at humor per se, but a repeat of the Good News and exhortations to behave appropriately—which is impossible in the absence of a joyful heart. Nevertheless 2 Thessalonians seems to lack the lightheartedness of 1 Thessalonians and therefore may be an especially controversial example for our purposes.

Whether Paul is the author of I Timothy, it contains the element of boastful weakness. For example, Paul describes himself as the foremost sinner (1:12–15). The letter also contains biting rhetoric: "By rejecting conscience, certain persons have suffered shipwreck in the faith" (1:19). But the letter also calls for seriousness (3:8, 11) and morally decent behavior toward oneself and others. All this in a way that seems to leave no place for humor of any sort we have described so far. It is no surprise that our

---

7. Martin, *Between Heaven and Mirth*, 213.

cadre of scholars promoting humor in the Bible has left this letter out of the collection.

Second Timothy is somewhat more celebratory and hopeful as Paul prepares for death, content in his evangelical efforts; "I have fought the good fight, I have finished the race, I have kept the faith. From now on there is reserved for me the crown of righteousness . . . the Lord will rescue me from every evil attack and save me for his heavenly kingdom" (4:7, 8, 18). A bittersweet ending, but one on the upswing of the U-shaped text.

First and Second Peter, though probably not from the same author, have in common a humorless, foreboding attitude that seems to give Christians little encouragement to act joyfully in this life. There will be suffering for Christians until the second coming and people should take it as Christ took it, without complaining. The effort to find humor here is beyond the scope of this book.

In 1 John there is an upbeat message about God's love. Indeed, the author claims to be "writing these things so that our joy may be complete" (v. 4). Except for the promise of joy, this letter offers little evidence of biblical humor.

Second John speaks of the joy of those who are faithful to the Word and to the Johannine community. But the better part of this brief letter is an indictment of false teachers and a command to treat them harshly. Not much humor here.

The author of 3 John expresses joy that "my children are walking in the truth" (v. 4), but emphasizes Diotrephes' failure to acknowledge authority and to practice appropriate hospitality. Again, perhaps partly because of its brevity, there is little to mine here for biblical humor.

The better part of the Letter of Jude is a warning to the faithful "to contend for the faith" against "people who pervert the grace of our God into licentiousness and deny our only Master and Lord, Jesus Christ" (vv. 3, 4). This warning includes a reminder of what awful things God has done to the morally corrupt. A joyful life may be coming for the faithful, but until then the emphasis is on moral purity, not joy and celebration.

Our list of outlying books may exist by design, rather than default. A brief attempt at finding humor in them has yielded little positive results. In some cases, as in the prophetic books, we have left open the possibility of fruitful attempts at further analysis. In other cases, such as the letters attributed to Peter, we have conceded that by themselves they belong on our

CONCLUSION

list of outliers. Of course, they still may have a proper place in the U-shaped structure of the entire Bible.

In any event, one hopes that this book has done its job warning against worshipping too somber a God and contributing to a long and rich conversation on that note.

Bibliography

Adams, Douglas. "Paul as Humorist." *Bible Today* 33 (1995) 84–87.
———. *The Prostitute in the Family Tree: Discovering Humor and Irony in the Bible.* Louisville: Westminster John Knox, 1997.
Alexander, Edward. "Banana Republics and V I Degrees: Rethinking Indian Folklore in a Post-Colonial World." *Asian Folklore Studies* 52 (1993) 177–204.
Alster, Bendt. "Two Sumerian Short Tales Reconsidered." Sumerian texts, English translations. *Zeitschrift fur Assyriologie und Vorderasiatische Archaologie* 82 (1992) 186–201.
Amarasingam, Amarnath. "Laughter the Best Medicine: Muslim Comedians and Social Criticism in Post-9/11 America." *Journal of Muslim Minority Affairs* 30 (2010) 463–77.
Anderson, Philip A. "Humor as Healing and Grace." *Chicago Theological Seminary Register* 77 (1987) 1–10.
Arbuckle, Gerald. *Laughing with God: Humor, Culture, and Transformation.* Collegeville: Liturgical, 2008.
Bard, Amy C. "Turning Karbala Inside Out: Humor and Ritual Critique in South Asian Muharram Rites." In *Sacred Play: Ritual Levity and Humor in South Asian Religions*, edited by Selva J. Raj and Corinne G. Dempsey, 163–83. Albany: State University of New York Press, 2010.
Bastien, Joseph W. "Humor and Satire." In *The Encyclopedia of Religion*, edited by Mircea Eliade, 6:526–28. New York: Macmillan, 1986.
Beasley-Murray, G. R. *Jesus and the Kingdom of God.* Grand Rapids: Eerdman's, 1986.
Beavis, Mary Ann. "'Like Yeast That a Woman Took': Feminist Interpretations of the Parables." *Review and Expositor* 109 (2012) 226.
Ben-Amos, Dan. "Jewish Folklore Studies." *Modern Judaism* 11 (1991) 17–66.
Berger, Peter A. *Redeeming Laughter: The Comic Dimension of Human Experience.* New York: de Gruyter, 1997.
Berkey-Gerard, Mark. "Woody Allen & the Sacred Conversation: If God Has a Sense of Humor, Who Gets It?" *Other Side* 33 (1997) 60–62.
Berkman, Joyce Avrech, ed. *Contemplating Edith Stein.* Notre Dame: University of Notre Dame Press, 2006.
Biddle, Mark E. "Are We Amused? Humour about Women in the Biblical Worlds." *Perspectives in Religious Studies* 34 (2007) 241–45.
———. *A Time to Laugh: Humor in the Bible.* Macon, GA: Smyth & Helwys, 2013.

BIBLIOGRAPHY

Binau, Brad A. "Humor Reconsidered: The Cultivation of 'Accurate Perception' as a Contribution to the Care of Soul." *Pastoral Psychology* 58 (2009) 667–80.

Biro, Adam. *Two Jews on a Train: Stories from the Old Country and the New.* Chicago: University of Chicago Press, 2003.

Biser, Eugene. "The Scales of the Spirit: Nietzsche's Battle with the Spirit of Gravity." In *Theology of Joy*, edited by Johan Baptist Metz and Jean-Pierre Jossua, 46–73. New York: Herder & Herder, 1974.

Blomberg, Craig L. *Matthew.* Nashville: Broadman, 1992.

Branson, Roy. "And Now . . . the Theology of Joy." *Encounter* 34 (1973) 233–45.

Braun, Adam F. "Reframing the Parable of the Pounds in Lukan Narrative and Economic Context: Luke 19:11–28." *Currents in Theology and Mission* 39 (2012) 443.

Brenner, Athalya, ed. *Are We Amused? Humour about Women in the Biblical Worlds.* London: T. & T. Clark, 2003.

———. "Who's Afraid of Feminist Criticism? Who's Afraid of Biblical Humor? The Case of the Obtuse Foreign Ruler in the Hebrew Bible." *Journal for the Study of the Old Testament* 63 (1994) 38–55.

Brisson, E. Carson. "Matthew 25:14–30." *Interpretation* 56 (2002) 307–10.

Burkey, Dean. *Holy Laughter: Humor in the Bible.* Self published, 2011.

Burrows, Millar. "The Literary Category of the Book of Jonah." In *Translating and Understanding the Old Testament: Essays in Honor of Herbert Gordon May*, edited by Harry T. Frank and William L. Reed, 80–107. Nashville: Abingdon, 1970.

Bush, Harold K., Jr. "Mark Twain's American Adam: Humor as Hope and Apocalypse." *Christianity and Literature* 53 (2004) 291–314.

Buss, Martin J. "Tragedy and Comedy in Hosea." In *Tragedy and Comedy in the Bible*, edited by J. Cheryl Exum, 71–82. Semeia 32. Decatur, GA: Scholars, 1984.

Bussie, Jacqueline. *The Laughter of the Oppressed: Ethical and Theological Resistance in Wiesel, Morrison, and Endo.* New York: Continuum, 2007.

Byassee, Jason. "Stand and Deliver: Performers in the Pulpit." *Christian Century* 126 (2009) 20–23.

———. "Zealous Skeptic: Bill Maher's Religulous." *Christian Century* 125 (2008) 13.

Cadwallader, Alan H. "The Building of Awareness of Hermeneutics through the History of Interpretations of the Bible." *Colloquium* 33 (2001) 8.

Calvin, John. *Commentary on a Harmony of the Evangelists: Matthew, Mark, and Luke.* Vol. 3. Translated by William Pringle. Edinburgh: Calvin Translation Society, 1846.

Capps, Donald. "Mother, Melancholia, and Humor in Erik H. Erikson's Earliest Writings." *Journal of Religion and Health* 47 (2008) 415–32.

———. "Religion and Humor: Estranged Bedfellows." *Pastoral Psychology* 54 (2006) 413–38.

Carpenter, John B. "The Parable of the in Missionary Perspective: A Call for an Economic Spirituality." *Missiology* 25 (1997) 166.

Carroll, R. P. "Is Humor Also among the Prophets?" In *On Humor and the Comic in the Hebrew Bible*, edited by Yehuda T. Radday and Athalya Brenner, 169. Sheffield: Almond, 1990.

Chan, Michael. "Ira Regis: Comedic Inflections of Royal Rage in Jewish Court Tales." *Jewish Quarterly Review* 103 (2013) 1–25.

Charles, David. "The Power of the Carnival Satirist: Taking Laughter Seriously." *Baylor Journal of Theatre and Performance* 2 (2005) 11–28.

Bibliography

Chenoweth, Ben. "Identifying the Talents: Contextual Clues for the Interpretation of the Parable of the Talents (Matthew 25:14–30)." *Tyndale Bulletin* 56 (2005) 61.

Chilton, Bruce. "Talents and the Art of the Parable." *Living Pulpit* 6 (1997) 19.

"Christians Get Apology from NPR." *Baltimore Sun*, December 23, 1995, 2D.

Claassens, L. Juliana. "Rethinking Humour in the Book of Jonah: Tragic Laughter as Resistance in the Context of Trauma." *Old Testament Essays* 28 (2015) 655–73.

Clarke, Shayne. "Locating Humour in Indian Buddhist Monastic Law Codes: A Comparative Approach." *Journal of Indian Philosophy* 37 (2009) 311–30.

Cohen, Anouk. "La Langue du Silence dans Le Maroc Urbain Contemporain." *Revue de l'Histoire des Religions* 228 (2011) 245–63.

Collum, Danny Duncan. "What Would Dilbert Do?" *Sojourners Magazine* 37 (2008) 48.

Commins, Gary. "Woody Allen's Theological Imagination." *Theology Today* 44 (1987) 235–49.

Craig, Kenneth M. *A Poetic Jonah: Art in the Service of Ideology*. Columbia, SC: University of South Carolina Press, 1993.

Davis, Dale R. "Comic Literature—Tragic Theology: A Study of Judges 17–18." *Westminster Theological Journal* 46 (1984) 156–63.

Delaney, Herbert: "Immortal Diamond: the Possible Dream." *Religious Studies* 19 (1983) 143–59.

Dempsey, Corinne G., and Sudarshan Durayappah. "The 'Artful Trick': Challenging Convention through Play in Upstate New York." In *Sacred Play: Ritual Levity and Humor in South Asian Religions*, edited by Selva J. Raj and Corinne G. Dempsey, 71–87. Albany: State University of New York Press, 2010.

Derby, Josiah. "The Funniest Word in the Bible: Purim Torah." *Jewish Bible Quarterly* 22 (1994) 115–19.

De Vries, Calvin. "Peter De Vries: The Vale of Laughter." *Theology Today* 32 (1975) 10–20.

Dipboye, Carolyn. "Matthew 25:14–3: To Survive or to Serve?" *Review & Expositor* 92 (1995) 507.

Djalili, Omid, and Bucky Garrison. "Laughing with the Infidel: Comedian Omid Djalili on Being Funny about Faith." *Sojourners* 39 (2010) 43–44.

Dodd, C. H. *The Parables of the Kingdom*. London: Collins Clear-Type, 1961.

Domeris, William. "Shades of Irony in the Anti-Language of Amos." *Hervormde Teleogiese Studies* 72 (2016) 1–8.

Dray, Stephen. "Good Theology." *Evangel* 22 (2004) 1–2.

Duke, Paul D. *Irony in the Fourth Gospel*. Atlanta: John Knox, 1985.

Durham, Israel A. "Richard Pryor: Melancholy and the Religion of Tragicomedy." *Journal of Religion and Health* 50 (2011) 132–44.

Easterbrook, Gregg. "A Hundred Years of Thinking about God: A Philosopher Soon to Be Rediscovered." *U.S. News and World Report* 124 (1998) 61.

Eberhart, Cy. *In the Presence of Humor: A Guide to the Humorous Life*. 3rd ed. Self published, 2006.

Efron, John M. "From Łódź to Tel Aviv: The Yiddish Political Satire of Shimen Dzigan and Yisroel Shumacher." *Jewish Quarterly Review* 102 (2012) 50–79.

Estepa, Pio. "Drinking from Comic Wells of Cultural Others." *SEDOS Bulletin* 41 (2009) 37–46.

Evans, C. Stephen. "Kierkegaard's View of Humor: Must Christians Always Be Solemn?" *Faith and Philosophy* 4 (1987) 176–86.

Bibliography

Exum, J. Cheryl, ed. *Tragedy and Comedy in the Bible*. Semeia 32. Decatur, GA: Scholars, 1984.

Exum, J. Cheryl, and William Whedbee. "Isaac, Samson, and Saul: Reflections on the Comic and Tragic Vision." In J. Cheryl Exum, ed., *Tragedy and Comedy in the Bible*, 5–40.

Feltmate, David. "The Humorous Reproduction of Religious Prejudice: 'Cults' and Religious Humour in the Simpsons, South Park, and King of the Hill." *Journal of Religion and Popular Culture* 24 (2012) 201–16.

Folarin, George O. "The Parable of the Talents in the African Context: An Inculturation Hermeneutics Approach." *Asia Journal of Theology* 22 (2008) 102.

Freeman, Helen. "Humor, Healing and Holiness." *Journal of Progressive Judaism* 8 (1997) 59, 67.

Friedman, Don, et al. "What's So Funny about Arguing with God? A Case for Playful Argumentation from Jewish Literature." *Argumentation: An International Journal of Reasoning* 29 (2015) 57–80.

Frye, Northrop. *The Great Code: The Bible and Literature*. San Diego: Harcourt Brace Jovanovich, 1983.

Galvany, Albert. "Distorting the Rule of Seriousness: Laughter, Death, and Friendship in the Zhuangzi. *Dao* (Binghamton, NY) 8 (2009) 49–59.

George, A. Raymond. "Ninurta-Paqidat's Dog Bite, and Notes on Other Comic Tales." *Iraq* 55 (1993) 63–75.

Giorgetti, Andrew. "The 'Mock Building Account' of Genesis 11:1–9: Polemic Against Mesopotamian Royal Ideology." *Vetus Testamentum* 64 (2014) 1–20.

Goldingay, John. "Are They Comic Acts?" *Evangelical Quarterly* 69 (1997) 93–107.

Goldsmith, Emanuel S. "The Divine Humor of Sholom Aleicheim." *Judaism* 35 (1986) 391–401.

Good, Edwin M. "Apocalyptic as Comedy: The Book of Daniel." In *Tragedy and Comedy in the Bible*, edited by J. Cheryl Exum, 41–70. Semeia 32. Decatur, GA: Scholars, 1984.

Gottwald, Norman. "Tragedy and Comedy in the Latter Prophets." In *Tragedy and Comedy in the Bible*, edited by J. Cheryl Exum, 83–96. Semeia 32. Decatur, GA: Scholars, 1984.

Greely, Andrew. "Humor and Ecclesiastical Ministry." In *Theology of Joy*, edited by Johan Baptist Metz and Jean-Pierre Jossua, 134–40. New York: Herder and Herder, 1974.

Greenspoon, Leonard J. "The Bible in the Funny Papers." *Bible Review* 7 (1991) 30–33, 41.

———. "The New Testament in the Comics." *Bible Review* 9 (1993) 40–45.

Gritsch, Eric. W. "Martin Luther's Humor." *Word & World* 32 (2012) 132–40.

Grossman, Cathy Lynn. "The Twible Delivers Holy Writ with Twitter Wit." *Christian Century* 130 (2013) 14–15.

Guesnet, François. "A Tuml in the Shtetl: Khayim Betsalel Grinberg's Di khevre-kedishe Sude." Translated by Bill Templer. *Polin* 16 (2003) 93–106.

Gunn, David. "The Anatomy of Divine Comedy." In *Tragedy and Comedy in the Bible*, edited by J. Cheryl Exum, 115–29. Semeia 32. Decatur, GA: Scholars, 1984.

Guppy, Shusha. *The Secret of Laughter: Magical Tales from Classical Persia*. London: Tauris, 2005.

Halkin, Hillel. "Why Jews Laugh at Themselves." *Commentary* 121 (2006) 47–54.

Hancock, Rebecca. "Psalms." Class lecture, June 14, 2018, from the course "A Time to Laugh: Humor in Scripture, Faith and Practice." St. Mary's Ecumenical Institute, Baltimore.

BIBLIOGRAPHY

Hand, Karl. "A Wicked Sense of Humor." *Theology Today* 70 (2013) 119–27.
Handy, Lowell K. "Uneasy Laughter: Ehud and Eglon as Ethnic Humor." *Scandinavian Journal of the Old Testament* 6 (1992) 233–46.
Harap, Louis. "Jews in American Drama, 1900–1918." *American Jewish Archives* 36 (1984) 136–50.
Harman, William P. "Laughing Until It Hurts . . . Somebody Else: The Pain of a Ritual Joke." In *Sacred Play: Ritual Levity and Humor in South Asian Religions*, edited by Selva J. Raj and Corinne G. Dempsey, 107–22. Albany: State University of New York Press, 2010.
Harrington, Daniel J. "Polemical Parables in Matthew 24–25." *Union Seminary Quarterly Review* 44 (1991) 287.
Harris, Henry F. "The Absence of Humor in Jesus." *Methodist Quarterly* 57 (1908) 460–67.
Haverluck, Robert. "When God Was Flesh and Wild: A Conversation with Bob Haverluck." *Arts: The Arts in Religious and Theological Studies* 5 (1993) 27–32.
Hiltebeitel, Alf. "Recontextualizing Satire of Brahmanical Dharmaśāstra in the Aggañña Sutta." *Religions of South Asia* 3 (2009) 77–92.
Holbert, John C. "'Deliverance Belongs to Yahweh: Satire in the Book of Jonah." *Journal for the Study of the Old Testament* 6 (1981) 59–81.
Honeycutt, Frank G. "Jester and Tester." *Journal for Preachers* 37 (Pentecost 2014) 33–35.
Hooke, Ruthanna. "Humor in Preaching: Life Touched by Grace." *Word & World* 32 (2012) 187, 189.
Hostetler, Jeptha R. "Is Laughter Really the Best Medicine? How Humor Can Help Sustain the Work of Social Justice." *Sojourners Magazine* 40 (2011) 34–37.
Howell, James C. "Trojan Horse." *Christian Century* 122 (2005) 19.
Huebner, Chris K. "Make Us Your Laughter: Stanley Hauerwas's Joke on Mennonites." *Mennonite Quarterly Review* 84 (2010), 357–73.
Hussey, L. M. "The Wit of the Carpenter." *American Mercury* 5 (1925) 329–36.
Hyers, Conrad. *And God Created Laughter: The Bible as Divine Comedy*. Atlanta: John Knox, 1987.
Iverson, Kelly R. "Incongruity, Humor, and Mark: Performance and the Use of Laughter in the Second Gospel (Mark 8:14–21)." *New Testament Studies* 59 (2013) 2–19.
Jacobson, Rolf, and Karl N. Jacobson. "'Everyone Who Hears Will Laugh with Me': Humor and Telling God's Truth." *Word & World* 32 (2012) 107–16.
Jarrard, James L. "Preaching and the Comic Side of the Gospel." *Christian Ministry* 18 (1987) 26–28.
Jenkins, Ron. "Sacred Laughter—Clowning and Ritual in Bali." In *Theater—Ritual—Religion*, edited by Ingrid Hentschel and Klaus Hoffmann, 163–77. Münster: Lit, 2004.
Jeremías, Joachim. *Rediscovering the Parables*. Translated by S. H. Hooke. London: SCM, 1963.
John, P. M. "Joke and 'the Punch Line': On Interpreting Myths in Indian Culture." *Religion and Society* 22 (1975) 63–76.
Johnson, Luke Timothy. "The Lukan Kingship Parable (Luke 19:11–27)." *Novum Testamentum* 24 (1982) 140.
Jones, Ivor Harold. *The Matthean Parables: A Literary & Historical Commentary*. Leiden: Brill, 1995.
Jones, L. Gregory. "Punch Lines." *Christian Century* 124 (2007) 33.
Kabat, Vicki M. "Nothing to Joke About." *Family and Community Ministries* 23 (2009) 56.

Bibliography

Kaminisky, Joel S. "Humor and the Theology of Hope: Isaac as a Humorous Figure." *Interpretation* 54 (2000) 363–75.

Kissling, Paul J. "Self-Defense and Identity Formation in the Depiction of Battles in Joshua and Esther." In *Interested Readers: Essays on the Hebrew Bible in Honor of David J. A. Clines*, edited by James K. Aitkiens et al., 105–19. Atlanta: SBL, 2013.

Kistemaker, Simon J. *The Parables of Jesus*. Grand Rapids: Baker, 1980.

Koppel, Michael S. "A Pastoral Theological Reflection on Play in the Ministry." *Journal of Pastoral Theology* 13 (2003) 1–12.

Krasney, Ariela. "The Badkhn: From Wedding Stage to Writing Desk." Translated by Erica Nadelhaft and Benjamin Greenberg. *Polin* 16 (2003) 7–28.

Kruger, Hennie. "Can the Phenomenon of Humor Serve as an Interpretive Key to Understand the Idea of Laughter in the Old Testament?" *In die Skriflig* 48 (2014) 1–7.

Kuschel, Karl-Josef: *Laughter: A Theological Reflection*. New York: Continuum, 1994.

Kynes, W. J. "Beat Your Parodies into Swords, and Your Parodied Books into Spears: A New Paradigm for Parody in the Hebrew Bible." *Biblical Interpretation* 19 (2011) 276–310.

Landover Baptist Church. Discussion Forum, Muslim Jokes. https://www.landoverbaptist.net/showthread.php?t=14227.

Landy, Francis. "Are We in the Place of Averroes?" In J. Cheryl Exum, *Tragedy and Comedy*, 131–48.

Langston, Douglas C. "The Comical Kierkegaard." *Journal of Religious Studies* 12 (1985) 35–45.

Lanyon, Walter Clemow. *The Laughter of God*. Moon, PA: Bookhaven, 1941.

Lapidus, Rina. "The Poetry of Hayyim Lensky and Its Affinity with Minor Russian Humorous Folk Genres." *East European Jewish Affairs* 41 (2011) 189–202.

Lauder, Robert E. "Woody Allen: Camus's Existentialism as Comedy." *Philosophy and Theology* 2 (1988) 362–73.

Lee, Agnes Chwen Jiuan. "Chuang Tzu's Wit and Wisdom." *Ching Feng* 36 (1993) 12–23.

Lewis, C. S. *The Screwtape Letters*. Rev. ed. New York: Macmillan, 1982.

———. *Surprised by Joy*. San Diego: Harvest, 1963.

Lindsey, Donald B., and John Heeren. "Where the Sacred Meets the Profane: Religion in the Comic Pages." *Review of Religious Research* 34 (1992) 63–77.

Lindtner, Christian. "'Madhyamaka'—the Philosophy of Great Humor?" *Journal of Indian Philosophy* 18 (1990) 249–60.

Linss, Wilhelm C. "The Hidden Humor of Paul." *Currents in Theology and Mission* 25 (1998) 195–99.

Lippitt, John. "A Funny Thing Happened to Me on the Way to Salvation: Climacus as Humorist in Kierkegaard's Concluding Unscientific Postscript." *Religious Studies* 33 (1997) 181–202.

———. *Humour and Irony in Kierkegaard's Thought*. New York: Macmillan, 2000.

Longenecker, Bruce W. "A Humorous Jesus? Orality, Structure and Characteristics in Luke." *Biblical Interpretation* 16 (2008) 179–204.

Ludlow, Jared W. *Abraham Meets Death: Narrative Humor in the Testament of Abraham*. London: Sheffield Academic, 2002.

Macy, Howard R. "Laughter on the Journey." *Word & World* 32 (2012) 141–48.

Maghen, Ze'ev. "The Merry Men of Medina: Comedy and Humanity in the Early Days of Islam." *Islam* 83 (2006). https://doi.org/10.1515/ISLAM.2006.014.

Bibliography

Markham, Ian S., and Samantha R. E. Gottlich. *Lectionary Levity: The Use of Humor in Preaching*. New York: Church, 2017.

Márkus-Takeshita, Kinga. "The Secret of Laughter: Magical Tales from Classical Persia." *Asian Folklore Studies* 66 (2007) 282–83.

Martin, James. *Between Heaven and Mirth: Why Joy, Humor, and Laughter Are at the Heart of the Spiritual Life*. San Francisco: HarperOne, 2011.

Martin, Janet Letnes, and Suzann Nelson. *You Know You Are a Lutheran If . . .* Hastings, MN: Caragana, 2002.

Masarik, Albin. "The Use of a Joke in Introductions to Anton Fabian's Homilies." *Expository Times* 128 (2017) 491–96.

Mather, Judson. "The Comic Art of the Book of Jonah." *Soundings* 65 (1982) 280–91.

Mattingly, Terry. "Doug Marlette: Tragedy and Bitter Laughter." *Christian Century* 101 (1984) 631–32.

Mazor, Yaakov. "The Badkhn in Contemporary Hasidic Society: Social, Historical, and Musical Observations." Translated by Glenn Dynner. *Polin* 16 (2003) 279–96.

McCaughey, Lane C. "The Fear of Yahweh and the Mission of Judaism: A Postexilic Maxim and its Early Christian Expansion in the Parable of the Talents." *Journal of Biblical Literature* 94 (1975) 235–45.

McClelland, Joseph C. "Doxology as Suspension of the Tragic." *Theology Today* 31 (1974) 114–20.

McDermott, Rachel Fell. "Playing with Durga in Bengal." In *Sacred Play: Ritual Levity and Humor in South Asian Religions*, edited by Selva J. Raj and Corinne G. Dempsey, 143–59. Albany: State University of New York Press, 2010.

McDonough, Sheila. "Canadian Muslims: Humour and Philosophy." *Touchstone* 25 (2007) 33–41.

McFadden, Susan. "Authentic Humor as an Expression of Spiritual Maturity." *Journal of Religious Gerontology* 7 (1990) 131–42.

Meredith, Christopher. "A Big Room for Poo: Eddie Izzard's Bible and Literacy of Laughter." *Bible & Critical Theory* 9 (2013) 61–77.

Metz, J. B., and J.-P. Jossua, eds. *Theology of Joy*. New York: Herder and Herder, 1974.

Miller, Justin. "Prophecy in the Fast Lane: A Psychological Typology of Jewish Wit." *Criterion* 29 (1989) 10–15.

Mir, Mustansir. "Humor in the Qur'an." *Muslim World* 81 (1991) 179–93.

Morison, D. N. *The Humour of Christ*. Newcastle, Australia: Self published, 1931.

Morreall, John S. "Is This Place Stuffy, or Is It Just Me?" *Word & World* 32 (2012) 178–85.

Morris, Ellen F. "Sacred and Obscene Laughter in the Contendings of Horus and Seth in Egyptian Inversions of Everyday Life, and in the Context of Cultic Competition." In *Egyptian Stories: A British Egyptological Tribute to Alan B. Lloyd*, edited by Thomas Schneider and Kasia Maria Szpakkowska, 197–224. Münster: Ugarit-Verlag, 2007.

Morrison, Robert. "Did the Buddha Have a Sense of Humour?" *ARC* 31 (2003) 75–98.

Morse, Benjamin. "Introduction to a Dandy, Part II: Qoheleth's Turn, with Duchamp at Monte Carlo." *Biblical Interpretation* 22 (2014) 233–52.

Nel, Marius Johannes. "He Who Laughs Last: Jesus and Laughter in the Synoptic and Gnostic Traditions." *Hervormde Teologiese Studies* 70 (2014) 1–8.

Nissan, Ephraim. "On Joshua in Pseudo-Sirach." *Journal for the Study of the Pseudepigrapha* 20 (2011) 163–218.

Novick, Michael. "'Almost, at Times, the Fool': Abimelekh and Genesis 20." *Prooftexts* 24 (2004) 277–90.

Bibliography

Oden, Thomas C. *The Humor of Kierkegaard*. Princeton: Princeton University Press, 2004.

Olson, Carl. "The Zen Clown Ikkyu: A Cross-Cultural Study of a Symbol of Disorder." *Journal of Dharma* 13 (1988) 147–63.

Ozgur, Iren. "Cafcaf: An Islamic Humor Magazine, No Joke!" *Contemporary Islam* 6 (2012) 1–27.

Page, Jake. "Spider Coming Down." *Journal of Religion and Health* 42 (2003) 111–16.

Palmer, Earl F. *The Humor of Jesus: Sources of Laughter in the Bible*. Vancouver: Regent College Publishing, 2001.

Palmer, Elizabeth Musselman. "God's Laughter: A Theological Reading of Woody Allen and Anne Sexton." *Word & World* 32 (2012) 149–56.

Park, Clara Claiborne. "Crippled Laughter: Toward Understanding of Flannery O'Connor." *American Scholar* 51 (1982) 249–57.

Parrill, Lloyd. "Concept of Humor in the Pseudonymous Works of Søren Kierkegaard." *Drew Gateway* 46 (1975–76) 116–17.

Paulson, Steve, and Pam Paulson. *Church Signs across America*. New York: Overlook, 2006.

Pelham, Abigail. "Job as Comedy, Revisited." *Journal for the Study of the Old Testament* 35 (2010) 89–112.

Phillips, J. B. *Your God Is Too Small*. New York: Collier/Macmillan, 1961.

Pickthall, Marmaduke William. "Of Suleymân the Dragoman." *Biblical Archaeology Review* 33 (2007) 68, 70.

Pieris, Aloysius. "Prophetic Humor and the Exposure of Demons." *Dialogue*, n.s., 31 (2004) 25–40.

Pintchman, Tracy. "Friendship, Humor, Levity, and Love in a Hindu Women's Ritual Tradition." In *Sacred Play: Ritual Levity and Humor in South Asian Religions*, edited by Selva J. Raj and Corinne G. Dempsey, 91–105. Albany: State University of New York Press, 2010.

Portaro, Sam A. "Holiness and Hilarity: The Reverent Irreverence of Mark Twain." *Criterion* 22 (1983) 22–25.

Portnoy, Edward. "Exploiting Tradition: Religious Iconography in Cartoons of the Polish Yiddish Press." *Polin* 16 (2003) 243–27.

Potella, Michael. "And God Created Laughter: The Eighth Day." *Interpretation: A Journal of Bible and Theology* 69 (2015) 156–68, 160.

Power, David. *Love without Calculation: A Reflection on Divine Kenosis*. New York: Crossroad, 2005.

Press, Michael. "'Where Are the Gods of Hamath?' (2 Kings 18:34 // Isaiah 36:19) The Use of Foreign Deities in the Rabshakeh's Speech." *Journal for the Study of the Old Testament* 40 (2015) 201–33.

Radday Yehuda T., and Athalya Brenner, eds. *On Humour and the Comic in the Hebrew Bible*. Sheffield: Almond, 1990.

Raj, Selva J., and Corinne G. Dempsey, eds. *Sacred Play: Ritual Levity and Humor in South Asian Religions*. Albany: State University of New York Press, 2010.

Raskin, Richard. "God versus Man in a Classic Jewish Joke." *Judaism* 40 (1991) 39–51.

Reis, Pamela Tamarkin. "Numbers XI: Seeing Moses Plain." *Vetus Testamentum* 55 (2005) 207–31.

———. "Uncovering Jael and Sisera: A New Reading." *Scandinavian Journal of the Old Testament* 19 (2005) 24–47.

Repp, Martin. "Buddhism and Cartoons in Japan: How Much Parody Can a Religion Bear?" *Japanese Religions* 31 (2006) 189–203.

Bibliography

Rizvi, Sajjad H. "Sayyid Niʿmat Allāh al-Jazāʾirī and His Anthologies: Anti-Sufism, Shiʾism and Jokes in the Safavid World." *Welt Des Islams*, n.s., 50 (2010) 224–42.

Robertson, David. "Tragedy, Comedy, and the Bible: A Response." In *Tragedy and Comedy in the Bible*, edited by J. Cheryl Exum, 99–106. Semeia 32. Decatur, GA: Scholars, 1984.

Robertson, David, and Robert Polzin, eds. *Studies in the Book of Job*. Semeia 7. Missoula: Scholars, 1977.

Rogness, Michael. "Humor in the Bible." *Word & World* 32 (2012) 117–23.

Rommer, Barbara R. "Hypothetical Letter: A Letter to: the Lord G-d Almighty a.k.a. Ha'shem, Allah, etc. From: the Jews: a.k.a. the Chosen People. Subject: Termination of Contract/Special Status (Chosen People)." *Journal of Religion and Psychical Research* 26 (2003) 3–5.

Roskies, David. G. "Major Trends in Yiddish Parody." *Jewish Quarterly Review*, n.s., 94 (2004) 109–22.

Samra, Cal. *The Joyful Christ: The Healing Power of Humor*. New York: Harper, 1991.

Sanford, A Whitney. "Don't Take It Badly, It's Holi: Ritual Levity, Society, and Agriculture." In *Sacred Play: Ritual Levity and Humor in South Asian Religions*, edited by Selva J. Raj and Corinne G. Dempsey, 37–56. Albany: State University of New York Press, 2010.

Saroglou, Vassilis. "Humor Appreciation as Function of Religious Dimensions." *Archive for the Psychology of Religion* 24 (2003) 144–53.

———. "Religion and Sense of Humor: An A Priori Incompatibility? Theoretical Considerations from a Psychological Perspective." *Humor: International Journal of Humor Research* 15 (2002) 191–214.

Schifferdecker, Kathryn M. "Of Stars and Sea Monsters: Creation Theology in the Whirlwind Speeches." *Word & World* 31 (2011) 357–66.

Schneider, Thomas, and Kasia Maria Szpakowska, eds. *Egyptian Stories: A British Egyptological Tribute to Alan B. Lloyd on the Occasion of His Retirement*. Münster: Ugarit-Verlag, 2007.

Schopen, Gregory. "The Learned Monk as a Comic Figure: On Reading a Buddhist Vinaya as Indian Literature." *Journal of Indian Philosophy* 35 (2007) 201–26.

Schultz, Brian. "Jesus as Archelaus in the Parable of the Pounds (Lk. 19:11–27)." *Novum Testamentum* 49 (2007) 105.

Sherwood, Yvonne. "Cross-Currents in the Book of Jonah: Some Jewish and Cultural Midrashim on a Traditional Text." *Biblical Interpretation* 6 (1998) 49–79.

Shore, Mary Hinkle. "Leave Them Wanting More: Humor in Preaching." *Word & World* 32 (2012) 124–31.

Short, Robert L. "Peanuts at 35: Distilled Love." *Christian Century* 102 (1985) 1022.

Smith, Christopher Colby. "Humor in Preaching: Who Needs Jokes?" *Word & World* 32 (2012) 186, 188.

Sölle, Dorothee, and Fulbert Steffensky. "Christianity and Joy in Sects & Fringe Groups." In *Theology of Joy*, edited by Johan Baptist Metz and Jean-Pierre Jossua, 113–125. New York: Herder and Herder, 1974.

Spencer, F. Scott. "Those Riotous—Yet Righteous—Foremothers of Jesus: Exploring Matthew's Comic Genealogy." In *Are We Amused? Humour about Women in the Biblical World*, edited by Athalya Brenner, 7–30. Journal for the Study of the Old Testament. Supplement Series 383. London: T. & T. Clark, 2003.

Spivey, Ed, Jr. "This Is Not about the Economy." *Sojourners* 38 (2009) 50.

Bibliography

Stackert, Jeffrey. "Introduction to Leviticus." In *The New Oxford Annotated Bible*, NRSV, edited by Michael D. Coogan, 141–43. Oxford: Oxford University Press, 2010.

Standhartinger, Angela. "Humor in Joseph and Aseneth." *Journal for the Study of the Pseudepigrapha* 24 (2015) 2–19.

Stark, Ryan J. "Are Laurence Sterne's Sermons Funny?" *Literature & Theology* 30 (2016) 456–70.

Steere, David. "Our Capacity for Sadness and Joy: An Essay on Life Before Death." In *Theology of Joy*, edited by Johan Baptist Metz and Jean-Pierre Jossua, 15–30. New York: Herder & Herder, 1974.

Stone, Lawson G. "Eglon's Belly and Ehud's Blade: a Reconsideration." *Journal of Biblical Literature* 128 (2009) 649–63.

Strange, Marcian. "God and Laughter." *Worship* 45 (1971) 2–12.

Sullivan, John. "Edith Stein's Humor and Compassion." *Spirituality Today* 43 (1991) 142–60.

———. "Some Instances of Edith Stein's Humor and Compassion." In *Contemplating Edith Stein*, edited by Joyce Avrech Berkman, 76–92. Notre Dame: University of Notre Dame Press, 2006.

Sutton, Eugene Taylor. "Humor for Preachers." *Perspective* 6 (1991) 9.

Suzuki, Keiko. "The Making of Tōjin: Construction of the Other in Early Modern Japan." *Asian Folklore Studies* 66 (2007) 83–105.

Szombathy, Zoltán. "On Wit and Elegance: the Arabic Concept of Zarf." In *Authority, Privacy and Public Order in Islam*, edited by B. Michalak-Pikulska and A. Pikulski, 101–19. Leuven: Peeters, 2006.

Tasker, R. V. G. *Matthew*. London: Tyndale, 1961.

Thoennes, Erik. "Laughing through Tears: The Redemptive Role of Humor in a Fallen World." *Presbyterion* 33 (2007) 72–83.

Thompson, Casey. "Living by the Word: Reflections on the Lectionary [M 18 2012]." *Christian Century* 129 (2012) 21.

Thysell, Carol. "Unearthing the Treasure, Unknitting the Napkin: The Parable of the Talents as a Justification for Early Modern Women's Preaching and Prophesying." *Journal of Feminist Studies in Religion* 15 (1999) 7–20.

Toorawa, Shawkat M. "Play in the Qur'an." *Journal of Qur'anic Studies* 5 (2003) 99–102.

Trueblood, Elton. *The Humor of Christ*. San Francisco: HarperSanFrancisco, 1964.

Valpey, Kenneth Russell. "Reflections on Ludic Dimensions in Hindu-Christian Scholarship." *Journal of Hindu-Christian Studies* 25 (2012) 51–54.

Van Eck, Ernest. "Do Not Question My Honour: A Social-Scientific Reading of the Parable of the Minas (Lk 19:12b–24, 27)." *HTS* 67 (2011) 1–11.

Van Heerden, Willie. "Why the Humour in the Bible Plays Hide and Seek with Us." *Social Identities* 7 (2001) 75–96.

Van Rensburg, Lee. *The Sense of Humor in Scripture, Theology and Worship*. Limoa, OH: Fairway, 1991.

Via, Dan O., Jr. "The New Testament and the Comic Genre." *Christian Century* 92 (1975) 901–4.

Vinokurov, Val. "'On the Brink of Tears and Laughter': Joy and Suffering in the Thought of Emmanuel Levinas." *Journal of Religion & Society* 6 (2004) 1–8.

Walker, Steven C. *Illuminating Humor of the Bible*. Eugene, OR: Cascade, 2013.

Walters, Jonathan S. "Gods' Play and the Buddha's Way: Varieties of Levity in Contemporary Sinhala Practice." In *Sacred Play: Ritual Levity and Humor in South Asian*

Bibliography

Religions, edited by Selva J. Raj and Corinne G. Dempsey, 123–39. Albany: State University of New York Press, 2010.

Ware, Amy M. "Will Rogers's Radio: Race and Technology in the Cherokee Nation." *American Indian Quarterly* 33 (2009) 62–97.

Webster, Gary. *Laughter in the Bible*. St. Louis: Bethany, 1960.

West, Mark, and Sunil Pokharel. "Questioning Caste: Performance, Parody, and the Political Economy of a Hindu State: An Interview with Sunil Pokharel." *Baylor Journal of Theatre and Performance* 2 (2005) 47–63.

Whedbee, J. William. *The Bible and the Comic Vision*. 1998. Reprint, Minneapolis: Fortress, 2002.

―――. "The Comedy of Job." In *Studies in the Book of Job*, edited by Robert Polzin and David Robertson, 1–39. Semeia 7. Missoula: SBL/Scholars, 1977.

Whitfield, Stephen J. "The Distinctiveness of American Jewish Humor." *Modern Judaism* 6 (1986) 245–60.

Wilcox, Lance. "Staging Jonah." *Bible Review* 11 (1995) 20–28.

Witetschek, Stephan. "The Dragon Spitting Frogs: On the Imagery of Revelation 16.13–24." *New Testament Studies* 54 (2008) 557–72.

Wolski, Nathan. "The Secret of Yiddish: Zoharic Composition in the Poetry of Aaron Zeitlin." *Kabbalah* 20 (2009) 147–80.

Wood, Ralph C. "Community of Laughter: Remembering Peter de Vries." *Christian Century* 110 (1993) 1006–7.

―――. "Marooned in Mercy: De Vries' Connubial Comedy." *Christian Century* 102 (1985) 491–94.

―――. "Talent Increased and Returned to God: The Spiritual Legacy of Flannery O'Connor's Letters." *Anglican Theological Review* 62 (1980) 153–67.

Wordsworth, William Arthur. *The Laughter of God: An Essay on the Indications of a Sense of Humour in the Son of Man with Some Verse*. N.p.: Farnham, 1925.

Wright, N. T. *Jesus and the Victory of God*. Christian Origins and the Question of God 2. Minneapolis: Fortress, 1996.

Yancey, Philip. "From Carnival to Mardi Gras." *Christianity Today* 37 (1993) 64.

Young, Brad H. *Jesus and His Jewish Parables: Rediscovering the Roots of Jesus' Teaching*. New York: Paulist, 1989.

Zakovich, Yair. "U and ∩ in the Bible." In *Tragedy and Comedy in the Bible*, edited by J. Cheryl Exum, 107–14. Semeia 32. Decatur, GA: Scholars, 1984.

Zuver, Dudley. *Salvation by Laughter*. New York: Harper, 1933.

Suject Index

Abbot (Bud), 81
Abel, 81, 134
ability, talent (currency) as, 147
Abimelech, 81–83
Abittai, Jonah son of. *See under* Jonah.
Abraham, 67, 75–77, 81–83
absurd, the, 107, 108
    theatre of, 111
absurdity, 15, 64, 68, 70, 105, 107
    comic. *See* under comic.
    of the disciples, 123
Achzib ("Lie"), the houses of, 96
actions
    arbitrary, 71
    comic. *See* under comic.
    ritual, 73
Acts, book of, xvii, 4, 61, 72, 114, 126–28
Adam, 43, 65, 81, 82, 156
adamah, 81
Adams, Douglas, 67–69, 115, 116, 122, 129–32, 149, 150, 156
Adams' Four Categories (of Jesus's humor), 115
adulteress, story of, 121
advents, two, 40
Aesop, 133
affirming the consequent, fallacy of, 33
aggada, Jonah as. *See under* Jonah.
Agrippa, 127
allegorical, parable of the talents as. *See under* parable of the talents.
allegory, parable of the talents as. *See under* parable of the talents.
Allen (Gracie), 81

ambiguity, fallacy of, 33, 34, 66
Ambrose, Saint, 56, 60
Amos
    biting sarcasm of, 95
    book of, 14, 88, 94, 95
analytic definition, 8
Ananias, 128
Anderson, Philip, 38
anger of Jonah. *See under* Jonah.
animal imagery in Revelation, 133
animal sacrifice, 14
animal, man the laughing, 46
animals in Jonah. *See under* Jonah.
animosity of Jonah. *See under* Jonah.
Annunciation, the, 116
antecedent (logic), 33, 34. *See also* consequent.
antidote, humor as. *See under* humor.
antihero, David as. *See under* David.
antilanguage, 94
appeal (to)
    authority, 44, 45, 54–58
    ignorance, 34
    reason, 25, 152
    unsuitable authority, 45. *See also* argument and argumentum.
apocalyptic, parable of the talents. *See under* parable of the talents.
Aquinas, Thomas. *See* Thomas Aquinas.
Arbuckle, Gerald, 66–68, 82, 83, 85–87, 89, 92–95, 97, 100, 101, 115–17, 119, 122, 124, 129, 131
argument
    against the person, 34

Subject Index

argument *(continued)*
    circular, 32
    deductive, 31–33, 35, 42, 43, 45, 46, 54, 56, 154
    inductive, 31
    sound, 28, 29, 35, 37. *See also* appeal and argumentum.
argumentum
    ad hominem, 34
    ad ignorantiam, 34
    ad verecundiam, 45. *See also* argument and appeal.
Arimathea, Joseph of, 126
Aristophanes, 71, 80, 133
arrogance, attack on 12
Artemidorus's dream book, 133
Aseneth, 81, 85, 86
atonement, xvi, 14, 153
audience in the parable of the talents. *See under* parable of the talents.
Augustine, 55, 60
authoritarianism, 20
authorities, 45, 56, 127
authority, appeal to. *See under* appeal.

Baal, 92
babayit, 101
Babel, tower of. See Tower of Babel.
baker (in Daniel), 66
Balaam's ass, 86, 87
banter, xvi, 65, 117–119, 122, 123, 125
Baptist, John the. *See* John the Baptist
Barnabas, 127
Barth, Karl, 7
Basil, Saint, 56, 60
Bastien, Joseph, 56
Bathsheba, 65, 92
bawdy riddles, 90
Beasley-Murray, G. R., 142
Beatitudes, 12
Beavis, Mary Ann, 141, 143, 148
beggar, the disabled, 128
begging the question, fallacy of, 32
Benedict, Saint, 60
    Rule of, 13
Benjamin, tribe of, 91
Berger, Peter, 47–49, 54, 55, 59

Berger's theology of the comic, 47–49, 59
Bernard of Clairvaux, 55
bestiary, diabolic. *See* diabolic bestiary.
Beth Aphrah, 96
biases, religion's and humor's, 57
Biddle, Mark, 8, 36, 47, 50, 59, 65, 83, 91, 101, 108, 115
Binau, Brad, 39
birthright, Esau's. *See under* Esau.
Biser, Eugene, 5
biting rhetoric of Paul. *See under* Paul.
biting roasting of Jesus. *See under* Jesus.
biting sarcasm of Amos. *See under* Amos.
blind leading the blind, 12, 118–19, 122, 124
Blomberg, Craig, 142
boastful weakness of Paul. *See under* Paul.
Branson, Roy, 73
Braun, Adam, 146
Brenner, Athalya, 64, 67, 100
Brisson, E. Carson, 143, 144
Burkey, Dean, 85–87, 96, 99, 100, 101
burlesque, 64, 67, 68, 110, 153
Burns (George), 81
Buss, Martin, 71, 73, 95
Bussie, Jacqueline, 9
butler (in Daniel), 66
Byassee, Jason, 15, 19

Cadwallader, Alan, 146, 147
Cain, 81, 134
Calvin, John, 142, 148
camel
    swallowing, 12, 119
    through the eye of a needle 119, 123
Cana, wedding in, 65, 116, 125
Canaanite woman, 122, 123
Capps, Donald, 55–57, 59
caricature, 67, 68, 95, 98, 99, 144
Carpenter, John, 141, 145
Carroll, R. P., 54
cartoon, Jonah as. *See under* Jonah.
catharsis as a corollary to humor, 8
cedar of Lebanon, parable of. *See* parable of the cedar of Lebanon.

Subject Index

celebration, xv, xvi, 5, 23, 44, 65, 70, 158
chairete, 114, 123
Charles, David, 40
Chawwah, 81
cheerfulness, 49
Chenoweth, Ben, 140, 142, 144, 145, 147
child's spirit, 12, 65
children, 5, 9, 12, 39, 97, 114, 119, 123
Chilton, Bruce, 141
Chronicles, I and II, 72, 155, 156
Chrysostom, John, xvi, 55, 60, 133
Church Fathers, 48, 60
church signs, 23
church, early, 55
Cicero, 15
circular argument. *See under* argument.
Claassens, Juliana, 9, 103
Clairvaux, Bernard of. *See* Bernard of Clairvaux.
Clement of Alexandria, 56, 60
clowning humor of Jesus. *See under* Jesus.
clowns, 68
Codrescu, Andrei, 19
coherence theory of truth. *See under* truth.
Colossians, 155–57
comedies, 6, 73
comedy, 4, 6, 8, 10, 59, 83, 85, 125
   Bible as, xvii, 4, 6, 10, 59, 61–158
   Daniel as, 102
   Esther as, 100, 101
   Job as, 98, 99
   integrative, 73
   Jonah as. *See under* Jonah
   parable of the talents as. *See under* parable of the talents
   slapstick, 84
   of creation, 81
   of reversal, 124
   of subversion, 73, 102
comic
   absurdity, 6, 70
   actions, 93, 94
   development, 156
   dialogue, 111

   distance, 111
   elements in the Bible, 71–79, 85, 98, 106, 117, 133, 155–57
   exaggeration, 104, 105
   incongruity, 91
   laughter, 55, 84
   markers, 65
   pairings, 81
   paradox, 4–6, 45, 70
   parentheses, 4, 5, 6, 45, 70
   phenomena, 48
   play, 100
   relief, 133
   reversal, 124
   salvation, 93
   satire, 104, 105
   seduction, Jonah's. *See under* Jonah
   speed, 127
   understatement, 104, 106
   views of life, 87, 155
   virtues, 71, 72
   vision, 84
   theology of the, 47–49, 59
concordance, 44, 54
conditional sentence, 33
consequent (logic), 33, 34. *See also* antecedent.
Coptic Gnostic Apocalypse of Peter, 78
Corinthians, I and II, 129–31, 145
correspondence theory of truth. *See under* truth.
Costello (Lou), 81
Craig, Kenneth, 103
croaking frogs, 133–35
cross, foolishness of, 130
crowd (s), 118, 123, 143–44, 147, 153
crown of righteousness, 158
crucifixion, tragedy of, 59, 114
cutting-edge satire of Jesus. *See under* Jesus.
cynicism, 5, 71

Damascus, Paul's escape from. *See under* Paul.
Daniel, book of, 71, 73, 96, 102
David, 4, 48, 50, 69, 70, 91, 92, 95
   as antihero, 91
   as rebel, 91

Suject Index

David *(continued)*
  Vacation Bible School, 50, 91.
Davis, Dale, 90
deduction, 27, 31
deductive argument. *See under* argument.
definition, types of, 8
  See also analytic definition; dictionary definition; ostensive definition; and stipulative definition
Delaney, Herbert, 43
delight, xvi, 15, 37, 41, 43, 64, 65, 75, 76, 82, 99, 116, 123, 138, 149, 151, 152
denarii/denarius, 138
Derby, Josiah, 101, 103
derision, 67, 68, 76
Deuteronomy, 71, 80
DeVries, Peter, 23
diabolic bestiary, 133
dictionary definition, 6, 8, 67, 145
digressions of Paul. *See under* Paul.
dinner, parable of the. *See* parable of the dinner.
Diotrephes, 158
Dipboye, Carolyn, 140, 142, 144, 147
disciples, xv, 68, 117, 118, 120, 123, 125, 126, 142–47
discipleship, 140, 147
divine foolishness, 105
divine humor. *See under* humor.
Dodd, C. H., 141
Domeris, William, 94, 95
Dowling, Elizabeth, 141, 143, 148
drachma, 138
Dray, Stephen, 40
drollery, 8
Duchamp, Marcel, 98
Duke, Paul, 126
dupe, Isaac as. *See under* Isaac.
Durham, Israel, 37

Easter, 66
Eberhart, Cy, 7
Ecclesiastes, 52, 96, 98
Eglon, assassination of, 88
Ehud, 88, 89
Elihu, 98, 99

Elijah, 92, 109
Elisha, 93
empirical
  evidence, 29, 30
  fact, 30
  objectivity, 29
enjoyment, xvi, 39, 57
Ephesians, 155–57
equivocation, fallacy of, 66
Erikson, Erik, 23
Esau, 81, 83, 85, 118
  birthright of, 85.
Esther, book of, 44, 72, 96, 100–103
Ethiopian, the puzzled, 128
Eutychus, 128
Eve, 43, 65, 81, 82
evidence, affirmative, 55
exaggeration, 12, 67, 104, 106, 116, 117, 120, 122
excreta, 82
Exodus, 72, 80, 86, 133, 134
Exum, Cheryl, 70, 84
Ezekiel, 48, 88, 94
Ezra, 155, 156

fairy tales, 6
fake prophet, Jonah as. *See under* Jonah.
fallacy/fallacies, 27, 32–35, 44, 45, 66. *See also*, argumentum; appeal; begging the question, fallacy of; equivocation, fallacy of; irrelevance, fallacy of
farce, 84, 110
Felix, 127
Feltmate, David, 20
Festus, 127
fish-belly religion, 106, 108
Flavius Joseph, 134
Folarin, George, 147
foolishness, 16, 52, 68, 69, 73, 82, 95, 97, 105, 130
fools, 48, 52, 60, 78, 85, 98, 130
foreskins, 69, 92
fox-hole religion, 106, 108
Friedman, Don, 77
frivolity, 78
frogs, 133–35

Subject Index

Frye, Northrop, 71
fun, xvi, 8, 20, 57, 70, 93, 101, 133, 143
funniness, 8

Galatians, 129, 131
gelos, 115
Genesis, 66, 72, 80, 81, 83–85
Gentiles, 144, 157
Gideon, 88–90
Gilgal, 14, 95
Giorgetti, Andrew, 82
glee, 95
gloom, 127, 128
Gnostic Gospels, 78
Goldingay, John, 127, 128
Goliath, 70, 92
Gomorrah, 67
Good, Edwin, 71, 73, 102
good Samaritan, parable of. *See* parable of the good Samaritan.
Gospels, xvii, 5, 45, 46, 61, 70, 78, 114–16, 119, 121, 123, 125
gotcha moments, 65, 66
Gottlich, Samantha, 15, 16
Gottwald, Norman, 71, 73, 87, 93, 155, 156
grace, 15, 38, 71, 105, 157, 158
grandmother letters, 129, 156
gratitude, 7, 157
Greeley, Andrew, 9
Gritsch, Eric, 38, 40
Grossman, Cathy Lynn, 23
grotesque, the, 64, 68, 69, 107, 108, 135
grotesqueness, 128
Gunn, David, 73, 74

Habakkuk, 88, 155
Haggai, 88, 155
Haman, 100, 101
    pomposity of, 100.
Hancock, Rebecca, 97
Hand, Karl, 115
Handy, Lowell, 89
happiness, xv, 4, 6, 7, 9, 10, 98
Hardy (Oliver), 81
Harrington, Daniel, 147, 148
Harris, Henry, 57, 58
Hartshorne, Charles, 151

hasty induction, 32, 34, 35, 44
Hauerwas, Stanley, 18, 19, 56
Hebrews, Epistle to, 132
Herod, 128, 139
hilarity, 23
Holbert, John C., 104, 107–109
Honeycutt, Frank, 126
Hooke, Ruthanna, 15
hope, 9, 47, 84, 104, 152
hopelessness, 152
Hosea, book of, 14, 71, 73, 88, 95
    mockery of, 95
hospitality, 158
Hostetler, Jeptha, 22
hostility, 57
Howell, James, 148
Huebner, Chris K., 18, 19
Hugo of St. Victor, 55
humility, 8, 28, 40, 71
humor
    abusive, xvi, 17–21
    acoustical, 64, 69
    antagonistic, 19
    as antidote, 39, 49, 90
    as means to truth. *See under* truth
    at the expense of outsiders, 127
    biting, 20
    black, 128
    divine, 86, 87
    integrative, 95
    mind-boggling, 116, 129, 131
    mocking, 82, 131
    non-abusive, 17, 21
    of love, 124
    of repetition, 12, 125
    pastoral, 41
    phenomenon of, 81
    presence of, xvi, xvii, 12, 25, 31, 36, 43–46, 50, 51, 53, 54, 56, 57, 64
    salty, 125
    stinging, 131
    subversive, 64, 82
    turned inward, xvi, 17, 22, 23
    turned outward, 17, 22

Subject Index

humor *(continued)*
  value of, xvi, xvii, 12, 16, 19, 22, 25, 36, 37, 40, 41, 43, 44, 46, 50–53, 140
  wry, 13. *See also under* Jewish; preaching; sermons; theology of.
humor in the Bible
  arguments against, 51–60
  arguments for, 36–50. *See also under* Luke, Gospel of; John, Gospel of; Mark, Gospel of; Matthew, Gospel of; Prophets; Revelation; scripture; Torah
Hyers, Conrad, 4, 37, 39, 71, 82, 104
hyperbole, 72, 94, 101, 120, 149
hypocrisy, 70, 105, 107

iconoclasm in Jonah. *See under* Jonah.
idleness, 52
idol(s), 23, 93, 95
ignorance, appeal to. *See under* appeal.
Imago Dei, 46
improbable, the, 104
incongruity, 8, 20, 38, 49, 50, 57, 65–67, 72, 83, 91, 98, 113, 116, 123, 128
inconsistency, 105
  fallacy of, 32, 35
inductive reasoning, 27, 31, 32, 34, 35, 43, 44, 54, 150
innocence, 102
integrative comedy. *See under* comedy.
integrative humor. *See under* humor.
invalidity, 28, 33, 35
inward, humor turned. *See under* humor.
irony, xvi, 12, 23, 47, 50, 59, 63, 64, 67, 68, 83, 94, 98, 116–18, 122, 125, 126, 129, 130, 153, 156
irrelevance, fallacy of, 33, 34
Isaac, 70, 72–74, 76, 81, 83–85, 90, 91
  as a dupe, 84.
Isaiah, 48, 88, 93
Islam, 24, 41
Israel, 14, 20, 21, 37, 73, 76, 87, 89, 90–92, 94, 96, 118, 142
Israelite(s), 14, 66, 86, 87, 89, 118, 133, 155, 156

Iverson, Kelly, 123

Jacob, 81, 83, 85, 118
Jacobson
  Karl, 11, 13, 14
  Rolf, 11, 13, 14
Jael, 88, 89
James, Epistle of, 132
Jarrard, James, 71
Jeremiah, 48, 88, 94
Jeremias, Joachim, 142
Jerome, Saint, 55, 60
Jerusalem, enemies of, 100
Jerusalem, Jesus in. *See under* Jesus.
Jesus
  ascension of, 146
  biting roasting of, 123
  clowning humor of, 116
  cutting-edge satire of, cutting-edge satire of, 116
  in Jerusalem, 79, 122, 124–26
  jousts of, 123
  ministry of, 117, 122–25 130, 144
  ministry of in Judea, 122
  mirth of, 72
  parables of. *See under* parables
  sorrowful, 59
Jewish
  Bible. *See* Tanakh
  Christian audience, 144
  humor, 21
  leaders, 127, 143
  literature, 133
  practice, 65
  purity movement, 109
  roots, 24. *See also* Judaism.
Jews
  God of, 44
  unbelieving, 127
Jezebel, 92
Job, xv, 31, 42, 72, 77, 96, 98, 99
Joel, book of, 88, 155
Johannine community, 158
John, Gospel of, 127, 133–35
  humor in, 125, 126
John the Baptist, 5, 124
John XXIII (pope), 49

Subject Index

John, First, 155, 158
  Second, 155, 158
  Third, 3, 155, 158
Johnson, Luke Timothy, 146
Joke(s), 13, 15, 16, 18, 19, 41, 57, 116–18, 122
Jonah
  aesthetic form of, 110
  anger of, 106
  animals in, 111
  animosity of, 105
  as aggada, 111
  as cartoon, 111
  as comedy, xvii, 9, 101, 103–112
  as false prophet, 133
  as history, 107
  as midrash, 111
  as non-satirical comedy, 110, 111
  as novella, 107
  as political cartoon, 27
  as satire, 104, 105, 107–109
  as unprophetic prophet, 104–105, 108
  book of, xvi, xvii, 27, 31, 45, 61, 72, 73, 88, 102
  comedic elements in, 9
  comic seduction of, 111
  iconoclasm in, 110
  not a sinner, 110
  prejudice of, 105
  psalm of, 108, 110
  son of Abittai, 106, 107
Jonathan, 92
Jones, Greg, 38, 40
Jones, I. H., 141
Joppa, 107
Jordan River, 122
Joseph, 66, 81, 85, 86
Joseph of Arimathea, 126
Joseph, Flavius. *See* Flavius Joseph.
Joshua, 88
Jossua, Jean-Pierre, 47, 49, 59
Jousts of Jesus's. *See under* Jesus.
joy
  call to, xvii, 1–25, 45, 61, 65, 70, 132, 153
  religious, 6
  spirit of, 152

  theology of. *See under* theology
joyful
  heart, 157
  life, 158
  mockery, xvi
  news, 114, 124
  noise, xvi
  relationship, 3
  tidings. *See under* tidings.
Joyful Noiseletter, 59
jubilation, messianic. *See under* messianic.
Judah (person), 81
Judah (place), 156
Judaism, 24, 41, 44, 148. *See also* Jewish.
Judas, 128
Jude, Epistle of, 155, 158
Judea, Jesus's ministry in. *See under* Jesus.
Judges, book of, 88, 89
judgment, 29, 72, 90, 142, 146

Kabat, Vicki, 41
Kaminsky, Joel, 83–85
Keystone Cops, 127
Kierkegaard, Sören, 12, 23, 68
Kistemaker, Simon, 142
komos, 70
Koppel, Michael, 39, 42
Kruger, Hennie, 81, 98
Kuschel, Karl-Josef, xvi, 38, 42, 44, 46–49, 55, 59, 60, 75–79, 97
Kynes, W.J., 100

Laban, 85
laborers in the parable of the talents.
  See under parable of the talents.
Lamentations, book of, 55, 96, 100
Landover Baptist Church, 19
Landy, Francis, 74
laugh, freedom to, 4, 5
laughter, 3–5, 7, 9, 10, 13
  affirmative, 47
  boisterous, 13
  comic. *See under* comic.
  infectious, 47
  involuntary, 8

Subject Index

laughter *(continued)*
  mocking, 47, 76, 97, 98
  of God, 44
  of superiority, 76, 97
  of unbelief, 75, 77
  proud, 47
  redemptive, 39
  revisited, xvii, 61, 63, 75, 99
  sick, 47
  theological, 18
  theology of. *See under* theology
  tragic, 9, 103
Laurel (Stan), 81
Lazarus, 60
Leah, 81
Lectionary Levity, 15, 16
Leviticus, 72, 80, 155, 156
Lewis (Jerry), 81
Lewis, C.S., 7, 39
lightheartedness, 132, 157
liminal stage of joking, 116, 117
liminality, 122
Linss, Wilhelm, 129, 132
logic, xvii, 25, 27–35, 59, 114, 152
Longenecker, Bruce, 73, 124, 149
Lord's Supper, 4
Lot, 81
love, humor of. *See under* humor.
love, Yahweh's, 73
Ludlow, Jared, 67
Luke, Gospel of, 79, 126–27, 136–39, 141, 143–44, 146, 148
  humor in, 123–25
Luther, Martin, 38, 40

Macy, Howard, 39
magnanimity, 71
Magnificat, Mary's, 65, 79, 114, 124
Maher, Bill, 19
Malachi, book of, 88, 155, 156
manna, 86
manure, human, 94
Mareshah ("inheritance"), 96
Mark, Gospel of, 71, 80
  humor in, 123, 124
Markham, Ian, 15, 16
Martin (Dean), 81

Martin, James, 5, 6, 7, 8, 55, 56, 60, 132, 149, 157
Martin, Janet Letnes, 20
martyrs, xv
Marx Brothers, 84
Mary, mother of Jesus, 65, 79, 114, 116, 123, 124
Marys, the two, 114, 123
Mather, Judson, 104, 110, 111
Matthew, Gospel of, 12, 119
  humor in, 122–24
McCaughey, Lane, 139, 143, 146
McClelland, Joseph, 71
McFadden, Susan, 38
meekness, 71
melancholy, 49
Mennonites, 18, 19
Meredith, Christopher, 82
Merriam-Webster's Dictionary, 8, 67, 145
Mesopotamian royal ideology, 82
messianic
  enthronement, 146
  jubilation, 79
metaphor, 128
  truth of. *See under* truth.
Metz, Johann, 47, 49, 59
Micah, book of, 88, 96
  as punster prophet, 96
Micah-Danite, 88, 90
Michal (Saul's daughter), 69, 92
Midianites, 90
Midrash, Jonah as. *See under* Jonah as
Ministry of Jesus's. *See under* Jesus.
mirth, house of, 52
mirth of Jesus's. *See under* Jesus.
misery, 60
mite, widow's. *See* widow's mite. 70
Moabites, 88, 89
mocker, sinner as, 77
mockery, xvi, 67, 68, 130, 131
mockery, Hosea's. *See under* Hosea.
mockery, joyful. *See under* joyful.
mocking humor. *See under* humor.
mocking laughter. *See under* laughter.
mocking of Christ, 48
mockumentary, 19
modus ponens, 33

Subject Index

Mohammed, 40
Mordecai, 100, 101
Morreall, John, 40, 44, 52
Morse, Benjamin, 98
Moses, 66, 70, 86, 87
mourning, 49, 52, 98, 111
Muslim joke, 21
mustard seed, parable of the. See parable of the mustard seed.

Nahum, book of, 88, 96, 155
Naioth, 92
Nathaniel, 118, 125
nativity, 78
Nazareth, 125
needle, eye of, 13, 69, 119, 123
Nehemiah, book of, 155
Nelson, Suzann, 20
Nicene Creed, 29
Nicodemus, 126
Nietzsche, Friedrich, xv, xvi
Nineveh, 104–109
Ninevites, 105, 109
Noah, 81, 82
nonabusive humor. See *under* humor.
nonsense, 30
novella, Jonah as. See *under* Jonah.
Novick, Tzvi, 82, 83
NPR, 19
Numbers, book of, 80, 86

O'Connor, Flannery, 23
Obadiah, book of, 88, 155
Onesimus, 132
oppressed, the, 22
oppression, 9, 95, 103, 104
oppressive
  discourse, 115
  master, 141, 148
  systems, 9
orthodox/orthodoxy, xvii, 29, 90, 153
orthopraxis/orthopraxy, xvii, 153
ostensive definition, 8
outsiders, humor at the expense of. See *under* humor.
outward, humor turned. See *under* humor.
overstatement, 12, 105

oxymoron, 3, 54

Palmer, Earl, 117–18, 120–21, 124–25
Palmer, Elizabeth, 38
parable of the cedar of Lebanon, 67
parable of the dinner, 124
parable of the good Samaritan, 70, 124.
parable of the mustard seed, 67
parable of the prodigal son, 67, 109, 115, 121, 149
parable of the pounds, 136–140, 146–148
parable of the talents, xvi, xvii, 61, 68, 135–50
  as allegorical/allegory, 140, 145, 147–48
  as apocalyptic, 145–48
  audience in, 140, 143–49
  laborers in, 142, 149
parable of the unjust judge, 116
parable of the vineyard workers, 120
parables
  Christ's, 68, 118
  Jesus's, 116, 121, 124, 153
paradox, xvi, 12, 66, 67, 100, 113, 116–19, 122, 124, 125, 153, 157
  comic. See *under* comic.
parentheses, comic. See *under* comic.
parodies/parody, 14, 64, 67, 68, 72, 82, 98, 100, 110, 129, 156
Parousia, 139, 146
Passion, the, 55, 123
pastoral humor. See *under* humor.
pathos, 121
Patristic period, 147
Paul, 48, 127, 132, 156–58
  as a sinner, 157
  biting rhetoric of, 157
  boastful weakness of, 157
  digressions of, 129, 130, 156
  escape from Damascus of, 127, 128
  letters of, 55, 126, 129–32, 156
  oppression of, 129
  preaching of. See *under* preaching.
Pauline texts, 71, 80
peace workers, 22
peaceful community, 129
peacemaking, 22

Suject Index

pearls before swine, 13
Pelham, Abigail, 99
Pentateuch, 156
Pentecost, 128
performative theory of truth. *See under* truth.
performative utterance, 30
perseverance, 47
Persian government, 101
pet owners, 37
Peter (apostle), 4, 66, 72, 78, 117, 120–22, 127, 128, 131
Peter
   First, 155, 158
   Second, 2, 155, 158
petitio principii, 32, 33, 35
Pharisees, 31, 68, 118, 121–23, 144
phenomenon of humor. *See under* humor.
Philemon, Epistle to, 129, 132
Philip (apostle), 118, 126
Philistines, 20, 69, 92
Philo of Alexandria, 134
piety, 83, 110, 111
Pilate's impotence, 48
play, 4, 5, 9, 10, 15, 37, 39, 41–43, 84, 100, 106, 130, 153
playfulness, 9, 57, 64, 65, 71, 82
pleasure, 47, 50, 67, 75, 98
Plutarch, 133
polemic, 90, 147
polemical parallelism, 134
political cartoon, Jonah as. *See under* Jonah.
political power, 95, 143
political revolutionary, 117
pomposity of Haman. *See under* Haman.
pompousness, 12
Poo, 82
Potella, Michael, 123
pound (currency), 137–39, 146–48
pounds, parable of. *See* parable of the pounds.
pragmatic theory of truth. *See under* truth.
prankster, 91
preachers, 16, 149
preaching
   humor in, 11, 15, 16, 23
   Paul's, 127
   Stephen's, 128. *See also*, sermons, humor in.
prejudice of Jonah. *See under* Jonah.
premise(s) (in logic), 27, 28, 29, 31–35, 152
preposterous imagery, 13
preposterous (ness), the, 12, 13, 68, 69, 116, 117, 119, 120, 122
presence of humor. *See under* humor.
Press, Michael, 93
pretensions, 9, 14, 101
probability, 31, 32, 43, 54
prodigal son, parable of. *See* parable of the prodigal son.
profane, the, 40
proof, 28, 34, 42, 59, 67, 86, 102, 112, 140
prophet, 67, 109, 115, 121, 149
prophetic books, 74, 87, 88, 155, 156, 158
Prophets, xvii, 61, 71, 72, 73, 80, 88, 155, 156
   humor in, 80, 87–96
proposition, 1, 25, 29, 30, 31, 36, 51, 61
Protestant Reformation, 56
Protestant reformers, 148
proud laughter. *See under* laughter.
Proverbs, book of, 69, 72, 96, 97
Pryor, Richard, 38
psalm, Jonah's. *See under* Jonah as.
Psalms, 5, 14, 55, 76, 96, 97
puns, 12, 65, 66, 72, 81, 86, 87
punster prophet, Micah as. *See under* Micah.
Puritans, 44

Qoheleth, 98
quail metaphor, 86

Rabshakeh's speech, 93
Rachel, 81, 85
Rahab, 65, 122
reaggregation, 116–17, 122
realism, 129
reason, appeal to. *See under* appeal.

Subject Index

reasons, objective and subjective, 59
Rebecca/Rebekah, 81, 83–85
rebel, David as. *See under* David
reconciliation, 38, 39
redemption, 37, 40, 71
  folly of, 48, 49
redemptive laughter. *See under* laughter.
Reis, Pamela, 86, 87, 89
Reiss, Jana, 23
rejoicing, 46, 77, 152–54, 157
Religulous, 19
repetition, humor of. *See under* humor.
resentment, 39
resistance, 9, 15, 104, 122
resolution, 106, 116
retort, 115
Revelation
  book of, xvii, 61
  humor in, 114, 132–35
reversal, 64, 66, 124
reversals, role, 67, 100
revisited, laughter. *See under* laughter.
revolution, 124
reward(s), 41, 42, 43, 66, 97, 137, 144, 149
riches, 157
riddles, 90
ridicule, 89, 93, 94, 101, 105, 111
ridiculousness, 130
righteousness, 5, 67, 83, 100, 121, 158
riposte, 115
ritual joking pattern, 119
Robertson, David, 71
Rogness, Michael, 64–69, 97
Romans, Epistle to, 129, 130
Rule of Benedict. *See under* Benedict.
rulers, 44, 75–77
Ruth, book of, 65

Sabbath, 23
sackcloth, 111
sacred, the, 9, 40
sacrifices of Abel and Cain, 134
Sadducees, 68, 127
sadness, 59, 114, 152
saltiness, 117
salty humor. *See under* humor.

salvation, x, 5, 72, 93, 106, 131, 150, 153
Samaritan woman, 125, 126
Samra, Cal, 59
Samson, 88, 90–92
Samuel
  First, 1, 88, 91, 92
  Second, 2, 88, 91, 92
Sapphira, 128
Sarah, 38, 67, 68, 75–77, 81–83
sarcasm, 14, 67, 68, 85, 90, 93–95, 129, 130, 131, 156
Sargon, 109
Saroglou, Vassilis, 57, 59
satanic triad, 133, 135
satire, 56, 64, 67, 83, 93, 104–108, 110, 111, 116
Saul, 69, 91, 92
Sceva's sons, 127
Schelling, Friedrich, 53
Schifferdecker, Kathryn, 99
schlemiel, 84
Schultz, Brian, 139
scoffer(s), 77, 94
Screwtape Letters, 39
Scribes, 121, 123
Scripture(s), 55, 75, 148, 150, 152
  humor in, xvi, 31
self-deception, 77
self-image, 40
senseless croaking, 134, 135
sentence (in logic), 27–30, 33
separation (as a stage in jokng), 116–17, 122
seriousness, 39, 53, 55, 82, 157
sermon of doom, 108
Sermon on the Mount, 67, 122
Sermon on the Plain, 55
sermons, humor in, 15, 16, 42. *See also* preaching.
servants, Abraham's, 83
servants, the three, 144, 146–47
sex, 82, 89
sexual harassment, 41
sexuality, 89
shambles, tragic. *See under* tragic.
shame, 14, 130
she-bears, 93

Subject Index

Sherwood, Yvonne, 104, 110, 111
Shore, Mary Hinkle, 15, 16
shortcomings, 50, 151, 153
Simon (Peter), 66, 122
sin, 14, 121, 147, 151
sinfulness, 52
sinner(s), 77, 79, 110, 157
    Jonah not a. *See under* Jonah
    Paul as a. *See under* Paul.
sins, x, 14, 48, 111, 150
Sirach, 24, 52, 78
Sisera, 88, 89
sitcoms, 20
    animated, 20
slander, 157
slapstick, 84
slave(s), 137, 38, 137–40, 142, 143, 146, 148–50
slavery, 86, 89
slothful induction, 32, 35, 44
slothful people, 148
small talk, 56
Smith, Christopher, 16
Smyrna Wesleyan Church, 23
snakes, 134
snappy comeback, 115
Sodom, 67
sojourners, 86
Sojourners Magazine, 22
solemn occasions, 9
solemnity, xvi
Solomon, Song of, 96, 100
somberness, 68
Song of Solomon, 96, 100
sorrowful Jesus. *See under* Jesus.
soulless opinions, 134
sound argument. *See under* argument
soundness (logical), 27, 28, 31
sounds in the Bible, 69, 70
Spencer, F. Scott, 65
spirit, 49, 54
    child's, 12, 65
    downcast, 97
    gifts of, 146
    happy, 98
    of gravity, 5
    of joy. *See under* joy
    of prophecy, 92

spirits, 133, 134
    evil 127
spiritual
    capacity, 141
    development, Luther's, 38
    healing, 38
    maturity, 37, 38, 40
    meaning, 145
Spivey, Ed, 22
spontaneity, 57, 65
sport, 42, 97
Stackert, Jeffrey, 156
Standhartinger, Angela, 85
Steere, David, 42
Steffensky, Fulbert, 39
Stein, Edith, 23
Stephen, Saint, 128
stereotype, xvi, 20
stewardship, 145, 149
stinging humor. *See under* humor.
stipulative definition, 8
Stone, Lawson, 89
Stooges, Three. *See* Three Stooges.
straining a gnat, 12
Strange, Marcian, 44, 71, 72
stupid people, 78
stupidity of false religions, 90
subversion, comedy of. *See under* comedy.
subversions, 115
subversive humor. *See under* humor.
suffering, 13, 158
suffering servant, 117
superiority, 20, 95, 130
    laughter of. *See under* laughter.
surprise, 8, 13, 64, 66, 105
Sutton, Eugene Taylor, 42
swallowing a camel. *See under* camel.
Synoptic Gospels, 45, 123
Syrophoenician woman, 119
Sölle, Dorothee, 39

talent (currency), 138, 140–42, 148
talents, parable of. *See* parable of the talents.
talk
    idle, 52
    obscene, 55, 156

of fools, 78
silly, 55, 156
small, 56
vulgar, 55, 156
Tamar, 65, 122
Tanakh, 74, 80
Tasker, R. V. G., 146
tears, theology of. *See under* theology.
tears, vale of. *See* vale of tears.
tension, 20, 37, 73
texts, Pauline. *See under* Pauline.
thanksgiving, 55, 156, 157
theological
　laughter, 18
　virtue, 49
theology
　deliberative, 152
　embedded, 152
　of humor, 47, 50, 59
　of irony, 47, 50, 59
　of joy, 47, 49, 59, 73
　of laughter, xvi, xvii, 25, 36, 46–49, 59–61, 63, 75, 78, 79, 152–54
　of tears, xvi, xvii, 25, 36, 50, 51, 59, 60, 152, 154
　of the comic. *See under* comic
Thessalonians
　First, 129, 132, 157
　Second, 155–57
Thoennes, Erik, 47, 50, 59
Thomas Aquinas, 7
Thomson, Casey, 66
Three Stooges, 84
Thysell, Carol, 148
tidings
　glad, 5
　tidings, joyful, 4, 5, 46, 114
Timothy
　First, 155, 157
　Second, 155, 158
tithes, 14, 95
tombs, 31, 69
Torah, xvii, 61
　humor in, 80–87, 96
Tower of Babel, 81, 82
tragedies/tragedy, 4, 6, 10, 13, 34, 59, 70–74, 87, 103, 104, 114, 152–54
tragic

heroes, 71, 99
laughter. *See under* laughter
shambles, 87, 155
virtue, 71, 72
transcendence, signals of, 48, 49
Transfiguration, 116, 117
transformative joking, 115, 116
triad, satanic. *See* satanic triad.
tribulation, 60
trickster(s), 72, 91
Trueblood, Elton, 11–13, 45, 55, 59, 65, 67–69, 114, 117–20, 138, 149
truth
　coherence theory of, 29
　correspondence theory of, 29
　humor as a means to, xvi, xvii, 1, 8, 11, 12, 15, 37, 61, 114, 115, 121
　of metaphor, 30, 31
　performative theory of, 30
　pragmatic theory of, 30
Twain, Mark, 23
Twitter, 23

U-shaped
　plot, 71, 72, 82, 84, 98, 125
　structure, 61, 153, 156, 159
　text, 158
　visions, 73
unbelief, laughter of. *See under* laughter.
unbelievers, 127
underdog(s), 70, 90–92
understatement, 12, 104–106
unexpected, the, 12, 57, 66, 67, 117, 120, 125
unjust judge, parable of the. *See* parable of the unjust judge.
unprophetic prophet, Jonah as. *See under* Jonah as.
unsuitable authority, appeal to. *See under* appeal.
uproariousness, 8
upside-down U, 74
utterance, performative. *See* performative utterance.

Vacation Bible School David. *See under* David.

Suject Index

vale of tears, 55
validity, 27, 28, 31
value of humor. *See under* humor.
Van Eck, Ernest, 148
Van Rensburg, Lee, 123–25, 130
vanity, 12, 70
Via, Dan, 71, 80
victims, 72, 85
vineyard workers, parable of. *See* parable of the vineyard workers.
vipers, brood of, 68
virtues
   comic. *See under* comic
   tragic, 71, 72
   warrior, 72
vulgar talk. *See under* talk.

wag, 40
Walker, Steven, 63, 64, 74, 81, 91, 101, 103–105, 126
warning, 12, 55, 77, 106, 144, 146, 155, 157, 158
warrior virtues. *See under* virtues.
wasf, 100
wedding in Cana. *See* Cana, wedding in.
weeping, 5, 60, 137

whale, 105, 106
Whedbee, William, 70–73, 81, 82, 84, 86, 90, 91, 98, 100
whirlwind speech, 99
widow's mite, 70
Wilcox, Lance, 104, 107, 109
Wiley E. Coyote, 101
wine, 4, 65, 99, 118
wineskins, 99, 118
wisdom, 69, 97, 98, 105, 150
Wisdom, book of, 133
wit, 24, 40, 65, 66, 90, 120
Witetschek, Stephan, 133–35
wordplay, 12, 65, 66, 72, 82, 84, 86, 87, 96, 104, 106, 153
worldliness, 52
wrath, 96, 101, 157
Wright, N.T., 139
Writings, the, xvii, 22, 61, 80, 96–102

Yahweh, 73, 94, 108, 109
Young, Brad H., 141

Zacheus, 70
Zakovitch, Yair, 4
Zechariah, 88, 155
Zephaniah, 88, 155

Scripture Index

GENESIS

1–11	72
2:23–24	82
2:23	65
4:13a	66
6:11–9:29	82
11:1–9	82
11:4	69
15–20	72
17	72
17:15–17	75
18:10, 12	75
18:12	67
18:25–32	67
20	82
20:2	82
21:6	76
24	83
24:17–22	83
27:22–23	83
27:43–45	85
28	122
29:11	85
31:38	83
35:29	83
37:19	85
37:26–28	85
38	65
40	66
40:19	66
41	85

EXODUS

4:10	86
7:26–8:11	133
20:1–17	23
34:6–7	86

NUMBERS

11	86, 87
11:21–22	87
4:13–19	66
22	86
22:22–35	87

JOSHUA

2 & 6	122
2	65

JUDGES

3:12–30	88
4:7–22	89
4:20	89
5:24–31	89
6:31	90
7:1–23	90
7:2	90
13–16	90
17–18	90
18:24	90

Scripture Index

1 SAMUEL

9–10	91
9:21	91
11:20–24	91
17	70
17:43–44	92
18:10–11	69
18:25–27	69
18:27	92
19:9	91
19:13	92
19:24	92

2 SAMUEL

1:25–26	92
2:1–4	92
11	65
19:24	92
6	48

1 KINGS

1	92
18:27	92
21	92

2 KINGS

2:23–24	93
18:34	93

ESTHER

7	101
7:10a	101

JOB

1:21	98
5:17, 22	42
9	77
9:23	77
32:19–20a	99
38	99

PSALMS

1:1	77
2	44, 68, 76
2:2–6, 12	76
2:4a	42
8	97
8:2	97
37	42, 44
37:13	76
59	42
59:8	76
65	5
65:8b	5
65:13	5
88	97
104	42
126:1–2a	42
137	97
138:6	66

PROVERBS

1:20–26	98
14:13	52
17:16	69, 97
17:22	97
19:24	69, 97
22:3	69, 97
23:9	69, 97

ECCLESIASTES

7:4	52, 98

SONG OF SOLOMON

7:1–10	100

ISAIAH

3:16–23	93
20	48
20:2–3	93
36:19	93
40–55	93
44:9–20	93
44:14–17	93

Scripture Index

JEREMIAH

19:1–13	94
19:9	69
20:7–8	94
27:2	48
28:10–16	94
30:12, 14	94
30: 17, 22	94

EZEKIEL

3:1–3	94
4	48
4:12	94
31	67

DANIEL

6	102

HOSEA

4:7–8	14
13:2	93, 95

AMOS

4:4	95
4:4–5	14
6:4–5	95

JONAH

3:5–9	109

MICAH

1:10	96
1:11	96
1:14	96
1:15	96

WISDOM

4:17–18	76
15:18–19	133
16:1–4	133
19:10	133

SIRACH

21:14, 15	78
21:15, 20	52
27:12–13	78

MATTHEW

3:7	68
4:12–18:35	122
5–7	67
5:3–5	118
5:21	147
5:43–46	71
7:3–5	72
7:6	13
7:34	122
11:18–19	5
15:14	122
15:21–28	122
16:18	66, 122
16:23	120
17	116
17:1	117
17:5	117
18:3	12, 123
19:1–20:24	122
19:24	69, 123
19:30	123
20:1–16	120
21	48
23	12, 70
23:1–12	118
23:3b	118
23:11, 12	118
23:24	72, 119
24:2	146
24:3–28	146
24:29–35	146
24:36–44	146
25:14–30	137, 144
25:17, 19	143
25:21, 23	137
25:24	137
25:29–30	137
27	48
28:9	114

MARK

2:21–22	118
4:30–32	67, 116
5:3–9	69
7:24–30	119, 123
7:27	119
7:28	119
8:14–21	123
10:15	123
10:25	119, 123
10:26	13
12:37	123
16:15	114

LUKE

1:26–39	116
1:41–44	79
1:44	65, 124
1:46–55	79, 114, 124
2:10	124
4:18, 19	79
6:25b	115
6:39	118, 124
10:17	124
10:21	79
10:25–37	70
10:29–37	124
14:15–24	124
15	115, 121, 125
15:11–32	115
15:11–12	67
15:29–30	109
16:17	68
16:19–31	150
18:2–5	116
19:1–10	70
19:3–4	72
19:12–27	137
19:12	137
19:13	137
19:14	137, 141
19:21, 22	141
19:21	137
19:25	138
19:26–27	138
19:27	141
19:36–38	79
20:21–26	125
21:1–4	70
22:26	125
24:1–53	125

JOHN

1:45–51	118
1:46	125
1:47	118
2:1–11	65, 116
4:7–26	125
6:5	126
8	121, 125
8:7	121
13:9	72
13–17	126
16:22	42
20:15	126
21:15–17	121

ACTS

1:18	128
2	4
2:12–15	4
2:13	127
2:15	128
2:15b	4
2:28	4
2:46	4
3:2–8	128
4:13–22	127
5:1–11	128
5:17–26	127
7:1–53	128
8:26–40	128
9:24–25	127, 128
12:14	72
12:19	128
12:23	128
14:18	127
14:19–20	127
19:13–16	127
20:9	128
24:25	127
26:24	127

Scripture Index

26:28–29	127
28:1–6	127
28:31	127

ROMANS

9:20	129

1 CORINTHIANS

1:16	130
1:18	130, 131
1:27–28	130
4	48
4:1–5	145
4:10	131
4:13	130
7	130
7:3–4	130
9:27	130
12:15–21	69
15:8–9	130
15:8	130

2 CORINTHIANS

4:7	131

GALATIANS

1:8–9	131
2:20	129
5:1–12	131
5:11–12	72

EPHESIANS

3:8	157
4:31–32	157
5:4	55, 156

PHILIPPIANS

4:4	46, 152

COLOSSIANS

1:24	157

1 THESSALONIANS

5	5
5:16–18	132
5:16–17	157
5:16, 18	5
5:18	157

1 TIMOTHY

1:12–15	157
1:19	157
3:8, 11	157

2 TIMOTHY

4:7, 8, 18	158

PHILEMON

11	132

HEBREWS

12:2	132

JAMES

James 1:2–4	132

1 JOHN

4	158

3 JOHN

4	158

JUDE

3, 4	158

REVELATION

13	69, 134
14:6–13	134
16:13–24	133
16:13–14	133

www.ingramcontent.com/pod-product-compliance
Lightning Source LLC
Chambersburg PA
CBHW051738230426
43670CB00012B/2073